The Shadow Scholar

The Shadow Scholar

How I Made a Living Helping
College Kids Cheat

Dave Tomar

B L O O M S B U R Y
New York   London   New Delhi   Sydney

Published by Bloomsbury USA, New York

All papers used by Bloomsbury USA are natural, recyclable products made from
wood grown in well-managed forests. The manufacturing processes conform to
the environmental regulations of the country of origin.

LIBRARY OF CONGRESS CATALOGING-IN-PUBLICATION DATA HAS BEEN APPLIED FOR.

ISBN: 978-1-60819-723-1

First U.S. edition 2012

1 3 5 7 9 10 8 6 4 2

Typeset by Westchester Book Group
Printed in the U.S.A. by Quad/Graphics, Fairfield, Pennsylvania

Many of the names and locations used in this text have been altered or fictionalized for
legal reasons or for the protection of those involved. While all of the events depicted in
this text did occur as described, certain specifics relating to participants, institutions,
businesses, or assignments have also been altered for the reasons stated directly here above.

FOR MY B.

Contents

Preface

On November 12, 2010, the *Chronicle of Higher Education* published an article titled "The Shadow Scholar," in which, using the pseudonym Ed Dante, I provided some detail on my career as a writer of student papers. The article was met with a colorful mix of outrage, empathy, and recognition. In fact, it went on to become the most read and commented-on article in the *Chronicle*'s history. This surprised the living hell out of me.

Apparently, people were shocked by the article's revelations concerning academic dishonesty, student treachery, and professorial incompetence. And here I thought everybody already knew about this kind of stuff. I never made any secret of it. If anybody ever asked me what I did for a living, I told them, "I help students cheat."

The article, though, touched off a far-ranging conversation: about academic integrity, about ethics, about the technological implications of cheating, and about the cultural context in which cheating occurs. One week after my article was published, Ed Dante, the Shadow Scholar, was notorious. Websites used hyperbolic phrases like "the Ed Dantes of the world" and "in the age of Ed Dante." Meanwhile, Dave Tomar continued to write in quiet obscurity, plugging away on album reviews and political diatribes that only his friends and a handful of Internet junkies would ever read. Even as the *New York Times*, the *New Yorker*, and the *National Review* offered their respective opinions on Ed Dante, even as radio personalities, television reporters, and independent film producers sought him out, Dave Tomar remained just another anonymous, struggling writer.

I had been helping students cheat for a decade. I wrote every day. I was paying the bills. I was making a living. I was a homebody, and sometimes something just short of a highly social shut-in. I wore the same thing every day: jeans and a wifebeater from a pack. I usually had weed resin under my fingernails. My hair hung down into my eyes. I was kind of grimy. I had a foul mouth and a ton of bad habits. In many ways, I was a writer out of the necessity to do something that didn't force me to interact too much with regular people.

So when Diane Sawyer called looking for an interview, it was almost more than I could handle. The evening that Sawyer's people called—the culmination of a week in which the CBC, NPR, and MSNBC also came looking for interviews—found me keeled over in my office chair with my face in my hands. I had expressed the sentiment to my agent that I really didn't feel comfortable doing any interviews just then. I wasn't ready. I had no formal training. What business did I have going on *Nightline*? On the last day of summer a few years earlier, I was walking down the boardwalk hand in hand with my girlfriend when a local newsman approached us with a camera. He asked us what we were doing to savor the last moments of the season. My girlfriend said some cute stuff about miniature golfing and ice cream. I made some nervous joke about seagull incontinence that totally bombed. They literally cropped me out and showed only her on the news. I don't blame them. She's much prettier than I am.

So I told my agent I didn't want to go on TV. She sent back an e-mail basically saying, "Tough titties."

I would be a fool to say no to Diane Sawyer.

Try to recall the moment in *The Matrix* when Neo is actually shown the Matrix and proceeds to hork green stuff all over the holodeck. That was me.

I was dizzy and queasy, and I could hardly bring myself to speak. One week before the "Shadow Scholar" article was published, the highlight of my career had been that TomJones.com published my review of Tom Jones's new album. I enjoyed a happy existence and had a rich inner life. I loved the woman I was going to marry. I loved my family. I loved my friends. I was physically active, had a lot of hobbies, and found plenty of time to travel, find adventure, and eat gourmet food. Despite a general sense that I wanted to be and had ostensibly failed at becoming a real writer, whatever that means, I always felt that I was living the sweet life. I answered to nobody. I wanted more out of life, for certain, but if this was it, and it never got any better . . . I supposed that it could have been a lot worse.

I wrote constantly, and nobody gave a shit. Things were going great. And as much as I really wanted to get out of it, as much as I needed to get out of it for my health, my sanity, and my integrity as a human being, I hadn't prepared myself for this sort of thing. I enjoyed my privacy. And, quite frankly, when I set out to write my article, it occurred only fleetingly to me that it might be controversial. It seems funny to say, but I'd been doing the work for a long time and I'd been frank about it with everybody. When I would tell people I got paid to write papers for students who cheat, most were fascinated and had many follow-up questions. But controversial?

My parents knew what I did. My grandmother knew what I did. My friends and their parents knew. The IRS knew. It wasn't a secret. I knew many of them had suspected I was wasting my talents, but they didn't let on about it in conversation. People are too polite for that.

Fortunately, the Internet is a really angry place filled with really angry people, many of whom come positively unglued when not subject to the social consequences of face-to-face interaction. So when I used the forum of the *Chronicle* to announce my intention to retire from the business, I was rewarded with every kind of response imaginable. There were those who lauded me for my confessions, those who rhetorically shook their heads in pity for me, and those who referred to me as the scum of the earth. There were those who read my attempts at self-effacing humor as arrogance, those who repurposed misconstrued, out-of-context moments from the article to opine from the safety of their blogs, and those who calculated my earnings per hour and (as if I didn't already know) observed that I was making a pittance for my efforts. There were those who referred to me as a sociopath and analogized my behavior to drug dealing and murder.

All good points.

Another point that was not as good, not as perceptive, and quite frankly kind of stupid was that Ed Dante was a sham, that the extent of his work had been exaggerated and that the deficiencies identified among students in his article were simply too extreme to warrant belief. This was a response I had not foreseen.

And yet—a lot of people seemed to believe it was true.

During the course of the entire year that I composed this book, you could enter "shadow scholar" into Google and the very first auto-fill response was "shadow scholar hoax." I don't know a thing about Google's secret algorithms, but it certainly made me wonder just how many people thought I didn't exist.

Perhaps we Google what we want to believe.

Ultimately, I did the Diane Sawyer gig. David Muir interviewed me. He was super nice. They put me in shadow and disguised my voice with that creepy *A Current Affair* drone modulator. During the interview, he asked me if I had any regrets. I told him I had learned so much in my years as a shadow scholar that I wouldn't have traded it for anything.

Indeed, I'm pleased to be in a position to share with you in these pages some of the things I've learned. Take them as you will. Skepticism can be wise, and doubt can be healthy. But denial is another thing altogether.

For the most part, schools would just as soon disagree with everything I have to say here. That's because they're afraid. It isn't greed alone that motivates them; they are afraid because they must change and there's no way of knowing what the future holds for them, or for any of us.

People are afraid and I don't blame them. I'm afraid too. I've done too much academic research not to be.

I'm afraid that schools are producing too many graduates and not enough opportunities. I'm afraid because we're producing graduates who are simply too deeply invested in themselves to receive an education commensurate to its expense. I'm afraid of what this means for an economy that is hemorrhaging white-collar jobs to the global marketplace. I'm afraid because the population of Americans on Medicare will soon be greater than the size of America's workforce . . . and because the United States has aggressively savaged the value of its own dollar . . . and because we're running low on the fossil fuels upon which our very way of life depends . . . and because we're facing enormous challenges that will call for the best and brightest of us to make the most of our lives.

I'm afraid that we're not up to the task.

If we all collectively agree that something is seriously wrong, then, of course, there will be response. There will be outrage. There will be hand-wringing and finger-pointing and filibustering. There will be grandstanding. And in the throes of election season, there will be politicians making commercials with slow-motion footage depicting themselves playing soccer with multiracial children.

Don't believe the hype.

If solutions are to be found in all of this, we need to be honest about the problems facing us. We all know that students cheat, but do we know why? Until we can answer that question with any kind of confidence, we can't even begin to stop it.

CHAPTER 1

On the Banks of the Old Raritan . . .

My left eye is twitching uncontrollably. The lid wanted to close so long ago. But I fight it off. I make another cup of coffee. I roll another blunt. I put on John Coltrane's *A Love Supreme*. I pull out a few of the hairs on the back of my neck. I slap myself across the face.

But the eye, it just wants to be done for the night. I close it hard, I jab my finger into the eyeball, and I press it there until all those little black spots start vibrating with color. I open my eye, shake out the blurriness, crack my neck, and hunch back over my computer. It's one A.M., and I have another five pages to go on a paper about the Baltic states of the former Soviet Union.

If that doesn't sound too bad, bear in mind that I woke up early this morning to a twelve-pager about Andrew Jackson, I had a three-page SWOT analysis of Chick-fil-A for lunch, and I spent the evening snuggled up to a seven-page paper on teaching English as a second language.

Once I'm done with my journey through the Baltic, it's back to America for a seven-pager on Ralph Ellison's *Invisible Man*, then a four-page lesson plan for an aspiring special ed teacher. That one is due by five A.M.

My face feels like it's going to melt. I admit I'm not bringing my "A game" at this point, but I've been here so many times before that I already know what's going to happen. I'm going to do the work. I'll finish with the sunrise. The dread that some experience just imagining themselves in this scenario—I don't have that. I just have hours and words.

I'm automatic. I go into a zone. Sometimes, while I'm writing a paper, my mind will start to wander. When it does, my hands just keep writing—stock academic phrases, mostly. At this hour, I'm just stringing words together to get to the end. So if I get distracted and my thoughts stumble off to the comfort of my bed or the items in my refrigerator, I start typing stuff like "insofar as this framework serves to contextualize the subject at hand, we can see the degree to which this may be remarked upon as an effective way of approaching the research addressed here throughout."

Seriously. My eyes just glaze over, I start thinking about how nice a sandwich would be, and my hands just keep typing academic nonsense. I'm a paper factory, a sweatshop of one, a warehouse of industrial machinery humming over an endless assembly line where the stack of incoming parts never gets smaller.

I'm self-employed, so I'm always on the clock.

One can find me huddled in a corner of the room punching out the last words of an essay before the start of a holiday dinner.

On a romantic getaway, I sneak in a last-minute assignment while the lady gets dressed for dinner.

When I ride the bus, I type furiously while apologizing to those around me for my flying elbows.

I write papers in crowded bars. I write papers in the midst of drunken debauchery, pausing between paragraphs to hit the blunt going around the room. Sometimes during my Thursday-night poker games, I write a few sentences every time I fold a hand.

Once I wandered through an antique garden in New Orleans searching desperately for a wireless Internet signal via which to submit my paper on toxicology. I battered my keyboard furiously at the edge of a hotel bed in Las Vegas, reasoning out an assignment on the cognitive psychology tool known as the Johari window just before the strippers showed up for a bachelor party. I wrote a paper on improving English curriculum design midflight to Chicago, buzzed on Valium, scotch, and acrophobia.

My laptop is a bionic organ always connected to my fingertips. I've had my current computer, a MacBook Pro, for just over three years now. The E, D, C, A, S, and L keys have all been rubbed clean of visible lettering. Deep grooves have forged into the plastic. N, I, O, and M are going fast. The acid from my palms has corroded the slick silver coating from the empty spaces on either side of the touch pad. When I do manage to get a few hours of sleep, I just put it on the floor next to the bed, its eerie glow casting visions of lapsing deadlines into my anxious dreams.

The computer before this one was a Dell. I absolutely murdered that piece of shit. I ran it ragged. I never shut it off. The lifestyle was simply too strenuous for it. By the end, the fan ran so loudly it was like writing on top of a dishwasher. It emitted a squalling white noise that sometimes moved me to nausea. Finally, the thing just refused to turn on anymore. I said good riddance and kicked it to the dumpster.

I have yet to find the computer that can keep up with me. I work almost every day of the year. Sometimes I'll squeeze in one hour. Sometimes, twenty hours. Sometimes I trudge through several twenty-hour days in a row, sometimes weeks of them. Every day is another three, four, or more deadlines. Every week, another hundred-plus pages. Every moment of my life for the past decade has been financed by and grounded in the unending march of assignments that might have enlightened a generation of students.

I started taking blood pressure medication in my mid-twenties to compensate. I don't recommend it.

But I have my reasons.

I have my reasons for making a living in a way that some would call objectionable, that many have called despicable, that others still would consider intolerable. I have my reasons for working at an hourly rate that many of my better-educated peers would no doubt consider embarrassing; for remaining in this field in spite of my greater aspirations as a writer; for participating directly in the wholesale destruction of American education. And I have my reasons for desiring to be done with it; for deciding to make a clean break from the strangely addictive game of writing papers; for choosing to resolve my long-standing grudge against America's educational system.

At no point while doing this job have I felt guilty. Don't flip through these pages searching for remorse. It isn't there. But I also have not felt particularly proud. A writer does not aspire to this profession so that others can be praised (or ridiculed) for his work.

In any case, this is how it happened. Take what clues you will from it. I spent ten years defrauding the educational system. It would be disingenuous to tell you that I did this out of some strict sense of principle. But the story below is told with principle. I have dedicated my adult life to exploiting the weaknesses in a deeply flawed system. I am no moral authority. But I permeate this flawed system, I feed off of its vulnerabilities, and I know what about it is broken. If you feel compelled to fix it, or simply to avoid exploitation yourself, let my story be instructive to you.

So how did I get to this place, and why does it matter?

Much of what follows is the story of America's schools. I assure you, I am not the only wasted potential out here in the wilderness. There is a whole generation of malcontents, swindlers, bunglers, cynics, pragmatists, mama's boys, basket cases, narcissists, and underachievers on the make. I have made my living off of a disaffected, insecure, and dependent generation with no sense of itself, its obligations, and the challenges ahead of it. It will inherit a fading empire, and it will have no concept of what to do with it other than blog its feelings on the matter.

I am often asked how I got into this line of work. I can assure you, it happened quite organically. I hated school and I was broke.

College was a combination of disappointments for me. I went to Rutgers University, the state school of New Jersey, which is often referred to as one of the best schools for your money. If that phrase isn't a euphemistic kick in the crotch . . .

Rutgers is a university of great cultural diversity. Its residents will have journeyed there for higher education from far-off places like Vineland, New Jersey; Manalapan, New Jersey; and Metuchen, New Jersey. A veritable melting pot, Rutgers has students from South Jersey and North Jersey. Often we were pushed to the boundaries of cultural tolerance on such heated battlegrounds as whether it should be called a hoagie or a sub and which turnpike rest stop had filthier urinals, Molly Pitcher or Joyce Kilmer.

If you were from in-state, the tuition was low enough that you might've had loan money leftover for 40s of malt liquor. Not me. I didn't manage my money well enough for malt liquor. I once went to a gas station a half mile away from my dorm. The attendant began pumping before he ran my card. He had gotten to a dollar and thirty-seven cents' worth of gas when my card came back declined. He stopped the pump and told me I had to come up with another way to pay. I told him I had my checkbook on me, and of course he insisted that the gas station did not take personal checks. I offered him back the gas, but he wouldn't take it. Finally, with no other option, he relented and accepted a personal check in the amount of one dollar and thirty-seven cents. Naturally, the check bounced, and that is the story of how I scored three-quarters of a gallon of gas for little more than the thirty-two-dollar NSF fee assessed by my bank.

I never bought a book during college. I couldn't afford them, and I certainly wasn't going to read them. Before college, I went to a fancy high school where the parking lot was sectioned off according to make and model. I parked behind the dumpster, an area specifically reserved for people who only had cars because some older relative had died. I had the same periwinkle Buick Century as the janitor. My high school was competitive, and the people who grubbed for grades there genuinely gave a crap. Truthfully, it was a lot more academically challenging than college. So I decided I could live without the books.

In terms of survival, though, I learned a lot at Rutgers.

College was a financially bleak time for me. My first stab at personal independence was marked by unpaid bills, undone laundry, and unpopped bags of popcorn for supper. So I was down-and-out in the ghettos of New Brunswick. And while I was down, Rutgers University kicked me repeatedly in the ribs and stood over me laughing while I tried to get my bearings.

It locked me out of my classes, so I switched my major. It shunted me from main-campus housing, so I lived on a periphery campus and took buses to my classes. I couldn't afford basic educational commodities like notebooks or Rutgers pep paraphernalia, so I got a job off-campus. When I applied for a parking pass, I was refused. I spent my first year of school looking for places to hide my car. When I accumulated a sufficient number of parking tickets, my transcript was withheld.

When I called the Office of the Registrar to have my transcript released, I was told to contact the Office of Academic Affairs. When I called the Office of Academic Affairs, I was told to contact the registrar. When I called the registrar back, they told me to consult the head of my major's department.

All of my classes graded for attendance. All of my classes were so big that the professors had to speak using microphones. All of my classes used multiple-choice tests with Scantron forms so that grading could be done by machine. All of my professors gave lectures with content lifted directly from the text. All of my courses seemed extraneous, unnecessary, and uninteresting. When I was counting down the last days of high school, I never imagined that freedom would be so mediocre.

Rutgers is like so many other schools of its size. It's a money farm. I didn't have a class with less than one hundred people in it until I was a senior, and by then I was too angry to care. One of the best schools for your money . . .

It's like saying that McDonald's has great deals on food. Just because it's relatively cheap doesn't mean you're getting a good deal. You could still develop heart disease.

I don't mean to complain. I've made peace with all of this. And it wouldn't be a big deal if it was just me. I could be nothing more than one loudmouthed jerk with a gigantic chip on his shoulder. But I got ripped off, and I don't think my experience was unique.

I was a young, aspiring, and arrogant writer. I was doing album reviews for the entertainment insert in our university paper. I was writing a weekly political humor column called The Monkey Goes Where the Wind Blows for the multi-campus publication the *Outside World*, which was founded by the future great sportswriter and my old high school mate Howard Megdal. I had a small but nerdy following.

I had written the manuscript for a novel but was unable to gain approval for an independent study at Rutgers. "There's nothing like that here," they told me.

At this age, I was fairly confident that I would soon be a long-awaited revelation to the world. My first book was going to be a monumental success, and it would force America to examine its own psyche. It would not be very long before I was sleeping atop a mattress made of money on a yacht crewed by beautiful naked women. You know, like novelists do.

Incidentally, I couldn't sell my work to pay for Q-tips. I started college in 1998 assuming that by junior year I'd be able to dispense with taking classes and move right on to the lecture circuit. But by the arrival of fall semester 2001, I regularly considered faking my own death to get out of paying campus parking tickets.

In 2001, the cost of getting your car out of tow in New Brunswick was ninety dollars. This was pretty close to a year's wages for me at the time. I indicated as much to Erin, my fellow communication major. We had three classes together, so we became study buddies. We'd check in for attendance, then sneak out to get high. One day, as we sat out on her roof passing a joint and listening to Bob Dylan, I lamented the loss of my car. I told her of my desperate predicament and the sad reality that I would probably never see my beloved periwinkle Buick Century—Slow Lightnin', I used to call her—again.

She offered to lend me ninety dollars. My friends were mighty generous to me in those days. But I refused. I couldn't even think of when I'd be in a position to repay that money.

"Hmmm," she reflected.

"Eh?"

"I'll give you ninety bucks to write my sociology paper."

Well, now. This was something new. This wasn't charity. Somebody was willing to pay for my work. My first commission!

Suddenly, everything changed. Would you believe it if I told you that people started begging to give me money for my writing?

Erin was happy with her paper, so she recommended me to a friend in a fraternity. He too expressed interest in paying money for my work. I established a formal pricing structure. I charged him ten dollars per page and an eighth of weed. He was thrilled to do business with me.

I came over to his frat house at eleven A.M. to gather up his text and the details for his assignment. He mashed up an OxyContin and snorted it through a twenty-dollar bill. He took a big gulp of Busch Light and said, "Hey man, there's a ton of guys around here that would love you."

Dude was right. I became quite the popular man around the fraternity. By the middle of the fall semester, I was carrying a significant portion of its course load. Word got around fast that there was a way to get out of doing work without being placed on academic probation. Giving a frat boy an easy way to cheat is like putting a preschooler in the priesthood. They were all over me.

Of course, this did not make me a suddenly wealthy man. But now I had money for malt liquor and even some food. Anytime I could top that off with a little action on the side . . . I am a simple man of simple needs.

My quality of life changed. I was getting less sleep but more of everything else. And finally—and really for the first time in my postadolescent life—I was actually doing homework. It wasn't mine, but I was doing it.

And I was writing for a living. So my name wasn't on the work. So what?

I was in high demand.

CHAPTER 2

Rich Kid Sid

My life in college was getting better. I was paying even less attention to my own studies and genuinely immersing myself in the work of others. My junior year marked a turning point. Rutgers was finally delivering on its promise as an academic institution. It had put me in touch with the kinds of people who could help me further my career.

My fellow scholars, my college mates, my traveling company along this road of enlightenment toward the Lyceum in Athens, the great library of Alexandria, and all the temples of Buddha.

Speaking of, here was my new client now, Sid.

"Sorry I'm late, bro. I was taking a shit."

"No worries. I've done that."

"So you're, like, a paper writer?"

"At your service."

"Sweet. I really need this. I mean, I don't need it like I couldn't do this shit myself. I could. But I'm not going to waste my time on this class."

Sid was talking about Expository Writing, the basic composition course that most Rutgers freshmen are required to take. It rivals Barney the purple dinosaur as an intellectual challenge and an instrument for teaching.

Sid was in crew. He was short but stocky. His head was almost perfectly square, and he had a crispy gel-helmet that told me right away he was from north of exit 10 on the New Jersey Turnpike. More than likely Long Island.

Sid was a particular breed, one that would fund my future profession.

Sid was, in a greasy nutshell, Generation Y's worst-case scenario.

Sid was an examplar of a very specific segment of Generation Y, an archetype that would become a constant presence in my life. Surely, in his generation as in all others before it, there are honest, ambitious, intelligent, and compassionate individuals. And in every generation before his, there have been Sids. But the opportunities, pressures, and challenges distinct to his generation have made it easier and more desirable for Sids to take the easy way out.

A Sid has no conscience. He has been coddled, prep schooled, propped up, and promised the world. He has been told that he is special. He has been assured that he is capable. He has been protected from any evidence that he might not be up to the challenges ahead of him. He should stink of self-doubt, but he is buoyed by his own sense of entitlement and the promise of lavish excess in his personal and professional life.

And the Sids aren't the only ones. According to a 2010 report by the Pew Research Center, "unlike the Silent Generation, Boomers and Gen X . . . Gen Y is the only generational cohort that doesn't cite 'work ethic' as a defining characteristic."[1] The Pew report notes that a majority of Generation Y respondents cited technology and pop culture as having greater importance in their lives. To put this another way, a statistically significant number of Millennials are more interested in tracking down a Dick in the Box ringtone than in solving the pickle of global climate change.

Not that this inherently makes Sid, or any of his contemporaries, a cheater. But it does mean that we are a legion of avid consumers. Today, more than was true for previous generations, formative experiences for the population of mostly white, middle-class and wealthy Americans who can afford to go to college and graduate school have increasingly come to center on social networking status and celebrity voyeurism. This is the retailer's most perfect fantasy come true: a demographic organism more consumer than human. Its rites of passage are virtual. Its accomplishments are tweeted. It no longer loiters in front of the convenience store. It loiters on Facebook. It needs to hang out in a place where it can talk about itself, where it can be validated, where it can be assured that somebody gives a shit. It expects schools to be that way too.

And if that means yet more consumption, so be it. New clothes to model on Facebook, new devices from which to tweet, new e-books for school. Sid was a consumer plain and simple. How far one like Sid might go to buy his way through life is generally a matter of resource and motive.

Sid was flush with resource and guided by the twin motives of deficiency and ambition.

I was introduced to Sid through my friend Bree.

I first met Bree at an interregional Jewish youth group event when I was sixteen and she fourteen. She was sitting with her sister on a bench between the bathrooms, a pretty little hippie chick with an indefinable exotic quality, a tulip-petal face, and the narrow eyes of her Russian great-great-grandparents.

Bree has situs inversus, a condition in which, relative to the average individual, all of one's vital organs are on the opposite side of one's body. The condition affects one in ten thousand, and its most significant medical ramifications for Bree are that she carries a special card to notify paramedics and pledges allegiance using her left hand. She also bats and throws lefty.

From almost the minute we met, we were inseparable, entrusted, and codependent, even romantic, but never actually involved. Our allegedly platonic friendship took on a type of physical intimacy that is only really acceptable in high school.

I went to Rutgers, and she followed two years later. There we remained close friends, part of the same weekend binge-drinking scene. She made mention of my services at a party one night, and this guy Sid was all over it.

I met Sid that first time in the lounge of his dorm, surrounded by his floor mates. He explained to me that even though he was perfectly capable, extremely intelligent, and generally a straight-A student as far as he could recall, he was above the degrading tasks that comprised Rutgers's Expository Writing course.

"So, I don't want you to think I'm stupid, dude."

"No, man, I don't think you're stupid," I lied.

"I just don't have the time for this crap. With my crew schedule and my poli-sci courses and everything, I'm not trying to worry 'bout Expos."

"Yeah, I agree. It's nonsense. I'd never do it if I wasn't getting paid to." I was fortunate enough to have tested out of this course in the summer before freshman year.

"Besides, it's not like it matters. I just need to do well enough to get outta here. I need to be going to a much better college before I start applying to law schools. I can do way better than this place . . . no offense."

"Hey, no, man. None taken. I've been to Chuck E. Cheese's that were more educational than this."

"Yeah, for real. Wait, really?"

"Forget it. Let's just get to the thing."

"K. I just wanted you to know why I wanted your help. I'm not stupid."

"Don't worry, man. I don't judge" . . . out loud.

Sid sent me home with some cash, some nugget, a textbook, and his in-class writing sample. We were supposed to take this sample and turn it into a passing paper. I got home, smoked his weed, and started reading over his work. Poor Sid. He really didn't know how far off the mark he was. Nobody had ever told him.

Sid's in-class writing assignment read like the really long name of a Chinese takeout restaurant. It was a jumble of words slapped together uncomfortably, standing next to one another with an air of remoteness, like strangers in an elevator.

Punctuation dotted the landscape of his work almost randomly, as though he had written the paper first and then gone back through it indiscriminately inserting dots and dashes. For all I know, he was a supergenius who had strung Morse code throughout his paper in order to subliminally impact the teaching assistant's grading process. Unfortunately for Sid, the TA had missed it entirely. His in-class writing assignment had received a No Pass, the mark indicating that a student needed improvement. Invariably, a large percentage of students received a No Pass on the first assignment or two in Expository Writing.

This was done so that students could be shown to demonstrate improvement and ultimately pass the writing requisite even when no improvements had been demonstrated at all. Starting at zero, most students would pass and some would not. Grading was arbitrary, and classes were instructed by TAs.

Sid felt that his No Pass grade was among history's greatest injustices. For although Sid lacked many things, confidence was not one of them. He thought the world of himself. He felt an incurable self-worth that could not possibly have been instilled in him by a teacher. It had probably taken a lifetime of little reaffirmations, of barely passable efforts reimagined as successes, of material and abstract gifts—all the tuition, dorm swag, and name-brand threads a kid could want. And you can be damn sure, whether they knew it or not, Sid's parents were paying for his papers.

Starting with Rich Kid Sid and extending through a line of customers that could wrap four hundred times around the trendiest, douchiest, most popped-collar club in all of Hoboken, I have come to know a portion of this generation that, I'm very sorry to say, suggests that *Jersey Shore* is the most realistic program on television.

My customers are rooted to the common ground of school attendance in the millennial era. As I have reflected on the thousands of commissioned, completed, and archived assignments in my personal library, I am inclined to argue that at least a portion of the college-educated future leaders of this generation will be undone by their narcissism.

Many of my clients believe that with little to no effort on their part, the world will be delivered to them on a platter. Of course, these assumptions are predicated on the idea that America will continue to produce more opportunities for the children of each succeeding generation. What distinguishes Generation Y on the whole, as opposed to that which distinguishes its least admirable subsets, is the reality that this generational cohort will experience fewer opportunities and a lesser standard of living than its parents.

A 2010 article in *Bloomberg Businessweek* reports that "Gen Y is in a tougher financial position than previous generations. The average salary for 25- to 34-year-olds, for instance, fell 19 percent over the last 30 years, after adjusting for inflation, to $35,100 . . . That's if they can get jobs: Unemployment among 19- to 24-year-olds stands at 15.3 percent vs. the overall rate of 9.5 percent, according to the Bureau of Labor Statistics."[2]

Combine these realities with salary expectations driven not just by the desire to own a luxury sedan with inbuilt ass warmers but also by the incredible expense of higher education, and you start to gain an understanding of why this generation isn't faring well in a tough economy. America's businesses are hitting the skids, and this is not a temporary recession. This is a leveling out. This is the great promise of globalization in all its glory. This is the backlash for a culture of utter selfishness, for a way of life that is ecologically unsustainable, and for a mode of consumption so voracious that we must make war on foreign nations to support it.

And we're counting on guys like Sid to lead us from this mess. I was meeting Sid in between classes at the Student Center to get details for his second assignment.

"Hey. Thanks again for doing this, bro. I really need this."

"No sweat, man. Business is business."

"Yeah, but I appreciate it. I mean, this shit's so unfair. I don't see why I should even have to take this class. I'm going to work in my dad's firm either way."

"Oh yeah?"

"Yeah, dude. Maybe we can get you a job, like, writing legal-type shit for the firm."

"Yeah, that sounds really great, man."

I knew exactly who Sid was through and through. He was a sign of the times. My higher education was happening in simultaneity with the Bush administration, with the War on Terror, with the proliferation of reality TV, and with the collapse of corporate America; on the cusp of a spike in oil prices, just before Hurricane Katrina, at the onset of baseball's steroid scandal, and in anticipation of the meteoric rise of pricks like Mark Zuckerberg and the precipitous fall of pricks like Ken Lay. We put Donald Trump and Paris Hilton on television to be the first impression we make on the alien races many galaxies away who might stumble upon our satellite transmissions.

Ah, the hideous faces of the fabulously wealthy in the last era of American privilege.

George W. Bush always reminded me of one of my customers, the kind who paid for their assignment and handed it in without bothering to read it. CEOs, chairmen of the board, and presidents of the United States pay others to do their research and writing. Then they stand up there and say stuff like "I've always believed . . . America . . . freedom . . ." and some crap about family values.

We know they aren't writing this stuff. We know they haven't done the research. We know they probably don't mean it and possibly don't even understand it. But these people are preordained to sit in the corner office with potted plants, big windows, and an incredible view while a staff of nerdly underlings scampers about gathering clever factoids and synthesizing comprehensive business reports. Schools are highly feudal. Legacies, mentorships, and cost-prohibitive hierarchies of learning denote that many people with considerably less ability than you and I are destined for a better life. I mean, sure, they may feel terrible on the inside (they also may not), but school is not a problem for them. It's just another corporation.

And it's a corporation that wants them to succeed in order to justify its own enormity. We promise that No Child will be Left Behind, so we nudge them through the shallow waters of public school education until they find themselves in the deep end of the pool, their lives of comfortable indulgence tied to them like ballasts of concrete.

We are raised to believe that we can be whatever we want to be, we can have whatever we want to have, we can do whatever we set our wallets to. Of course, we are also raised to compete. As Marx notes about a capitalist society, in order for one to have, another must have not. The grading curve is an excellent demonstration of this principle. You can't get a good grade unless you're better at something than your classmates. So there is a basic, obvious flaw in the idea that everyone is entitled to a good grade if they work for it. My customers are people whose work ethic (and often intellectual tools) should make them have-nots, but whose aristocratic means convince them otherwise. Nobody bluntly confronted these people with their own limitations or found a way to encourage them to overcome these limitations.

That's a real shame, because the challenges before this generation will be truly humbling. A generation that insists on updating its online status every time one of its members takes a dump doesn't know the meaning of the word "humble." So it lives in denial, expecting that it can always spend the dollars, make the purchases, and be awarded the customer service to succeed in life.

Later on in my career as a paper writer, I would come to know intimately this sense of entitlement, which came spewing out of the occasional disgruntled client.

Here, an unhappy customer asks for a revision of an assignment I've completed.

> The paper is not Master's level, is poorly written, does not follow APA format and does not include all the necessary criteria that I submitted . . . Sentence structure is awkward and reads as if written by someone whose first language is not English . . . APA format is not followed, see sources cited within the paper . . . The structure of the information is disjointed and difficult to read . . .

It goes on for a while, actually. She really takes the time to write a well-thought-out, rationally organized, and essentially accurate essay about how my essay sucked. All of a sudden, she was this brilliant writing critic. And her response to my work revealed her to possess the traits of another of Generation Y's great archetypes: the pragmatist.

The values, the ethics, the feeling of satisfaction that one is supposed to have in a job well done? These exist. But they are simply factors in a decision that every student makes. They are not everything, they are not encompassing, and for many students, they are in the minority, grouped with other reasons not to cheat, such as the fear of getting caught and the lost opportunity for personal enlightenment. In the majority are the pressures to get good grades; the need to hide one's deficiencies; the importance of receiving a degree; the necessity of justifying the considerable expense of one's education; the need to compete for a job in a difficult market; the desire for the attainment of status; the aim of achieving personal freedom; the perception that ethics are secondary to success; the pressure placed upon one by family and friends; excessively heavy workloads; sheer laziness; and a greater interest in sports/drinking/ recreational drugs/promiscuous sex/Magic: The Gathering/fill-in-the-blank than in one's studies. Naturally, these are not all of the elements of the equation, but this is the nature of the decision that all students make when they determine how they will approach their studies, if at all.

Sid was at least somewhat pragmatic, which is why he needed me. He would not see his transfer to a better school sidetracked by a basic compositional writing course. Rutgers is on the Raritan River, a primary source of drinking water for the region and a historically popular dumping ground for toxic and industrial waste. I imagine that rowing on it is a harrowing experience. Sid needed this transfer. Expository writing, and school in general, would not stand in the way of his future.

He was destined for a more reputable school. He was destined for a higher professional post. He was destined to row on a river more water than feces.

I had already written three papers for him, and, of course, he was totally hooked. I think Sid was probably giving his TA a lot of credit in assuming that he was actually reading the assignments, but I wasn't about to blow it with a repeat customer.

"I've been getting pretty good grades, bro. Keep up the good work."

"Don't mention it, buddy. I'm happy to help."

"Yeah, so, how much would you charge for a little tutoring, then?"

"Like, what kind?"

"Well, I have to do an in-class writing test at the end of the semester, and it's supposed to show my progress."

"Have you been making any progress with the in-class stuff?"

"No. My peer-review partner is a fucking bitch."

"Hmmm."

Sid pulled a wrinkled sheet of loose-leaf from his folder and handed it to me. It had been savaged by the red ink of disapproval.

"Here! Look!" He thrust it into my hands and smashed a particularly dense cluster of red markings with the tip of his index finger. "Now just what the hell is wrong with this sentence? What does she mean, 'Fix phrasing'?"

I read the sentence over a few times. I had no idea what it meant. No idea. At all.

This guy was beyond my help.

But I did my best to help him anyway. I continued to write his papers, but I also trained him for his in-class final. I charged him for both. I taught him the standard formatting for an expository essay. I broke it down in simple terms. I told him how to write an introduction by funneling down from a general statement on his subject to a specific thesis argument. I told him to use the thesis to outline three pieces of evidence from the text to support his argument. I explained that he should use these three pieces of evidence as the basis for the three supporting paragraphs. I told him to use a quote from the text in each paragraph and showed him how to cite the source text. I explained that the conclusion should be a restatement of the main idea and an explanation of how the argument was either confirmed or refuted by the supporting paragraphs.

He said, "Nobody ever explained it like that to me before."

I doubted that it would really matter, though. He'd gotten this far without ever learning how to write. It was all a means to an end, anyway. That end is different for each student, but it is rarely the accumulation of knowledge for its own sake.

So suggests a recent cheating scandal making headlines in Sid's own backyard. In September 2011, Great Neck North High School graduate Sam Eshaghoff was arrested on charges of falsifying his identity in order to take the SAT college entrance boards on behalf of paying customers from his affluent Long Island region. Also arrested were a number of his customers. Since then, according to an article in the *New York Times*, "the Nassau County district attorney's office has broadened its inquiry into suspected cheating on college admissions exams to at least 35 students in five schools, including students believed to have paid for a stand-in to take the ACT, a standardized test that is growing in popularity in the Northeast, as well as the more common SAT."[3]

The scandal, which at the time of this writing was still under investigation, demonstrates both students' sense of the importance of performance in college entrance exams and the kind of emphasis that they place upon it. First, to the sense of importance, it is evident that students who were willing to invest various large sums of money and risk personal and professional ruin felt that they were under significant pressure to succeed. Second, as to the kind of emphasis, the students perceived that a score that might make the difference between a poorly funded state school and a vaunted private university was easily worth the investment of several thousand dollars.

According to a 2011 news report, Eshaghoff's prices started at fifteen hundred dollars and went up from there. The report also notes that "on an exam whose perfect score is 2400, he delivered the goods for his customers. 'Some of the scores,' Nassau County District Attorney Kathleen Rice said at a newsconference, 'were 2220, 2180, 2170.' "[4] Most of the students accused of paying for Eshaghoff's services defied the odds of their poor classroom performances during high school and went on to prestigious colleges. And according to an article produced by Reuters, the highest reported payment accepted by Eshaghoff was a sum of thirty-six hundred dollars.[5]

That the widening inquiry on this subject envelops a region filled with wealthy, high-performing student demographics demonstrates the infiltration of certain consumerist principles into the process of college entrance. And because higher performance on college entrance exams does carry significant and potentially lifelong implications for one's earning potential, both the investment made and the risk taken by the offenders ensnared by this inquiry—as well as by those countless others who have most assuredly exploited without ever being caught the vulnerabilities of a system too highly staked on standardized testing—can be defended, if not as ethical, at least as rational and pragmatic.

For many people of the Millennial generation, there is a rational pragmatism to cheating that did not exist for previous generations. Certainly the accessibility created by the Web strengthens the argument in favor of cheating. But quite frankly, there are a good handful of arguments in favor of cheating that speak to the logic of this generation's experience. Its experience suggests to many of its members not only that they are entitled to certain outcomes but also that this entitlement makes pragmatic and arguably necessary certain behaviors that traditional ethics tell us are wrong and evil.

Sid never for a second questioned the value of my services. And I suspect there was no reason he should have. The last time I saw him was at a party the week after our tutoring session.

"Yo, bro! Come have a drink with me. You are awesome!"

"Hey man, I take it your in-class final went well?"

"Oh, fuck that shit. I already got my transfer, man. Found out the day before. Shit, I don't even know what I wrote. Hah!"

Suddenly, I knew the gratification that Sid's teachers must feel.

So Sid went off to NYU the next year, and probably, thereafter, to a reputable law school and a job in a corner office with potted plants, big windows, and an incredible view. I stayed at Rutgers, where the view could be described as gritty at best. But at least I was getting my career off the ground.

Pragmatism abounded at Rutgers. By my senior year, I had developed a pretty streamlined system, including a set of rules that I stated to all of my clients at the outset. I was to be paid in total up front. The assignment would be delivered by the requested due date and according to the specifications made by the client. Cost would be determined per page and based on how long I had to complete the assignment. If the client received the work and was not satisfied that the specifications had been met, I would be willing to grant an edit. However, once the work was handed in to a professor, all bets were off. I could not personally endorse the act of plagiarism and therefore would note that I did not recommend handing in the custom-written "study guide" for a grade. Thus, I did not guarantee grades. No refunds would ever be issued on the basis of a grade.

I began receiving phone calls from strangers who had heard of my service. I received the calls with total professionalism. I posed a standard line of questions to each individual. How long is the paper? When is it due? What is the subject matter? Are any specific source texts required? Can you provide said texts? Based on these answers, I would quote a price, and we would set a meeting time and location for the exchange of materials.

During one such phone call, which occurred in the moments before the start of my Basic Acting elective, I leaned on the edge of the stage recording the details of a new assignment. When I hung up the phone, a pretty blonde girl from the class approached me. How exciting. What could this lovely lady want?

"Do you write papers?"

Oh. Of course.

"Sure. What do you need?"

"No, actually, I don't need a paper."

Oh? Sweet.

"No. I wanted to tell you, my boyfriend . . ."

D'oh!

". . . my boyfriend works for a company online that writes papers for students. He makes, like, thousands of dollars a month from it."

"Really?"

"Yeah. You should e-mail him. There's a lot of money in this."

Indeed. It was the fall of 2001 when I entered into the nerdly realm of the academic underground. By the approach of my graduation in the spring of 2002, I had long since dispensed with any illusions about doing my own work. I showed up for and passed tests. That was all. I was far too busy doing other people's work. Perhaps my wealthier classmates had the luxury to care about their grades. I cared about getting by with the only marketable skill that I had. We're a generation of pragmatic opportunists, and I would be damned if I was going to give away the only thing I had for free.

CHAPTER 3

The RU Screw

I am not a homicidal maniac.

But I swear, in my weaker moments at Rutgers, I would be cruising through the parking lot, and I'd see one of those meter maids out there with his dumb-ass badge and his pad of tickets, and I'd think to myself, "There's nobody here. It's just me and him. All I have to do is jerk the steering wheel to the right, swerve into him, and mash him up into that Ford Taurus he's about to write up."

No one would know. No one would miss him. But then, of course, another one would just spawn from the oozing sludge he left behind. I never did kill a parking attendant at Rutgers, but I might have been a folk hero if I had.

I wish this were a tangent. I wish that parking tickets had less of a defining role in my experiences at college. Problem is, Parking and Transportation Services was the most efficiently run department in the entire university. It was as if all of the school's resources had been dedicated to punishing scofflaw parkers, and the manpower and resources left for meaningful academic assistance, quality control, and psychological counseling had been utterly depleted.

No department was as well organized as Parking and Transportation. The school couldn't issue you a schedule without two overlapping classes. It couldn't approve your financial aid without losing your paperwork. It couldn't print your transcript without accidentally faxing your medical records to the student listserv. But if your meter had expired twenty seconds ago, you could be damn sure that a parking attendant was already writing your ticket out nineteen seconds ago. Such graceful efficiency.

Rutgers is big, old, and unfriendly. It's like going to school in Dick Cheney.

Rutgers is also, like most colleges, a business. And that's fine and important. But colleges are a special kind of business. It's not simply that some colleges are structured more like corporations than like places of learning. It's that many colleges are shitty businesses that don't give a crap about customer service or quality assurance. They function like your conglomerated cable providers and your giant cell phone carriers and all those other companies that happily take your business but also let you know in no uncertain terms that you need them more than they need you. And when a whole oligarchy of these shitty businesses gets together and agrees to keep prices prohibitively high, classes vastly impersonal, and opportunities for entrance locked into a universally streamlined admissions process, the result is a college experience not unlike a five-year afternoon at the DMV.

Rutgers University treated its students like it didn't really need their loyalty or affection. Those who gave it freely must have found what they were looking for at the sprawling, ghetto-bound school. I can't speak to everybody's experience there. And quite honestly, some of my friends even reflect warmly and nostalgically upon their time there.

But those who had difficulty finding what they were looking for—and I would count myself among them—experienced Rutgers as a preview for a callous, indifferent, infuriating, and inconsiderate world. Surveys suggest that this inhospitable quality is a constant presence.

According to the Princeton Review, which surveys students from 373 college campuses, in 2010 Rutgers ranked eleventh for "Least Beautiful Campus." Just down the turnpike a shade, New Jersey Institute of Technology was tops in that category. In response to the prompt "Are Your Instructors Good Teachers?" Rutgers got the ninth-lowest marks. NJIT got the seventh-lowest. In the category of "Financial Aid Not So Great," Rutgers ranked third, just behind Penn State and two spots ahead of Villanova.

Rutgers ranked eleventh in the category of "Class Discussions Rare." And in a list of 373 colleges, only the University of Toronto ranked worse than Rutgers in terms of the accessibility of professors. So according to the Princeton Review, the professors at Rutgers had the worst office hours of any professors in America.

Of course, I didn't know any of this when I signed up to go there. And it probably wouldn't have mattered if somebody had told me. I was a resident of New Jersey, and it was the only school I could afford that wouldn't have been considered a huge sociological embarrassment given my academic abilities and my 98th percentile SAT scores. As per the advice of my high school guidance counselor, I applied to five schools. I got into three. I had the financial means for only one. And I knew it all along. The admissions process was a charade, so I despondently resisted doing any real research on the subject.

All I really knew was that community college would have meant another year living with my parents. At the time, I'd have robbed a convenience store and turned myself in to the cops just to get out of their house. And so, I was New Brunswick–bound.

For the cost of tuition, room, and board, Rutgers delivers you into the brutal clutches of its bureaucracy and never lets go. Once your check is cashed, they bend you over and start thrusting, and they tell you you'll have to fill this form out in triplicate and submit it through the proper channels just for the reach-around.

They have this really cute thing at Rutgers University called the RU Screw. They probably have it at other colleges as well. It's like a syndrome, a catchall diagnosis for any number of things that are likely to go wrong over the course of one's time at the school owing to the incompetence, negligence, and bureaucratic inefficiency of the university and its personnel, as well as their very genuine indifference toward the student body. I spent more time at college trying to repair scheduling errors, attempting to navigate the endless maze of automated phone systems, standing in lines, filling out forms, haggling with Student Services, and wishing I had simply studied abroad than I did on my schoolwork and my binge drinking combined (and they usually were combined).

Even if I'd wanted to be a diligent student, even if my classes had been compelling, it would have been this way. This college, which I still pay for every single month, was a straight scam, the fourth-largest university in the nation at the time and boasting the leanest staff of administrative personnel this side of the American embassy in Samoa. At a discount price compared to many other universities but a total rip-off when you compared it to something you could actually use, my Rutgers education came with a major caveat to the emptor: You are on your own.

Hence, the RU Screw. This is every symptom of a sick system; every consequence of designing an institution of learning to function like a multinational business; every demonstration of the university's commitment to its corporate sponsors at the expense of its student body; every bit of evidence that the educational goals of the school are secondary to its vitality as a firm. As a client of any type of business, you would like to think that you'd stand up to such shabby treatment, that you'd be indignant, that you'd be all, "I don't have to take this crap."

But with colleges, you really do have to take this crap. As much as you're paying for the experience, it is you—not the college—who is constantly being evaluated. Say you buy a vacuum cleaner from Sears and take it home, and instead of vacuuming, it sends a power surge through your house and blows up all of your kitchen appliances. Suddenly, this shitty vacuum cleaner has cost you a ton of money. So you bring the vacuum cleaner back to Sears to complain. While you're waiting in line, a customer service representative walks up to you with a report card and says, "Based on what we've seen from you during your limited time in the store among several thousand other customers, we think you're a C– shopper."

"But what about my defective vacuum cleaner?" you ask.

To which your customer service representative replies, "There's nothing wrong with the vacuum cleaner. You're just too stupid to know how to use it. By the way, we misplaced your original payment on the vacuum cleaner, and your account with us is now delinquent. You'll be hearing from our attorneys."

It's ludicrous to think that as a customer, you would stand for such an arrangement. But such is the nature of the RU Screw, except that your vacuum cleaner costs somewhere between twenty-four and thirty-six thousand dollars per year, and you'll be paying for it until your Social Security benefits kick in.

Now, I've spent a number of years distancing myself from the day-to-day, bang-your-head-against-a-brick-wall frustration of being a student at this type of institution. So I thought it'd be fun, like a trip down memory lane, to call over to my old friends at Rutgers Parking and Transportation.

I push a few buttons to get through to the Parking Department. Somebody answers and immediately asks me to hold.

"Sure thing," I say.

A female robot voice says, "Thank you for holding. Somebody will be with you in just a moment." Cue the Muzak. Synthetic beats farmed from the opening credits of a motivational film and a jazz flute like Ron Burgundy with a frontal lobotomy.

The sound triggers something terrible and evil inside of me.

I'm tumbling into a well of bad memories the way that a motorcycle backfiring in the distance might take a guy back to 'Nam. I can see a younger version of myself flailing his arms and wantonly spewing profanities in tremors of apoplectic fury, knowing that ol' Charlie Rutgers has gotten the drop on him again.

I remember in an instant the absolute misery that was the school's matrix of automated phone services, understaffed offices, and disgruntled employees.

Now a male robot voice comes on.

"We appreciate your patience while holding. Please continue to hold for just a moment longer so that your call can receive the time and attention it deserves."

The first smooth-jazz abomination fades out, and another one comes in. This one has more of a 1980s-porn-soundtrack feel, with a backbeat that seems almost to thrust over the top of the lead synthesizer and a bass line that just kind of hangs there like a botched boob job.

This whole thing feels really familiar.

I used to skip classes, clear my schedule, and stock the house up with food as if a nor'easter were approaching anytime I had to accomplish something that would require administrative assistance. Nobody in any of Rutgers's offices of Academic Affairs, Student Services, Financial Aid, or Resident Life wanted to be there, and only a fraction of the staff seemed to know their job function . . .

unless that function was to create a maddening hedge maze of bureaucracy where nothing was ever accomplished and absurdity lurked at every bend. If that was the function, the personnel at Rutgers were as utterly brilliant, and as temperamental, as trained seals. Through a workforce of button pushers that could outbitter you on the day that your puppy died, Rutgers University found every way possible to separate the student from his dollars without giving him the recourse to defend himself.

I suffered lost documentation, registration holds, course-credit snafus, and sudden new expenses. I watched my classmates endure disappearing professors, unexplained course de-registrations, and prerequisite lockouts. Putting aside the school's accidental inefficiencies, I could not, for the life of me, figure out why Rutgers was so damn mean.

The female robot voice comes back on.

"We apologize for the delay. Please stay on the line. We will be with you very shortly."

They say that the purpose of Muzak is to provide an innocuous and inoffensive soundtrack that uses lowest common denominator science to achieve universal accessibility. It functions as background noise that doesn't cause you to think too hard about anything of meaning when you're fondling produce in the grocery store, minding your own business in an elevator, or eating in the food court at the mall.

But when it's piping directly into your earhole, it has a whole other purpose. It is designed to piss you off and make you hang up the phone. Four and a half minutes have passed.

The male voice comes back on.

"Thank you for your patience. You will be assisted momentarily. Please stay on the line."

Now I realize that the male and female robots are alternating. They're in on it together. And they're so wretchedly polite.

Another minute and she comes back on.

"Please hold so that your call may receive the time and attention it deserves. Please stay on the line."

It has only been five and a half minutes, and I'm seething anew with long-buried hatred for my archnemesis. I begin to remember the literally thousands of dollars that they took from me. I'm glad this is all coming back to me. I'm calling to find out what they did with all my money.

According to an article in the Rutgers University student-run newspaper the *Daily Targum*, as of 2006, Rutgers was grappling with roughly $3 million in unpaid parking tickets. And in the year 2005, the school had collected $1.3 million in paid parking fines. But things never seemed to get better. Everything was a Kafkaesque exercise in the ridiculous.

There were never new parking spaces. Commuters desperately circled the lots of New Brunswick in search of a place to stow the car before the start of class, sometimes finding none and returning home with no education to speak of for the day.

There were never enough buses. The class periods were close together and the campuses far apart. In the middle of a weekday afternoon, when people were mashed together on an intercampus bus like it was the last transport out of Saigon, you got the feeling that nobody but you really gave a shit about what happened to you and your little education.

It was hard to shake the feeling that they were plotting against you, that this was all part of some absurd conspiracy designed to waylay you on your path to mere adequacy, that your mission was to somehow obtain an education in spite of their best efforts to stand in your way.

No one was better at this than Parking and Transportation.

The people who worked there were a special breed. Among heartless bureaucratic soldiers, these were the Green Berets. They were taught to have rhinoceros skin, to breathe hate cloaked in onions. They were indoctrinated by self-flagellating monks to feel not the twinge of remorse, to know not the ache of compassion, and to fear not the wrath of our indignation. They were trained in tiger cages, poked with cattle prods, told that they were as replaceable as their own undergarments, and forced to listen to Celine Dion on full blast until they actually liked it. By the time we came to them angry and defeated, they were carved from stone. We were nothing to them but a source of revenue.

To be sure, the school prioritized Parking and Trans above education, as though the reason we were there was to defy all laws of physics by parking matter where no space existed. According to the university's current website, "Unpaid tickets and late fees"—a crime of which I was guilty on any occasion when I chose to spend money on food and toilet paper instead—"will result in a university hold barring students from":

Class registration
New parking permits
Receiving grades
Receiving transcripts
Permit refunds—ticket and late fee amounts will be deducted
Graduation

So, pretty much everything. The successful completion of your education depends on whether or not you've paid your parking tickets. I want to know why this is.

Seven minutes on the phone.

The robot guy tells me, "Your call is very important to us. You will be assisted as soon as possible. Please continue to hold."

My mind starts to wander. I wonder how close the robot man and woman are. Are they friends? More than friends? Do they share a loveless marriage and a few bratty robot children? Whatever the status of their personal relationship, they're a great tag team. Between the two of them and the smooth jazz, it only takes seven and a half minutes before I start to think about hanging up, eight and a half before I start to think about killing myself, and nine before I start to think about killing somebody else. I wish I had outgrown these feelings, but . . . I had a bad experience.

Why should the school so aggressively victimize its own students? Is the financial situation at Rutgers so dire that it has no choice but to carry out this aboveboard form of extortion.

Gimme all your money or the transcript gets it!

Well, it seems that every year, Rutgers stands before the New Jersey Legislature with its hat in its hands, begging for more public assistance. The poor public educational institution, the victim of cold governmental indifference, Princeton's talent-deprived neighbor.

Well, maybe there's something to that. According to an investigative report conducted by the *Bloomberg News* website in 2011, the History Department at Rutgers is so cash-strapped that its professors were forced to surrender their desk phones in 2009. The move was designed to save the school twenty-one thousand dollars annually.

Bloomberg reports that the History Department also shrank its doctoral program by 25 percent. The department has cut the number of Ph.D. candidates that it can field annually down to between twelve and fourteen, from sixteen to eighteen.

And with the recession worsening, leading to budget crunches at the state level, the university was forced to place a freeze on professor salaries. Professors were also instructed that they should give fewer tests to save money on photocopies. Professors were told in an e-mail in December 2010 that they could be billed personally for failing to cut down on photocopies. And professors are now being asked to pay for access to electronic journals that, until this point, they have had at their disposal for free. (It bears noting, here, that some of the paper-writing companies for which I have worked provide their contractors with access to such journals free of charge.)

According to the *Bloomberg* article, "state funding for Rutgers in the three fiscal years ending in June 2012 fell $29 million, or 10 percent, to $262 million . . . Tuition and mandatory fees jumped 7.3 percent over the same period to $12,755 for state students. The 2,800-member faculty hasn't received a raise since January 2010, according to Patrick Nowlan, executive director of the professors' union."[1]

With some professors departing for better-paying work, academic resources have become yet scarcer. In my experience, the school's overcrowding was apparent at every turn, with stuffed lecture halls and students getting turned away from classes at registration. So as I wait on the phone for a human being, I consider that Rutgers may have financial imperatives for the way it behaves. Maybe it's not just a crappy heartless corporation. Maybe it's a victim of the times.

"Thank you for holding. We appreciate your patience. Somebody will be with you in just a moment."

Eleven minutes.

So it would appear that Rutgers is struggling. It would be surprising to find out, then, that Rutgers is tops among all state universities in providing financial subsidies for its athletics programs.

What?

That doesn't sound right. The same Rutgers that's always asking its professors to tighten their belts? The same Rutgers that's always forcing its students to make sacrifices for the greater good? The same Rutgers that continues to inherit the catastrophic financial problems of its parent state? That Rutgers? That can't be right.

Let me check it again.

According to *Bloomberg*, "at Rutgers, of the $26.9 million given to subsidize athletics in fiscal 2010, $18.4 million came from university coffers, top among state schools in the Atlantic Coast, Big East, Big Ten, Big 12, Pac-12 and Southeastern Conferences.

"The other $8.4 million came from student fees, where Rutgers ranks fifth."

In a totally unrelated matter, Rutgers University raised its tuition fees by 8.5 percent in 2008 and proposed another 3.6 percent increase in the summer of 2011.

According to Newark's *Star-Ledger*, Rutgers has spent more than $115 million in university subsidies and student fees on athletics since 2006. The *Star Ledger* identifies this amount as the "highest of any public school and nearly twice the subsidy of the next highest college among the power conferences."

The recently departed* Rutgers football coach Greg Schiano, who amassed a 68–67 record across eleven seasons with the university, made $2.03 million after bonuses in 2010, when the average salary was $142,000 for full-time professors, $96,000 for associate

---

*Schiano was hired as head coach of the NFL's Tampa Bay Buccaneers following a 2011 season that helped him eke out a career winning record at Rutgers.

professors, and $49,000 for non-tenure-track instructors, accord-ing to the professors' union.[2] This is to say nothing of the forgive-ness of $100,000 in home loans that the university gifts to the coach annually. The school also pays $500 a month for women's basketball coach Vivian Stringer's recreational golfing activities.

According to the *Bloomberg* article, Rutgers Athletics reported a *net operational loss of $2.2 million in 2010.*

Now, I'm a sporting gent. I enjoy a spirited match. I appreciate a good competition. But this just strikes me as a shitty business model, the kind that deprives the university of personnel for simple functions like helping new students register for classes or helping returning students develop independent studies . . . or . . . or an-swering the fucking phone at fucking Parking and Transportation!

"We appreciate your patience while holding. Please continue to hold for just a little longer so that your call receives the time and attention it deserves."

"Answer the fucking phone!" I shout into the dark Muzakal nothingness.

"Thank you for holding. Please stay on the line. We will be with you very shortly."

Twelve and a half minutes and, suddenly, a human being on the other end.

"Hello." She already sounds pissed off. *She's* pissed.

"Hi. I'm conducting an independent study, and I'm hoping you can help me out. I just have a few questions about revenue from Parking and Transportation."

"Mm-hmm. Hold, please."

"Ummm."

Back to the robot lady.

"We appreciate your patience. Please be assured that your call will receive the time and attention it deserves when we return to the line."

The human being comes back after five minutes and offers me an e-mail address, one of those generic administrative e-mail ad-dresses with an abbreviated job title but no name.

"Is there a name of somebody that I might address it to?"

"No. But e-mail that address and it will get to the right person."

Of course. I had forgotten. It was a rule of thumb at Rutgers that you never got anything done in fewer than three tries. And if you couldn't get it done in three, you'd never get it done and that was that. I took down the e-mail address along with her assurance that somebody would actually respond to me.

I wrote the following e-mail:

To Whom It May Concern:

I'm a Rutgers Alumnus and I'm conducting an independent study for a book about the costs of college for today's student. I was hoping that you could answer a few basic questions about Parking and Transportation policies and revenues at the university. Please provide me with whatever information is available. Your assistance is most appreciated.

I thank you in advance for your prompt and thoughtful responses.

Thanks so much and I will look forward to hearing from you.

Very Truly Yours,
Dave Tomar

What is your position/title at Rutgers Parking and Transportation?

What are some of the projects that the revenues collected from parking tickets are used for at the university?

Could you tell me about some specific projects conducted or completed using parking ticket revenue? Please include dates, project costs and any other details that might be relevant.

How much revenue has PATS [Parking and Transportation Services] collected from paid parking tickets for each of the following years?

2010?
2009?
2008?
2007?
2006?
2005?

What are some of the projects that the revenues collected from university-issued parking permits are used for at the university?

How much revenue has PATS collected from student/faculty-purchased parking permits for each of the following years?
2010?
2009?
2008?
2007?
2006?
2005?

How many employees does PATS employ?

In years past, it was possible to negotiate a reduced settlement of large balances in unpaid fines. Recent investigation indicates this is no longer true. Has this reduced settlement policy changed and if so, why?

Student Facebook pages report consistent incidences of "double-ticketing" or even "triple-ticketing," in which students have received multiple tickets simultaneously for a single offense such as an expired meter. What is PATS' policy on double-ticketing and triple-ticketing?

Thanks again for your thoughtful responses.

Three days later, I followed up, forwarding my original e-mail and adding this message:

At your nearest opportunity, please reply to confirm that you have received this correspondence.

Thanks so much,
Dave Tomar

I was surprised to receive the following message within the hour:

Dave Tomar,

This has been received but we are in our busy season already so this will take a little while to get back to you. You have requested a lot of information that is not readily available.

Sincerely,

[name excised] AICP/PP–Director
Rutgers University–Dept. of Transportation Services
Administration and Public Safety Division
55 Commercial Avenue, New Brunswick, NJ 08901

Well, some of the information is readily available, anyway. Here are the revenues and revenue increases produced by Rutgers Parking and Transportation Services as presented in the university's 2010 annual financial report:

RUTGERS UNIVERSITY PARKING: NET REVENUE

Year	Revenue	Rate of Increase from Previous Year
2005	$5,643,000	/
2006	$5,762,000	2.10%
2007	$6,085,000	5.60%
2008	$6,468,000	6.30%
2009	$6,994,000	8.10%

There's not a lot of context here. We don't know, because they wouldn't tell me, how much money the school spends on making parking available, or how that figure compares to its budget for anything else. All I can really do with this information is observe that $7 million is a fuckload of money and that, for some reason that I'm sure has nothing to do with the school's alleged financial problems, students were victimized by Parking and Transportation at a rate that increased by 23.9 percent between 2005 and the end of 2009. Have students simply become more irresponsible with their cars, or is there a concerted initiative on the part of PATS to increase the school's revenues by fleecing its students? According to the 2010 financial report, the university recorded a revenue from parking that was $1,927,000 greater than that reported for the collection of loan payments from students and employees.

Now I had even more questions for the AICP/PP–director.

I replied immediately.

Mr. [name excised]

Thanks so much for your reply. Any information that you are able to locate would be most appreciated. Can I expect that you will be my primary contact for this?

I will await a response at your convenience.

Dave

Technically, that was my third attempt. I'll let you know when I hear from them.

I never got any answers when I was there. Why should it be any different now? I should have my head examined for even attempting to jump back into it. I made it out in four years, which at Rutgers is like getting out early for good behavior.

That is because there is a pattern at Rutgers that is perhaps even more insidious than the bureaucratic misery, the constant administrative bungling, and even the parking gestapo. This is the unabashed lie that Rutgers is a "four-year college." I was a communication major for one reason and one reason only: It cost less. As soon as I realized I was getting ripped off at my college, I did everything in my power to graduate as fast as possible without spending an extra cent. I sat down with my adviser in my sophomore year, and course by course we laid out everything that I would need to do to graduate on time. And I did it. No summer courses, no winter-break courses, and four years on the nose. I was one of the lucky ones, and in a shrinking minority, both at Rutgers and elsewhere.

A 2009 article in *USA Today* quoted the conservative think tank American Enterprise Institute as reporting that "nationally, four-year colleges graduated an average of just 53% of entering students within six years, and 'rates below 50%, 40% and even 30% are distressingly easy to find.' "[3]

I think I know why this happens. And it is no accident.

At Rutgers, you never knew what it was going to be. But you knew that at any given moment, the RU Screw could swoop in and derail your progress.

The kinds of technicalities exemplifying the RU Screw were amazing and rampant during my time at Rutgers, and they often overshadowed the simple need to focus on one's studies.

The school was huge and seemed to have fairly modest standards for the types of students that it would admit. But try getting into a class that you desperately needed to stay on track in your major, and suddenly it was like trying to sneak into a country club through the service entrance.

And really, I hate to sound paranoid, but I'll never forget this moment.

I had finally done it. I was graduating. I had two more finals to go, but my grades were all pretty solid. My credits were all in order. I had already RSVP'd a xerox of my butt to the graduation party committee. Time to go.

Then I got a phone call from a woman at the Office of the Registrar.

"Is this David Tomar?"

Oh crap.

"Yes."

"Hi. David. We've been reviewing your file . . ."

"Yeah? And?"

"Yes. We've been reviewing your file, and though you are slated to graduate, it appears that you are three credits shy of completion of your major."

"Bullcrap! I have 123 credits!"

"Yes. I understand that, but you are three credits shy of completion of your communication major."

"Impossible! That's not possible!"

"Mr. Tomar, there's no need to shout!"

"Absolutely there's a need to shout! Don't tell me, two days before I graduate, that I'm three credits shy! I've been following the same course agenda for three years. I made it with my adviser. I did everything I was supposed to do, and I never failed a class!"

"What it appears happened, if you'll just calm down, what it appears has happened is that one of the required 300-level courses in your major was moved to a different course category, so that one of the humanities that you took no longer counts as a humanities prerequisite. So you'll need to review the course catalog and pick an appropriate course to compensate."

"The hell I will! You call me now? Right now? And you tell me that a course I took two years ago, in the time since I completed it, is no longer a prerequisite in my major? And you think that makes sense? You think that's OK?"

"Don't worry. You'll still be allowed to walk in graduation. You'll just need to take this course during a summer session."

"Allowed? I graduated. It's my right, lady. There's no way, there's no way this is for real! Where were you two years ago? Forget that. This can't even be legal. You can't retroactively change that shit up on me and come at me looking for more money. If you want more of my money, go talk to the people at Parking. They've got all of it. But this is crap, and I will call a lawyer if I have to."

"Sir. There's no reason to lose your temper."

"Oh, it's lost. After all the crap I've put up with at this school, I'm finally done. And I did everything I had to. I will not be screwed by this university again. You have no right. How can you call me up like this, not even apologize, and start telling me that I have to put my whole life on hold because of a clerical error?"

"Well, sir, you can just review the course catalog . . ."

"Don't tell me to review the catalog. You review it. Review a law book. You can't do this to me. I mean, what is this?"

"Pardon?"

"I mean, what the hell is this? Is this a conspiracy? Are you conspiring to keep me from graduating? Is this a scam?" I know I sounded paranoid, but I couldn't think of any other explanation. I was yelling and spitting, and I figured I probably sounded pretty crazy. But I couldn't help it. I kept going. "Answer me! What are you trying to do to me? *Is-this-a-scam!?*"

"Hmm. I'm so sorry. It appears that we made a mistake."

"Huh?"

"Yes. Actually, I'm looking now, and we have made a mistake. Your credits will all apply to your major."

"So, wait. So, now I am going to graduate?"

"Yes. Everything is in order. Sorry for the confusion. Thank you for your time."

Click.

I was mystified. It wouldn't even be the last clerical error of the school's that I dealt with. I didn't go to graduation, so they actually sent me the wrong degree in the mail. I called and told them, and they just issued me another one. Now I have two. If I'd had any doubts before, now I knew for sure that it really was just a piece of paper, an insanely expensive piece of paper. Still, if anybody asks, I'm a double major. Believe me, I've earned it.

CHAPTER 4

The Quarter-Life Crisis

Just out of school, I was angry. I guess a lot of kids are, really. I had always had this Holden Caulfield–ish suspicion that everything was bullshit. I basically figured that the world is filled with frauds, and many of them are so worried about being figured out that they'll never stop to scrutinize you. I realized I could fake my way through anything.

Such was the nature of the world into which I had been thrust. The Bush administration was a travesty. The wars were a disgrace. The corporate scandals were outrageous. And here I was, like so many students, hurled into adulthood like a screaming, naked infant with a terrible debt-to-income ratio.

I moved back to my parents' house in South Jersey. This, of course, made me want to kill myself. I didn't even unpack my stuff from college. I just kept my boxes all stacked up and unlabeled in the garage. I no longer had a car. It was summer in the suburbs, and I was trapped. You couldn't walk around my neighborhood if you weren't a middle-aged mother in swooshy nylon jogging pants. A sweaty young man with long hair and a beard wandering the sidewalks of my parents' neighborhood? You could see anxious suburbanites peering through curtains at you, trying to decide if you warranted pity or a call to the cops.

I couldn't really go anywhere. I found a folding chair in the garage, brought it up to my room, and worked on my sister's old, hissing desktop PC. My student loan repayment began immediately. Again, I thought about faking my own death. This time, I got as far as a vaguely formed plan involving a wheat thresher and a mannequin that I would steal from Macy's. I was going to start over again in Canada with a big wooly coat and a brand-new name. Let the plastic shards of mannequin worry about student loan debt.

I told my parents about my plan. My father, rational thinker that he was, suggested that a med school cadaver might be more convincing. I respect my parents. They believe in tough love. They would lend a hand here or there, but my relative desperation was my own problem. They cared enough to let my body occupy the room they aspired to make into an office and storage place for luggage. I had my friends over for marathon weed-smoking sessions just down the hall from them. We would open the windows, towel the door, and turn my bedroom into an Allman Brothers concert.

I would stay out late, come home, accidentally wake the dog, and disrupt the quiet state of the house. There is zero living compatibility between a college graduate and his parents. They had a nice lifestyle to which they were entitled, and I had a seedy lifestyle that could not realistically be pursued under their roof. I had to get out. Problem was, I was the only one of my local friends who had finished school in four years. Some were heading on to graduate school. Some were preparing for super-senior status, awarded to those who needed at least one more year (sometimes two or three) to finish their chosen course of study. Some were still toiling with summer courses and inching toward completion.

All I could do was send out my thin résumé with my worthless degree(s) and my nonsense transcript to anybody who would read it. In the meantime, I was firing out writing of any kind. I was writing album reviews. I was producing humor pieces on relevant cultural issues. I continued to write my weekly political humor column for the *Outside World*. And for a salary of "exposure," I gave my writing to anybody who would post it.

I was also turning out as many papers as I could in the dead of summer. Pickings were slim. There are summer courses, schools on trimester schedules, and multi-semester research projects. You might have five to ten assignments to choose from at any one time. Any of the desirable ones, I was learning, go fast during the slow season. Desirable assignments are papers related to organizational theory, human resources, sociological theory, philosophy, history, political science, psychology, or any of those other fields where you can substitute fancy words for research and get away with it. Assignments requiring financial analysis, graphing, computer programming, or comprehensive scientific elaboration tend not to go as fast. So sometimes you simply have to take on a terrible, lengthy, and painful assignment just to keep the bucks coming in.

And it was my only source of income, so I knuckled down and wrote some shit that I was less than qualified to write: stuff about genetic coding, the behavior of certain proteins in the body's immune system, and euclidean geometric theories; detailed logistical evaluations of health care legislation and deconstructions of the language used in *Beowulf*. (Just for the record on this last one: Stop making kids learn *Beowulf*. *Beowulf* makes me feel like I'm retrieving an account of history as scrawled by twelve different ancient nationalities on a series of crumpled-up cocktail napkins and ATM receipts. I'm not saying it's culturally irrelevant. I'm saying it's an exercise in sadism.)

I admit, I took on many bits of work that, in the wee hours of the night, I would come to regret. But there is no way out. Once you've taken the assignment, it's yours and it must be completed. With every piece of work I completed, I squirreled away another few dollars for my eventual escape.

So this was the summer after graduation, filled with all the promise and anticipation of waiting in line to use a public toilet.

It wasn't until my buddy Mickey finished his summer semester that I finally had a real job prospect. Mickey was a few years younger, not yet graduated and only home for the summer. But his cousin had a stake in a family-owned business called Crackerjack Cleaning Company that specialized in industrial cleaning supplies. His cousin's partner, Mr. Lewis, was a guy who had spent a year in the can for white-collar crimes. He swore that he had been set up by the government, and quite frankly, I actually believed him, even though he was a habitual bullshitter.

Mickey would pick me up, and we'd drive across the bridge into Pennsylvania, then past Philly, through strip mall country, and into Conshohocken. We packaged products, shipped orders, and fielded angry customer complaints. I used about 1 percent of my brain while I was there, most of it on finishing the daily crossword puzzle during bathroom breaks.

I continued to write papers on the side, often piecing assignments together during the course of a workday, popping onto the computer whenever Mr. Lewis wasn't looking and punching out a few sentences. Still, I implored my new boss to use my writing skills. I told him that this was truly where my abilities would best be put to use.

He immediately put me to work bottling fluids. We made industrial-power odor neutralizers, designed for use in morgues and crime-scene cleanup. We had a spray that was designed to remove and destroy the most unpleasant odors. We called it "dead people spray," and we had to bottle and cap it manually in two-ounce containers drawn from a drum about the size of a Chrysler. We used it to cover the smell of weed when we smoked in the car on the weekends.

With respect to writing, my boss did have me edit some of his e-mails. So glad I went to college for that.

I suppose there were other jobs out there. I couldn't get them. It's for the best, too. I learned a lot at that little company. I learned a lot about business.

I could come down on my boss, but it wasn't just him.

I learned that in the mainstream, everybody is dishonest everywhere. The clients we dealt with, the industry we were in, the business that we sustained . . . all crooked. Every day was a combination of deceptions, little white lies, misrepresentations, slight bendings of the facts, and dramatic distortions of reality. And this was in a business that had no reason, conceptually speaking, to behave unethically.

Still, at Crackerjack we misled our customers as a matter of course. We told them products were shipping out when we hadn't even received the materials to make them. We hadn't received the materials because we had defaulted with our creditors. We usually told our creditors stuff like "I sent that payment last week. Let me check the FedEx tracking number and get back to you."

As for the working conditions, our paychecks got bounced, we were instructed to lie to clients, and the boss even peppered our conversations with the occasional ethnic slur.

It wasn't all bad, though. As bosses go, he did more damage to his own company than he did to me. I worked with relative freedom. A guy like that doesn't look over your shoulder while you're working. He's way too busy looking over his own shoulder.

He had a lavish lifestyle, ate heartily, drank aggressively, and was actually entertaining company at a party. I admit, outside of the office, I actually liked the guy. So this was the business world.

And then Enron, and WorldCom, Adelphia and Tyco, Martha Stewart and Bernie Madoff, etc., etc., etc. The whole straight world, it seemed to me at the time, was a lot of self-righteous grandstanding. No one was really straight.

I actually felt better about the papers I was writing on the side than I did about the work I was doing on the grid. I didn't feel especially honest doing it, but then again, I didn't feel especially honest when I was bottling dead people spray, either.

Still, after three months on the job, I had saved up enough for half a deposit on an apartment. Just as Mickey went back to school for fall semester, my old high school buddy and freshman-year college roommate, Ethan Tabernacle, finished his last summer session. His mother had just moved to Florida, so we bought a bunch of roach traps and went in on a place in South Philly together. I got Ethan a job at the industrial cleaning supply company, and we carpooled to work.

So now I was working full-time as a fluid bottler and part-time as a hack writer. With respect to my college education, I had graduated with nothing but financial regrets. College had bankrupted me, and every month it came knocking on my door.

Ethan and I lived on South Street, a place that had once fancied itself an East Coast Haight-Ashbury, teeming with hippie boutiques, art galleries, performance venues, and restaurants.

In 1963, Philadelphia natives and proliferators of the dance sensation the Wah-Watusi the Orlons hit number three on the *Billboard* chart with "South Street," a place where "all the hippies meet."

At the height of its popularity, in the sixties and seventies, South

Street was a bohemian mecca in a blue-collar town, attracting independent businesses, pedestrian nightlife, and all manner of street busking.

By the time of our arrival there in late 2002, your options were pretty much "Bennie and the Jets" on repeat coming from the speakers in front of Johnny Rockets or a mid-fifties homeless guy playing abominable Jimi Hendrix covers on his Stratocaster knock-off in front of the Subway hoagie shop. Anytime I walked by on my way to Repo Records or the cheesesteak joint under Fat Tuesday's, he would smile at me and slaughter Cream's "Sunshine of Your Love."

The popular haunts that had once drawn a flourishing nightlife had largely been moved, sold off, dismantled, or abandoned. Empty storefronts and aging For Rent signs pockmarked the main drag between Front and Eighth Streets. Zipperheads was gone. Punks would have to go elsewhere now for their gigantic safety pins. The Book Trader had closed up and relocated to the more fashionable Old City. It had been a cavernous place with staircases, crawl spaces, and piles organized according to precariousness. You could spend a day in there and buy nothing. It was replaced by a baggy-pants store.

Directly across the street from our apartment was a swingers' club called Karma Sutra. My friend Minnie, who was in the real estate business, had been inside and said there was one big room upstairs filled with mattresses and lord knows what manner of parasites. One of our favorite pastimes was to stand on our second-floor deck stubbing out cigarettes and guessing which people were about to enter Karma Sutra. The smart money was always on a middle-aged couple, he with a Mr. Clean haircut, she with a high leather skirt and exposed cottage cheese thigh. They almost always carried little handbags that we imagined had all kinds of awful gadgets in them.

Eventually, Karma Sutra closed and—I say this in truth and not for cheap laughs—was replaced by a fish restaurant called Bottom of the Sea. To everything there is a season.

Both before our arrival and during our time there, South Street was in a steady decline. By weekday, it was a barren place where

you had to walk carefully to avoid stepping in whatever the previous evening's last-call revelers had expelled onto the sidewalk. By
weekend night, it was a playground for roving flash mobs from
Camden, New Jersey—often ranked as the most dangerous city in
America and just a charming ferry ride away.

South Street was in a sorry state. We fit in like pigs in shit.

We took turns forgetting to pay bills. I'd let the cable get turned
off, apologize, and promise to get it switched back on. He'd let the
electricity get turned off, apologize, and promise to get it switched
back on. It was a good system.

A lot of mornings, we drove in silence to the little one-story
facility out by the railroad tracks. The sign near the entrance to
the parking lot said Dead End. That isn't symbolism. That is just
literally the last thing you would see before walking into work.

Working at a place like this only intensified my interest in paper writing.

The world was a crooked place, and I was no Boy Scout. There
are more evil things that one can do than defraud a university.
And at the time, I really felt that it was one of the finest things
that I could do. My university had defrauded me.

It had sold me on Walden Pond and given me Walmart instead.

At the time, I didn't attempt to rationalize what I was doing. I
just genuinely felt that I was defrauding an institution that deserved it. Boo-fucking-hoo for the schools. They were still getting
paid. They were still cranking out students. And to a certain extent I still believe that they couldn't have given a steaming pile of
shit whether the work was genuine or not.

Besides, I wanted to do something subversive. I didn't want to
be some schmuck in a cubicle, and the way I saw it, that's all that
my college had aspired to prepare me for. I wanted to give a huge
middle finger to the system. What's more, I saw that the system was
wounded. I wanted to salt my middle finger, stick it in the wound,
and twist it around. I was like the child of a neglectful parent.
You'd do anything to get attention from your parent, but you'd really like for it to be negative attention. You'd really like to be able
to hold yourself up to them and say, "You see? You see what you
made me do?"

I wanted to fuck shit up. I wanted arrogant professors to be undermined. I wanted schools to experience the true consequences of their stagnation. I wanted lazy students to enter life without preparation and always suffer the uncertainty and insecurity that comes with the fear of getting caught. I hoped that all the dishonest slobs who made up the world would give me their money, just a couple of dollars at a time, to gain their education.

And I wanted to learn. I wanted to know things. I wanted to be well-rounded. I wanted to engage in a complex, even revelatory exploration of those things that might help me to better define myself and those things that might be used to improve the life I was leading. I wanted all those things that I'd thought I was paying for when I went to college. I had left school with a need, and for all the pressure that my parents applied to the contrary, I knew that this need would be met neither through graduate school nor through the continuing accumulation of debt. The idea that I could somehow justify taking out more loans for more schooling . . . well, that just seemed ridiculous to me.

I didn't always intend to leave my crappy job to start writing papers full-time. I looked for other jobs, sent out writing samples, and interviewed when granted the opportunity. A job did not readily present itself.

I picked up my newspaper one morning. An article professed to offer some advice on how graduating college kids should prepare for the frigid job market. The number-one piece of counsel that the article had to offer was "Lower your expectations."

One would be better served, the article asserted, working below one's level of educational attainment. Check.

According to the article, I had no reason to go out and look for another job. What a relief.

This job was unbearable, it was humiliating, and I was getting dumber every day that I spent there. Use it or lose it, as they say. If I hadn't been writing papers on the side, I would have been making a real good future for myself as a manual bottler of fluids. Not trying to impress you, but I never took any classes to do it.

Bubbling under this layer of discontent, and hiding behind the long brick wall that runs along the whole north side of South Street between Seventh and Eighth, a tiny little business was in its first year of operation. I had referred Ethan to the paper-writing company I had worked with since college. He had never really written before, but he was a sharp guy. He threw together a quick writing sample and got the job. Now the unofficially named South Street Paper Company was a collective of two freelancers, two cats, and a grab bag of trash-picked furniture and twice-moved pieces from Ikea.

In college, a space half the size of our apartment would have been shared among four guys—one of them almost always a deranged psychopath or a person with severe hygiene deficiencies. So the two-floor cookie cutter one flight of stairs off of street level was like a palace to us. And as we had just departed from New Brunswick, Newark's even less impressive little brother, the beer-can- and pizza-crust-littered thoroughfare of South Street might as well have been a canal in Venice.

We had two bedrooms, one and a half bathrooms, a garage whose door didn't close, and a semifunctional washer-dryer set. As far as we were concerned, this was what the Jeffersons were singing about. We finally got a piece of the pie.

The first floor of our pie slice contained a galley kitchen with a doorway on either side; the space was narrow enough that the stove opened into the adjacent cabinets and short enough that you could enter and exit in the same stride. There was also one big room and one small room. The big room had only one thing in it: a pool table that my friend Donovan Root had no other place to store. We didn't really have room for it either, but priorities being what they are to a couple of intermittently single men, we broke it down at Donovan's place in Boston and reconstructed it in Philadelphia.

There was about a foot and a half of space on either side, enough for a nonportly individual to pass through. Eighty percent of shots were short-stick shots.

This left the small side room, probably intended for a credenza and a few folding chairs at most, to serve as our office. We took turns throwing on records, ridiculing our customers, and occasionally glancing over resentfully at one another for making disruptive accidental sounds like throat clearing and sneezing.

Every few hours, a double-decker tour bus would drive by. A person at the front of the bus would stand with microphone in hand telling people where stuff used to be when there was stuff down here to see. It would pass right by our windows, so that we were eye-to-eye with visiting midwesterners and their camera lenses. We kept one of those disposable cameras between our desks so that when they took their invasive pictures of us in our natural habitat, all they got were some dudes taking pictures right back at them.

At four A.M., a thirty-foot semi would park in front of the Domino's Pizza directly across from our place and leave its engine running, lower its mechanical ramp, roll its clattering skids across the sidewalk and into the store, roll the skids back to the truck, raise the mechanical ramp back up, and then do it all over again. This process usually ended at around five twenty. Fortunately, it only occurred five nights a week. I slept like a baby . . . in a bowling alley.

This was life at the South Street Paper Company.

The website that we worked for used a "writers' board" system. Every writer the company hired would select a user ID and password. This would allow the individual access to a bulletin board.

The bulletin board was where all customer orders showed up. Every time somebody's credit card was approved for the purchase of a nine-page paper on racial profiling or a five-page explanation of yoga's spiritual implications, the new item would appear on the board. Each item was assigned a corresponding ID number so that the customer, the writer, and the customer service department could keep track of it.

The following is an example of how an assignment that might show up on the board would be presented to a potential writer:

ID: 112123
Subject: Bovine Mating Behaviors
Writing Level: College (4th yr)

Pages: 6
Sources: 8
Citation: MLA
Pay: $72
Due Date: Sept. 7
Details: Write a paper detailing bovine mating behaviors, in-
    cluding courtship, gender dynamics, and the actual physical
    procedures relating to hot cow-on-bull action . . .

Next to the assignment was a button that said "Write It." Once
a writer clicked the "Write It" button, he or she was committed
to completing the assignment by the indicated deadline. An automated e-mail would be sent to the writer containing the selected
assignment's details, including a link to the "source board," where
faxed journal articles, scanned classroom handouts, and pdfs sent
by the customer could be downloaded for reference. From this
point forward, any correspondence between writer and client would
take place through the personal message board provided on the
company's website.

A line item would also appear on the writer's personal board,
starting with the assignment's ID number. The writer's personal
board would also keep a monthly tally of the number of completed
papers, the number of assignments submitted late, and the amount
of money earned. When ready to submit a completed assignment,
the writer would click on the line item and upload the paper, which
would then be sent directly to the customer. The customer's credit
card would be charged, and the writer's account would be cred-
ited for the amount earned. We got paid monthly by way of direct
deposit.

Which means that whatever I'd submitted by 11:59 P.M. on the
last night of the month, that's what I would have to live on for the
next thirty days. So historically, you could find me, on the thirtieth or the thirty-first of a month, occasionally gasping for air before dunking my head back down and bobbing for more papers.

And my company had an excellent system, so much so that I
immediately became addicted to taking on assignments, more than
I could handle, really, while also working a nine-to-five. Anytime I

finished an assignment, there were two more or five more or ten more on the writers' board. At most times, aside from in the dead of summer or during winter vacation, there was rarely anything less than forty papers to choose from. During midterms and finals, this number would rise into the eighties and nineties.

I barely looked at deadlines, and I almost never finished reading an assignment's directions before clicking "Write It." I looked at the length and the pay and scanned well enough to confirm that the assignment didn't call for any quantum mathematics. This told me all I needed to know. At this early stage in my career, I always kept five or six assignments waiting for me on the schedule.

Ethan, too, found that he had a penchant for the charms and challenges of life as the perpetual student. In the morning, we would carpool in miserable silence to our day job. In the evening, we would actually apply our college education while those around us simply wrote about it on their résumé.

Ethan tended toward English literature, political science, and philosophy, the last of which he really had a knack for. He had a great sense of humor and carried a tremendously dark place inside of him that was perfectly suited for paying gigs about nihilism and the rationalizations given for acts of institutional evil.

With our backs to each other, Miles Davis bouncing recklessly off the drywall in the little space, a bowl of weed passed constantly and wordlessly between us, burnt coffee and stale fart hanging in the air, we sold away our intellectual property, bits and pieces at a time.

CHAPTER 5

Twenty Years of Schooling and They Put You on a Day Shift . . .

In my early twenties, I discovered the perfect recipe for seasonal depression. Start with a mindless day job. Preferably, it should be something highly repetitive, emotionally thankless, and intrinsically empty. Also, it's a big help if you can find a place with fluorescent lights, bright white walls, and machinery that constantly hums.

Now try leaving every morning for your job while the sun is still hiding behind a wintry mass of clouds. Stay indoors until five P.M., preferably taking your lunch inside an empty or otherwise impersonal room. Leave for home thirty minutes after the sun has gone down and get your only dose of vitamin D from the can of tuna you have for dinner.

Working my nine-to-five felt like life in Alaska during those months when the sun is so briefly out that you could take a dump and miss it.

And once that was over, once I was home and fed, I would immerse myself in history's greatest sources of misery.

Write a ten-page paper on AIDS in Africa; a six-pager on the Manson Family murders; a dozen pages on the connection between violent video games and chronic masturbation. Explain the wanton criminal behavior of the Bush administration; the brazen corruption of the Bulgarian government; the gross hysteria of the Salem witch trials. Whip up a quick reflection on the massive human suffering created in the impoverished former states of the collapsed Soviet Union; the psychological complexity of the Nuremberg

Trials; the disturbing failure of EuroDisney to excite discerning Frenchmen.

Detail the ethnic cleansing in Bosnia and Herzegovina; the ecological destruction wrought by ExxonMobil; Wall Street's dismantling of the American economy; the spiritual indiscretions of pedophile priests; the nearing extinction of the world's seafood; the proliferation of obesity, juvenile diabetes, and McDonald's; the connection between tooth decay and methamphetamines; and the dangers latent in our own drinking water.

Explain why Palestinians and Israelis hate each other; why Tutsi and Hutu hate each other; why the Chechens can't stand the Russians; why the North Koreans don't care for the South Koreans; why Ireland loathes England; why India despises Pakistan; why everybody seems to hate the Kurds; why the Nazis hate everybody; and why everybody loves Raymond.

I have to tell you, this is one hell of a way to spend your evenings. I was probably getting laid less during this period of time than during any other in my young adult life. Note: It is never productive to bring up the tragic plight of ethnic Albanians while attempting to pick up a girl at a bar. Even if she's intrigued, this conversation won't lead to sex.

It was a dark time in my life. I was adrift in a sea of bleak opportunities. I was alone. I had Ethan around. But he was alone too. Such is the nature of growing up, standing on the terrifying threshold of adulthood with a childlike sense that nothing has prepared you properly for this moment. Only your future failures will suffice to teach you a thing.

I spoke quite rarely to my parents after moving out, a state of affairs that I think resulted from our mutual embarrassment over what I appeared to be becoming. Perhaps it was too soon to call me a failure. But certainly, I was a disappointment. A handful of squandered talent, all the straight As that a third grader's mother could want, all the ambition to learn, to know, to become more. Now I was just an angry jerk with a shitty job, just barely affording a crummy apartment.

I was born into a world of good fortune, like a lot of Americans my age. I was born into comfort, into sweeping promises of opportunity, into a host of assumptions about the successes that must surely be ahead. I hope never to take for granted the things that I have, and I recognize the infinitesimal odds, when one considers the distribution of global wealth, that I would be one of the relatively few people, compared to the whole world's population, who as a child never had to worry about where a meal was coming from, whether I'd have clothes on my back, or whether there would be a roof over my head.

And school is a gift, at least when you're getting it for free. Either way, that I should be in a position to access the resources, minds, and communities that accumulate around schools is tremendous. Not everybody gets to be in this position.

I know these things, and I consider myself blessed. Even on the way to a job that was chewing up little pieces of my brain and spitting them out like chicken fat, I had time to appreciate that my situation could have been far worse.

Ethan cracked before I did and quit the industrial cleaning supply company. He wallowed in partial employment, and I jealously detested him for it. The jolting squeal of public transportation now awaited me every morning.

During my ride out to the burbs, I would look out the window of the commuter train and into the guts of Philly: the old factories and warehouses lined with cracked and blackened windows like a thousand punched-out eyes and crowned by graffiti on the outside walls of the highest floors, inscribed by god knows what kind of brave scaffold-less souls; people hanging out on stoops in the early part of the day drinking 40s and throwing dice; boarded-up bodegas jutting grotesquely from barren sidewalks, flanked by grassless lots; basement storm windows gone so that crackheads could slither in and out as they pleased.

One-hundred-year-old homes, once inhabited by ambitious families with jobs in nearby textiles factories, collected no rent from the rats, roaches, and squatting junkies. Piles of rubble and endless stretches of charred remains told the city's story of twelve-alarm fires and police-sanctioned plastic-explosive detonations.

Row homes like the one I lived in as a child had no doors, only gaping black portals to inspire a sense of morbid wonderment. What kinds of scenes awaited the beam of a flashlight in such damp, unlit, paranoid, and foreboding places?

Of course, these damp, unlit, paranoid, and foreboding places were homes. People's whole worlds were in these places. So believe me, I know that a lot of middle-class bitching and moaning can seem sort of empty. Real poverty exists somewhere close by no matter where you are, and it's much worse than a bunch of post-adolescent psychic discontent.

The world's smallest violinist would be playing for all the discontented college graduates right now, but instead he's waiting tables at Denny's to pay for his art institute loans.

Still, the fact that some people have it much worse than college graduates is hardly a compelling justification for ripping off tens of millions of our allegedly best and brightest.

Indeed, the most alarming reality of my situation, in retrospect, was not the psychic struggle at all. It was not the existential crisis, even if this was an imposing presence as well. It was a larger financial crisis, the early makings of an educational bubble that has now swelled to the point that many experts are forecasting an impending burst.

Not to exaggerate my own personal problems to the proportion of a national crisis. I'm just saying—my struggles were typical of a system that was beginning to rot.

Today, many journalists are making this claim on my behalf.

Even as I write these words, the fervor of the Occupy Wall Street movement has reached Philadelphia. In October 2011, hundreds of protesters carried signs to City Hall calling for the federal government to make accountable the bankers and corporate CEOs who swindled us to the brink of economic collapse in the Wall Street crash of 2008, only to be rewarded with billions in government-sponsored bailouts.

Bankruptcies, bailouts, and bonuses have inflamed millions of frightened Americans who make no claims to militancy. The protesters in the Occupy movement have come out to express their desperation. They are struggling to find jobs, pay student loans, and become homeowners. But only millionaires and billionaires are eligible for bailouts.

During fiscal year 2003, I was a twenty-six-thousandaire, with forty thousand dollars in debt. I'd have given up a Learjet or two for a bailout.

I've been eligible for an occasional deferment on my federal loan for financial hardship, though I still accrue interest each month. After taking that option roughly five times, I have succeeded—in ten years of paying a monthly check to some bank in Wisconsin—at reducing the sum total of my debt by about a thousand dollars.

I don't mind saying that the very thought of it makes me want to find seventeen-year-old me, beat him senseless, throw him on a boat to anywhere more interesting than New Jersey (read: any-where), and tell him to get a job there cleaning public toilets. Poor stupid seventeen-year-old me wouldn't have believed it, though. He wanted college to be so much more than it would turn out to be, and he was pretty sure that from a socioeconomic standpoint, it'd be worth the money. Poor gullible bastard.

His college obligations follow me everywhere.

Student loans are the one debt that cannot be declared away. And according to an October 2011 article in the *Guardian*, the Occupy Wall Street movement is fueled significantly by students with little earning power who are carrying the burden of this fail-ing economy on their narrow shoulders. The movement describes itself as representing the 99 percent of the population that has been betrayed by its government, its corporations, and, oh yes, most especially its schools. And according to the *Guardian*, "student loans have been stripped of nearly all basic consumer protections that every other type of debt enjoys, including bankruptcy protec-tions and statutes of limitations. So, while you can have your business, credit card, mortgage and even your gambling debts dis-charged or restructured in bankruptcy court, student loan debt is with you for life—and sometimes beyond."[1]

An article in *Mother Jones* from the same week reports that what is so remarkable about this mass of outstanding debt is that most of it has been accrued in just the last four years. All the student loan debt that's ever been created in the history of U.S. education amounts to roughly $1.5 trillion. As of late 2011, the amount of outstanding student loan debt was verging on $1 trillion. The *Mother Jones* piece says that at best estimate, there are roughly sixty million Americans with outstanding student loans.[2] How many of these people will drag stagnant debts behind them into careers, homes, and families will depend largely on the ability of the American economy to reward their investment with opportunity.

The Occupy Wall Street movement vocalizes mounting evidence that for a great many Americans, the investment has not been and will not be rewarded thusly. The *Washington Post* observes that as protests have spread to Philly, to Houston, to Washington, to Boston, to Chicago, to Baltimore, to Los Angeles, to the downtown financial district or commercial center or university campus of every major city in the United States, an outrage that is neither radical nor countercultural nor liberal in nature has become impossible to deny. There is a sense, the *Post* surmises, that we have been told that if we follow the rules, work hard, and do the right things, if we go to school, study diligently, and get good grades, we will be rewarded with homes, jobs, and security.[3]

In exchange for their ethical malfeasance, their revolting avarice, and their irresistible influence, those who have conspired to perpetrate one of the greatest wealth transfers in history have been rewarded with bankruptcies, bailouts, and bonuses. Oh yes, and zero convictions.

According to the *New York Times*, the Wall Street executives of Lehman Brothers, Bear Stearns, AIG, Washington Mutual, and Goldman Sachs (to name just a few) who created the subprime mortgage crisis that precipitated the economic unraveling of 2008 have been either acquitted or preemptively spared scrutiny by the Financial Crisis Inquiry Commission. As the *Times* reports, "The recent financial crisis has failed to produce any criminal cases against big-name bankers or other top corporate executives, unlike the financial scandals in the last decade, when there were signature prosecutions of chief executives like Bernard J. Ebbers of

WorldCom and Jeffrey K. Skilling of Enron. And although the commission is said to have referred a handful of cases of potential wrongdoing to the Justice Department, it seems doubtful that these will lead to criminal charges."[4]

I know guys who have spent at least one night in the can for public intoxication. A couple of slurred syllables and the apparent intent to urinate into a street-corner honor box get you a holding-cell slumber party, but the billions of dollars that used to gird our economy suddenly disappear, vanish into thin air, and nobody spends the night in jail. Nobody gets a fine. Nobody is accountable.

And what's more, the bankers, CEOs, politicians, and lobby groups who created this momentous decline have been paid the highest rewards that our society can bestow: riches beyond our wildest imagination, immunity from the laws that govern us, shelters from the taxes that we must pay, protection from the terms of borrowing that we must endure, and lives bound to be longer due to access to better doctors, safer foods, softer pillows, and weird rich-person shit like oxygen bars and botulism parties.

According to a 2011 report by the Board of Governors of the Federal Reserve System, the chaotic looting of Wall Street contributed to the depletion of the median American household's net worth by 23 percent in just the two years between 2007 and 2009.[5]

And yet, reports the website *CNNMoney*, with its profits down by nearly 75 percent from 2010 to 2011, Goldman Sachs allocated ten billion dollars in the first three quarters of 2011 to its bonus pool. Though down by 25 percent from 2010, this pool results from a one-year increase—from 43 percent to 44 percent—of total company revenue.

Citigroup experienced no profit gains from 2010 to 2011 but did report a 6 percent increase in overall employee compensation. And Bank of America, losing 22 percent in profits over that one-year span, raised its employee expenses by 7 percent, and this in the shadow of plans to cut thirty thousand jobs. According to *CNNMoney*, we have to stand here and suck it while the investment bankers who did this to us get anything from modest bonus cuts to raises.[6]

Well, if I'm a kid paying for business school and harboring

dreams of a mahogany desk and a car that makes people question the size of my penis, this doesn't seem like a half-bad way to go. Cheating on a few tests along the way strikes me as perfectly good practice.

And what is your reward, on the other hand, for following the rules?

Why, a tremendous job, of course, with all the health benefits and vacation days and large-breasted secretaries you could want.

But let's pretend for a second that this isn't guaranteed. Let's pretend that we are today graduating more college students than ever before, that far too few well-paying jobs exist, and that even as these contradictory patterns continue to intensify, the cost of entry into the educational institutions making possible the tre- mendous opportunities mentioned above continues to rise pre- cipitously. Let's pretend that the first things that greet you on the other side of this ever more costly and risky investment are soul- sucking jobs, cans of tuna fish, and twenty-year repayment plans.

If all of this was true, you'd be a sucker to follow the rules. You'd be an all-day, everyday sucker. Not only that, but you'd be among millions of other suckers who work not because they are educated, but because they must pay for their education. And if all of this makes sense to us, then we aren't really learning a thing.

In the midst of America's economic collapse, a million and one sure things have backfired on us. A stalwart vertebra of our econ- omy's spinal column, the auto industry, is resting on a herniated disk. Once the only guarantee even in uncertain times, the real estate industry is double dipping for its second bottom-out in half a decade. And even now, after all of this has become unmistak- ably clear, a sucking silence envelops the shit-hill of student loan debt that we claw through every day with no real end in sight.

How my parents ever got to a place where they could pay off their loans, I'll never understand. Neither will the millions of other Gen Xers and Gen Yers who scan Craigslist Jobs daily won- dering what the hell all that money was for. Education—one of the surest ways to invest your money for the future, we've been conditioned to believe—is today a gamble with worse odds than a sports championship in Cleveland.

As CNN reported in June 2011, the rise in costs for college education has contrasted so dramatically with the negative shifts in our economy that the middle class is being gradually priced out of its public universities.

According to the report, college tuition costs have surged by roughly 130 percent over the past twenty years. In 1988, the average public university tuition, adjusted for inflation, was twenty-eight hundred dollars annually. By 2008, that figure was sixty-five hundred a year.[7]

The Economic Policy Institute reports that in 1988 the average hourly earning for a male college graduate was roughly $21.50. In 2010, it was $21.77. This denotes a 1.3 percent increase over twenty-two years. The average hourly earning for a female college graduate was roughly $17.75 in 1988 and $18.43 in 2010. This denotes a 3.8 percent increase over twenty-two years.[8]

Factor in a 130 percent rise in the cost of a college education (to say nothing about the failure to narrow the gender gap), and 1988 America is kicking our sorry twenty-first-century asses. It makes me yearn for the days when it was cool to sew a Def Leppard patch on your backpack.

Incidentally, it was no longer cool but still somewhat socially acceptable to sew a Def Leppard patch on your backpack in 1992, the last time the federal government approved a raise in the amount of financial aid that could be awarded to a college-bound student. The number is holding steady at twenty-three thousand dollars for a four-year degree.

That said, the *New York Times* reported in April 2011 that two-thirds of all bachelors were now graduating with debt, compared with slightly less than half of all students in 1993. Based on the increasing number of students graduating in debt, the rising cost of tuition, and the stagnant job economy, there is cause to believe that a significant portion of this generation's students will still be paying for college even as they start saving to send their children there.

One result is an increasing trend toward acquiring two-year degrees and enrolling in community college. While these may be a better investment, they are creating a workforce with lesser skills. A *CNNMoney* report speculates that in an American economy where we are simultaneously struggling to create jobs and fill jobs, the continued erosion of American skill sets is intensifying this seeming contradiction.[9]

The Bureau of Labor Statistics reports that the unemployment rate for twenty- to twenty-four-year-olds was roughly 15.2 percent as of late 2010. And this picture remains bleak even as young workers get older. The BLS goes on to say that for those age twenty-five and over with a high school diploma, unemployment was at 9.7 percent in September 2011; for those with "some college or associate degree," 8.4 percent; for those with a bachelor's degree or higher, 4.2 percent. While this demonstrates a long-observed trend connecting higher degrees of educational attainment to better employment prospects, there is considerable evidence that in addition to relying on historical patterns of fading pertinence, this claim hides many of the economic fallacies driving the education bubble to grander proportions.

According to the BLS, individuals holding a bachelor's degree or higher in any age bracket experienced a 3.1 percent unemployment rate in 1993, a 1.8 percent rate of unemployment in 2001, and, as recently as 2007, just before the crash of 2008, an unemployment rate hovering just under 2 percent. So if 4.2 percent unemployment doesn't seem like much, don't forget that the rate has more than doubled since 2007 and continues to rise. This is closely proportional to the doubling of the national unemployment rate, which the BLS places at 4.7 percent in 2001, 4.8 percent in 2007, and 9.6 percent in 2010.[10]

This appears to suggest that the average individual who has invested in a bachelor's degree has been no more protected from the rising scourge of unemployment than the individual without a staggering sum of student loan debt. It seems likely that this is at least one reason for the fact that, according to the *New York Times*, as of September 2011, student loan default rates had reached the all-time high of 8.8 percent. According to the *Wall Street Journal*, as of August 2010, Americans shared roughly $826.5 billion in revolving credit debt just as the total amount of student loan debt reached roughly $828.8 billion. As projected, the latter number would exceed $1 trillion by the spring of 2011.[11]

I know we don't like to think of our schools as ripping us off. Somehow, the schools are different from the corporations, the investment firms, the banks, the auto manufacturers, the energy companies, the politicians, and the lobby groups. I'd hate to speculate baselessly that the student loan industry is just another suit-wearing pirate trying to board your ship.

Fortunately, I don't have to. According to the blog *Zero Hedge*, Education Finance Council president Vince Sampson is so concerned about the plight of recent and upcoming graduates that he told a panel at a global finance and investment conference in Miami in October 2011 "that lenders are no longer pushing loans to people who can't afford them."[12]

Well, that is downright responsible, isn't it?

Wait. Come again. "*No longer* pushing loans to people who can't afford them"?

As in, this seemed like a really good idea three years ago, in the immediate and horrifying shadow of the subprime mortgage crisis, but now, after a couple years of surveying the carnage, it seems like a less good idea? I'm pretty sure this qualifies as admitting that colleges have been girded by a practice of predatory lending for a while now, using to their advantage the ingrained cultural philosophy that without a college degree, you might as well just sell your body to science for research. This is an admission that no small number of students have been hoodwinked into keeping aloft temporarily an economy that will ultimately squash them flat. This is an admission that the schools and the loan agencies are in on the looting of America's economy too.

Of course, I can't claim to have known this stuff when I started writing back in 2001. Frankly, when I started my job as a paper writer, there was a lot I didn't know. I didn't know how hard it would be to make a living as a writer. I suppose I could have guessed how hard it would get financially: how many checks I would bounce, how bad my credit rating would get, how many times I would default on my loans. But I am fortunate in that I never realize I've reached a low point until I'm looking back on it. I had no idea how low my odds were, not just in terms of succeeding in my chosen craft but in terms of simply finding a way to be happy and make a living at the same time. As I would learn in time, neither option was particularly accessible on its own, let alone in simultaneity with the other.

I was hardly alone in this predicament. The *Wall Street Journal* reports that between 2002 and 2007, hourly wages for men between the ages of twenty-five and thirty-five with bachelor's degrees dropped by 4.5 percent; for women in the same demographic, by 4.8 percent.

I'm sure those numbers were much worse for those of us dumb enough to aspire to careers in the arts. Still, at no point did I ever stop believing that I'd be a success—if not a distinguished one, at least one who could eat without food stamps. Even as I began to write according to the terms of a thousand morons, at no point did I ever cease writing on my own terms as well. While a character named Ed Dante was cultivated in the endless pages of academic material that might only hint at my personality, Dave Tomar enjoyed quiet anonymity and some level of prolificacy.

Like any artist, like any musician, like any poet, I was consumed by conflicting impulses of self-doubt and egomania. I e-mailed editors, I subscribed to writing pools, I submitted articles to websites, I mailed away printouts of my best fiction, I connected myself with a few music publications and wrote album and concert reviews. If you think writing term papers sounds like a low-paying gig, you should try being a legitimate writer. At twenty-five dollars a pop for concert reviews, I usually spent half my earnings on parking.

And every morning, I'd roll over and open my eyes with a day at the industrial cleaning supply company staring back at me, like some unwanted thing in my bed that had looked a lot better the night before with a few drinks in me but that now revealed itself as a terrible mistake that I was bound to make every weekday for the rest of my life with no end in sight but the sweet, icy embrace of death. (Or, I suppose, unemployment. But stay with me here.)

And this was after only a year and a half there. Seemed a lot longer at the time.

At least I had a job, right? Sure, there's that. Scant consolation to a swindled investor. My returns came in the form of a position that did not require a college degree and that I got only because I knew a guy. Otherwise, I would have had to beg for this terrible, degrading job. (On a related note, the *New York Times* reported in May 2011 that the number of college graduates between twenty-five and thirty-four now working in restaurants, bars, and other food-service areas had risen by 17 percent just between 2008 and 2009. Similar or more pronounced trends had emerged at gas stations, liquor stores, and taxi services.)[13]

As it turned out, helping students cheat on papers was the only available job for which my college had prepared me. More than that, I was suddenly receiving an education. My god, the thought hadn't even occurred to me until right then. I had taken this job because it had found me. It had been the one job in my field that had responded to my habitual claim: "I can write anything. Just give me a chance."

This job had taken me up on my offer, embraced my talents, and found more outlets for them than a normal occupation could possibly have dreamed up. I was learning more stuff in a week than I'd learned in four expensive years of college. It was like kindergarten all over again. Suddenly, I was learning without the hassle of grades, the dictates of dickhole professors, or the looming pressure to declare myself a major and imagine a career therefrom.

I had no obligation to a course of study, no registrar's office to tell me a class was full, no admissions process to navigate. I was interdisciplinary, unregistered, and unadmitted. And without all the artifices, impositions, and expenses, all the things that made me hate school from the very first rumble of pubescent angst to the day I had packed up my last Yaffa Block, I rediscovered a love for learning that really only travel and psychedelics had satisfied for quite some time.

Suddenly, I was composing my own time line for human history. You cold-stitch together my essays on the Bronze Age, the Mongolian invasion of the Caucasus, the spread of the Black Plague, the French Revolution, mass European immigration to the United States, the Cuban Missile Crisis, and Central American autocrats and the women who loved them, and you can trace the evolution of the species to present day.

As I wrote this history, I gave little reflection to the implications of writing it under these conditions, so that those who must know history lest they be doomed to repeat it could go out and get drunk on the weekends instead. Truly, the clientele were a thing about which I thought little in those first years. I really felt the strongest contempt for them, actually. So I put them out of my head and concentrated on my personal education.

I'd go to work grumpy and wordless on the outside, rattling with new ideas on the inside. The contradiction finally got to me on a Wednesday afternoon in late August. My boss was in some other country with our new international clients. He'd left me in charge, and I'd quickly found out exactly what it was like to be him.

I was receiving an angry phone call every few hours, from somebody who had been given my name and who insisted on collecting a payment, product, or apology, and specifically from me. Some I had dealt with before. With many, I had even achieved a decent relationship.

Others only knew that my name had been given to them as Crackerjack's contact in my employer's absence. One such individual, a creditor, called that afternoon. The secretary buzzed me, and I picked up the phone.

"Where the fuck is my money?!?"

"I'm sorry. Who is this?"

"You know damn well who this is! You told me you sent the check last fucking week! What kind of an asshole do you take me for?"

"I think you've got the wrong guy. I'm not sure what you and Mr. Lewis discussed, but I'll do whatever I can to help you."

"Is this Dave Tomar?"

"Umm. Yes."

"Then you're the guy I'm supposed to talk to. I-want-my-fucking-money!"

"OK. I understand now. I'll get this taken care of right away. I'll call you back in ten minutes."

I phoned the boss at his hotel. I'd been trying his cell phone all week with no luck.

"David! How are you?"

"Not so good, Mr. Lewis."

"What's wrong?"

"What's wrong is that you left a big pile of crap for me to deal with here, and you gave my name to a bunch of angry fuckers, and there's nothing I can tell them."

"Who's angry?"

"Well, for one, I got this guy from Trans-Pacific calling me every ten minutes . . ."

"Fuck that asshole!"

"Well, what should I tell him, then?" I was pissed off, and the insolence of my tone finally hit my boss, so he got angry too.

"I don't give a fuck what you tell him! Just handle it!"

Click.

Okeydoke. I called the guy back in ten minutes as promised.

"Listen, man, I don't have your check. Mr. Lewis never sent it out. He just told you that to stall you until he got out of the country. He won't be back until next week, so you'll have to wait at least that long for your check, but probably longer. He's pretty tough to reach, but I think he's staying at the Hilton. If you don't get him in his room, I'd have them try the bar in the hotel lobby. Have a great Labor Day."

So school was a scam, and work was a scam too. It was at this exact moment that I determined unequivocally that my money had been wasted at school; that my nonexistent opportunities did not justify the cost; that the debt I had accrued was for somebody else's enrichment and not mine; that schools were not innocent victims; that instead schools were part of a deeply entrenched institutionalization of the young predicated on the accumulation of personal debt; and that, sadly, even that institutionalization, with all the promised comforts for which we compromised, was becoming harder to access.

It was at this exact moment that I determined that I really had nothing to lose, that the grading system and the promotion system and the student loan system were all conspiring to make me think I had invested far too much at this point to withdraw myself from the mainstream job market.

It was at this exact moment that I found myself at a crossroads. This was the moment when I was expected to retire the notion of being a writer, a notion that my university and my employer were collaborating to demonstrate was unrealistic. Nothing made it more so than my student loans.

But writing was what I had set out to do, and no alternative would suffice.

Mr. Lewis returned to the office on Monday, at which point I gave him my two-week notice. I didn't get to use any of the clever or cutting indictments that I had thought of over the weekend in response to his angry questioning. There was no angry questioning. He didn't want to know why I was leaving, where I was going, or what I would do. I had spent just under two years in his daily employ, and there was no evidence that he gave a crap either way. He simply thanked me, told me he thought I had done a good job, shook my hand, and wished me luck. And suddenly, now that I wasn't working for him, I didn't even think he was such a bad guy. I'm not even sure he knew he was doing anything wrong. I wouldn't have taken a business class with him as my instructor, but outside of the office he was a good husband, an attentive father, and a warm human being. He was just another sign of the times.

And just like that, I was on my own forever.

Now, if I was going to sully my good name, it would be on my own terms.

CHAPTER 6

Use Me

Going full-time with the paper mills was the only decision I could have made at the time.

My life changed overnight. The self-esteem that refused to show its face anywhere near the industrial cleaning supply company quietly crept back into my life. Never again would I work for somebody else's dream. (Unless that dream was turning in a paper without having to write it.)

I was finally producing a commodity with value that couldn't easily be outsourced to India. In fact, India's best and brightest were outsourcing to me. And not just India's but China's, Korea's, the Philippines', Indonesia's, Saudi Arabia's . . . you name it. If you could find an Internet café in your hood, barrio, or *wasti*, I was at your service.

I was starting to make a little loot. Not much but just enough to buy a buggy Dell laptop. The company I worked for charged customers a rate per page that varied, depending on how tight the deadline was. I could make a bunch of money taking on "rush orders," which were assignments due in twenty-four hours or less. And I was learning little tricks for working faster, for getting more in, for turning minutes into dollars. Really, though, it wasn't about the little tricks, like fluffing sentences with unnecessary clauses or adding gratuitous lines summarizing previous claims. These tricks help to shave off seconds as exhaustion begins its gloaming. But really I was improving with practice, getting more efficient with each passing assignment. It was dribbling a basketball for a thousand hours and taking ten million free throws and bounce passing against a cinder block wall until these foundational elements of the game were encoded into muscle memory, until I no longer needed to be completely awake to analyze themes of insanity in *Hamlet*, until the creation of new intellectual property was truly nothing more than pushing buttons.

And once I reached this point, the idea of protecting my personal copyright seemed ridiculous.

Ethan and I lived the ascetic and meditative life of bachelors. Defrosted burritos for dinner, pitchers of Yuengling at Manny Brown's for dessert, and hours upon hours spent turning blank pages into cheap intellectual property. The Internet made us brokers of knowledge based on no greater credential than the ability to create supply where we perceived demand. It was pure market science.

It wasn't always easy to explain my job to people. It relied so heavily on technological and cultural conditions specific to the early twenty-first century that if you weren't up to speed, it just wouldn't even seem possible. Lord knows I tried fruitlessly to make sense of it for my grandmother.

During one of our regular visits to her apartment in South Jersey, my sisters and I brought Grandma dinner from the prepped-food aisle at the supermarket. It was just easier than cooking in her kitchen, where she'd constantly pop up, hobble over, and insist upon helping, this in spite of the fact that she hasn't been able to open a pickle jar since Ed Sullivan last had a show on television.

I brought my laptop, my travel hard drive, and my mobile wireless card from Verizon, which allows me to access the Internet from anywhere, even 1953, which is where my grandmother's apartment is located.

I usually queue up a list of her favorites on iTunes while we hang out: Frankie Laine, Vaughn Monroe, Perry Como. Nothing with a pulse. I don't mind it, my sisters tolerate it, and my grandmother, who smoked cigarettes through her forties, sings along with every song. Of course, all of this is possible through the magic of the interweb.

My grandma . . . well, she's a trip. Everything makes her cry, but not in a sad way. It's what Jewish seniors call "kvelling." She wells up, her voice rises three octaves, and she sort of quakes. She does this when she sees us on holidays. She does this when we call her to thank her for the ten-dollar checks that she sends every birthday without fail. She does this when we help her set the VCR to tape her "programs." She loves COPS.

She's a cool old lady. She laughs at swear words, and if you say any particular word frequently enough in a short space of time, she's bound to accidentally say it herself. My grandmother has actually started out sentences by saying, "Fart, I mean . . . oh, dammit."

She's never thrown anything out. She still has every bottle of laundry detergent she ever bought. Her freezer is like a tour through history: "If you look to your left, you'll notice a loaf of bread that dates back to the second Roosevelt administration. As part of the New Deal, Roosevelt brought food rationing and price controls to the market so that Grandma could purchase this bread at seven cents a loaf."

That night I was hanging a picture for her, and I asked her for some nails. She produced a yellow cardboard box with an illustration of a little boy hammering. It was in perfect condition and at least fifty years old.

"Grandma," I said, "these are actually the original nails. This box could be worth something."

My grandmother has absolutely no understanding of how the Internet works, what it is, or what makes it possible. I have attempted tirelessly to explain it even though I suspect that the Internet is probably a dangerous place for somebody like my grandmother. It's not that she'd start giving her bank account and routing numbers to every Nigerian prince or friend allegedly stranded at a PO box in Scotland. Quite to the contrary. If she received an e-mail like that, she'd call the police, move the couch in front of her door, cancel all her credit cards, and throw her computer off her balcony. The Internet is a big place, and I'm not sure she'd be comfortable there.

"So, how's work? Are you still with the cleaning supply people?" she asked.

"Actually, I graduated from there."

"*Ohhhhhhhhhhhhhhhhhhh*. I'm so proud of *youuuuuuuu*."
High-pitched wailing and sobbing.

"Yeah, and I've got corporate headhunters all over me, so really, anything could happen now."

"I love you so much!"

"I love you too, Grandma."

"And how's your book-writing going?"

"Well, I'm not really working on a book right now."

"What are you working on?"

"Well, I'm helping students with their homework. Remember? I told you about this."

"So you're tutoring the students?"

"No. Grandma. I'm helping them cheat. I write papers for them, and they pay me."

"Ohhhh," she said somewhat gravely. "Does that pay well?"

"It pays me well enough. Actually, it pays me better than the cleaning supply company."

"Oh," she said, giggling a little bit. "So how does that work? Do you go to the students, or do they come to you?"

"No. Grandma, it's all over the Internet." I pointed to the computer and showed her the website while I explained. "They send their assignments through the company that I work for. I write them and send them back."

"But how do you find the students?"

"Well, they find me. I should say, they find the company that I work for, they use their credit card to pay for a paper, then the company puts the paper online, where I can look at it and decide whether to write it."

"But how do you write their papers? You don't do the research, do you? Where do you find everything?"

"Grandma, you have to understand, it's very easy to find stuff on the Internet. You just type in the thing you're looking for, a page comes up showing you all the different websites where that thing might be, and you just click on them."

"OK." She didn't understand.

"OK. It's like, imagine if you were in a library, and you wanted to find every page in every book that mentions Tony Bennett."

She lit up at the thought of Tony Bennett. These were the first two words she'd understood in about twenty minutes.

"So imagine that you can walk into this library and type in the words 'Tony Bennett' and that all the books that mention him fly off the shelves and land in front of you with bookmarks for all the pages on which you can find his name."

"Your grandfather and I met Tony Bennett when he was performing in Atlantic City. He's very tall in person."

Talking to my grandmother about the Internet was like going back in time and trying to explain to an Andrews Sisters fan club why people like Lady Gaga.

I knew she didn't really understand what I meant by anything. I had tried so many times to explain it to her. I had even showed her on numerous occasions, scrolling through websites about Eddie Cantor and demonstrating how easily I could look up all of Jeanette MacDonald's movies just like that. But she couldn't possibly comprehend the way that facts are so accessible, the way that we communicate with one another, the speed at which information careens, replicates, disseminates, distorts, and disappears into the virtual ether, never to be googled again.

This is a cultural game-changer that makes no sense whatsoever to my grandmother. How could it? When she was in school, if she wanted to know who had invented the cotton gin, she'd just ask around until she met somebody who'd known Eli Whitney. If my parents wanted to know, they'd go to a library and do, well, god knows what. I went to libraries when I was a kid, and all I did was read *Mad* magazine and leaf through issues of *National Geographic* looking for native boobies.

Ethan and I tried to go to the library once, just once, in order to conduct research. I was looking for a book by Hunter S. Thompson. It was readily available on the Internet, and the assignment was easy enough. But it seemed like as good a reason as any to get out on a sunny day. And really, you have to get out of the house once in a while, or a job like this could turn you into a freak.

The Central Library occupies multiple city blocks, rises several stories, and descends some number of moldy levels underground.

It is a hulking behemoth, impressive in its own way but also a monument to something from a long time ago.

After entering, ascending the wide marble steps, regrouping to catch our breath, emerging in the wrong section of the correct floor, receiving directions from an unsmiling lady librarian, and finally arriving at our destination, we found that the book was not in its proper spot. I logged in to the library intranet at a computer terminal and learned that the book was not checked out. I inquired with the old cardigan-wearing gentleman at the desk, who said that the book was "in the stacks."

"I can send somebody down there. But you'll need to have a seat."

He called for an old lady who walked with an excruciating, disjointed, and slow gait that suggested one, maybe even two prosthetics. He sent the poor thing down to the stacks. Ethan and I sat down and agreed that book or no book, it was simply a victory if she didn't die down there.

Thirty minutes passed, and to our relief, she returned. She had had no success locating Mr. Thompson's text, though. I'd have to go elsewhere for my gonzo. I went home, my sunny day now more than half over, with nothing but a soft pretzel from a stand downtown to show for it. I googled the book and wrote the paper in an hour.

I haven't a fuck's clue how to do research if my Internet is down and my phone battery is dead.

My grandmother can't make sense of the Internet. Me, I can't make sense of the world without it. If it weren't for the Internet, I would have no idea how to make a living as a writer. I paid all that money for that Writer's Market book. I sent out a billion self-addressed stamped envelopes so that magazine editors could throw my manuscripts in the trash and reuse my postage stamps . . . probably. I submitted samples to the too-cool-for-you hipster papers that circulated the city for free. I got by on encouraging rejection letters and constructive critiques.

Nearly every cent I've ever earned as a writer was made online and not just without the help of gatekeepers but in spite of them.

I suppose I can credit my college for training me thusly. Books were so goddamned expensive there that I just learned to get by on whatever I could find on the Internet. Everything is googleable.

A great wealth of knowledge is available for free to those who know how to massage a keyboard. For a master masseur and an indigent scumbag, it was a no-brainer. I could never afford books, not any good ones, anyway. I always had a copy of Shatner's *TekWar* lying around.

Ironically, though, thanks to my job I was now getting awesome books, and some terrible ones, for free. Many of my clients would not only buy syllabus-required books that they had no intention of reading, but also bundle them up and FedEx them to me so I could do their coursework. Thousands of dollars' worth of brand-new texts, many of them gorgeous hardback editions. I did a whole course on American constitutional history once for a client. This kid sent me *The Federalist Papers*, *The Anti-Federalist Papers*, Alexis de Tocqueville's *Democracy in America,* Abraham Lincoln's *Great Speeches, Selected Writings* by Thomas Jefferson, Benjamin Franklin's *Autobiography and Other Writings*, Thomas Paine's *Common Sense*, and John Locke's *Two Treatises of Government*.

All of them were shrink-wrapped editions with glossy covers that make my shelves look positively stunning.

Naturally, I could find any one of those texts on the Internet for free, and I generally have. Frankly, cutting, pasting, and properly citing reference materials from websites takes a lot less time than retyping them from physical texts. Still, it's fun to get shiny new books and put them in my personal library. It makes me look well-rounded. Most of my clients never ask for their texts back.

It's just as well. The best of them I usually read in the bathroom, anyway. They are flagged.

Frankly, if it weren't for the tactile pleasures of holding a text while on the toilet, I would only read on the Internet. Such is the crime of my generation. We are killing the book. The book shouldn't take it personally, though. We are also killing the record, the newspaper, and the magazine. Someday soon, we'll have nothing with which to swat flies.

I can see the bind that professors are in, though. Many of them make a good side piece hustling their own books in class. I had a class called Politics and Culture in my junior year of college. The summer before the class, the professor published a pet project about the spy novels of John le Carré. When we showed up in class, the required readings were five le Carré spy novels and the professor's book analyzing them. There was a mutiny. Half the class dropped immediately. But it was so hard to get into a requisite-fulfilling class that the other half of us simply remained behind and harangued the professor deep into the semester about how any of this crap related to politics or culture.

Don't tell me that selling books isn't a priority for educators.

Professors and schools are gatekeepers of intellectual property, arbiters of that which is valid and that which is not. But capitalism cares nothing for their prejudices. Capitalism helps those who help themselves. Enter the paper mill.

There are a few things that people will not want to hear about the company for which I began working all the way back in college. Here they are:

- This is one of the best and most ethical companies that I have ever worked for. I won't tell you its name. It wouldn't matter anyway. It's just one of many, at least hundreds and possibly thousands.
- The company never bounced a check to me, and it never paid me late. I always got paid exactly what I'd earned. It was never a question. If I was on the right side of a dispute with a customer, the company went to bat on my behalf. If I needed an advance, the company would approve it. If there was a change in company policy, it would be reported on the writers' board in due time for writers to prepare.
- The company revamped its website format every few years, always working to improve the flow of traffic and ease of use. It remained abreast of advancing Web-design and e-commerce technologies, created a highly streamlined work flow that required very little oversight, and still engaged in regular testing and maintenance of the system.

- When customer service or employment issues came up, I rarely waited more than an hour for a response from one of the two customer service representatives to whom I was assigned. They were always friendly, polite, professional, fair, available, and appreciative.

Having been the recipient of bounced paychecks, having been verbally condescended to, having been falsely promised opportunities for advancement in past jobs, I saw the paper-writing company as one of the first trustworthy entities I'd yet met in the crooked world.

And not just with me. It was judicious and fair with its customers, too. The common impression that many of the paper-writing companies online are scams demonstrates a critical misunderstanding of how the paper-mill economy works. Some may indeed be scams, but many are simply service companies. Repeat business, good word of mouth, and consistent results are very important to success in a service industry. Therefore, it behooved my employers to run a fair, equitable, and trustworthy practice. A paper-writing company has natural enemies, and no need for conflict from other sources.

I followed this example to the best of my abilities. I used a personal honor system when dealing with customers. Revisions are a common part of the job. Writing papers is not an exact science, of course. After I've sent out a paper, there's no way to know if I'll ever hear another word on the subject. I might complete an epic masterpiece and receive a five-page diatribe detailing with bullet points and headings exactly what I did wrong. I might puke a bunch of barely related words onto a page and receive an e-mail praising my work and promising the customer's vote if I ever run for president. Beauty is in the eye of the somewhat literate beholder. No way to know.

But when revision requests came in, I would try really hard to be fair about it. If the completed essay really hadn't adhered to the customer's initial instructions, I would provide the requested rewrite. And the company would expect me to do so. But it was objective about this, and so was I.

I've gotten lord knows how many assignments phrased like this: "In three pages, tell your life story, complete with the most embarrassing thing you ever did in a public bathroom and how it felt the first time you had an inguinal hernia examination." The student might supplement this with additional information such as the following: "Please make this essay awesome. Thnx."

The customer presumes that whatever deeply personal anecdote or complex set of emotions I select from the annals of his or her memory will do just fine. Some paper-writing companies will inflate the accomplishments of their independent contractors, claiming to employ staffs of Ph.D.s and retired professors. But telepathy is another skill entirely, and as far as I know, my employer never claimed I had it. Why so many customers had the impression that I could explain their internal strengths, describe their greatest fears, and rifle through their personal memories without much more than a credit card receipt, I'll never know.

I tended to use assignments like this as an opportunity to flex my sometimes neglected creative-writing muscles. Prompted to describe a life-changing experience and how it related to my eventual career aspirations—a standard multipurpose academic essay that I've written at least thirty times—I might tell the story, from the perspective of the customer, of course, of the morning I woke up to find that I'd been bitten by a radioactive praying mantis and would thenceforth travel the world using my special powers to fight crime in a fluorescent green spandex bodysuit.

In the event that I got any complaints from Praying Mantis Man, my employers would probably review the initial instructions and agree that I'd been left with little choice but to improvise. Who's to say what's true and what's not?

On the other hand, if I wrote this same essay in response to the question "What are the three primary causes of climate change over the continent of Antarctica?" my employers would most assuredly request that I edit the assignment with closer attention to the initial instructions. And because they were so judicious and fair, I would always defer to their mediation in such matters.

My company had a disclaimer that appeared at the top of every completed order. The basic gist of it was that the customer bore sole legal responsibility for any undue usages of the material in question; the material could be used in the individual's own work only if proper citations were made; and it was expressly illegal to reuse, resell, or otherwise claim the work in question without proper crediting. The company would even provide the customer with a bibliography to be used in the event of citing the completed "study guide," "research supplement," or whatever the hell other euphemism you wanted to give it.

This was the basic legal measure taken to protect the legitimacy of the paper-writing company. Not every company takes this step, but the better ones that are likely to be around for a little while all offer a similar disclaimer. The disclaimer was, of course, not really designed to prevent the student from turning in the assignment. It was to prevent him from blaming us for whatever consequences came of this action. The disclaimer was sufficient to preemptively inform the student that we would take no responsibility for grades received for submission; that we held no accountability for punitive measures, such as probation, censure, or expulsion, resulting from the assignment; and that in such instances, if we really wanted to, we could actually sue the student for improper usage of our intellectual property.

Not that we ever would. Suing your own customers is poor business practice. Just ask the music industry.

Also, not unlike in the music industry, one offshoot of this arrangement was that the customer didn't have a whole lot of recourse for buying a crappy product. If you buy a Michael Bolton record and then walk around complaining to everybody about how bad it is, you're really just incriminating yourself.

Like many companies, some paper mills simply sell a shitty product. It is incumbent upon the buyer to make informed decisions, as one would when choosing a car or a laptop or a doctor. Referrals are a pretty big part of the business for the company of quality.

The company I worked for was successful and strategic and perfectly poised to enjoy the realities of intellectual property law and globalization and that magical series of tubes* known as the Internet. And thus, I and my fortunes as a writer were bound to these tubes, which suspended the limitations of time and space, which sent my writing over lakes, rivers, and oceans, which erased the once impenetrable imaginary borders between countries but did little to erase the language barriers, which in fact created one vast virtual Babel where you could also find great deals on flights.

The Web was a place so unlike school in its versatility, its accessibility, and its mystery. My classes had been rigid and often dedicated to the assertion of one perspective. But here, where no gatekeepers existed, I was free to use and create intellectual property in a way that school had never ventured to teach me.

That's because the fundamental role of the professor has changed very little since the time when my parents went to school, or even since the time when my grandmother went to school. Our relationship to information is in a state of constant evolution, and our relationship to our professors remains stuck in a hundred-year holding pattern. Even through the occasional scrutiny and reform of pedagogy, the professor remains the single great channel for knowledge, the funnel through which years of singular education are condensed into ideas conveniently framed by a textbook and a semester of lectures.

Unfortunately, students have other ideas altogether about acquiring information. They find it themselves, they make it themselves, and they share it with each other.

In November 2010, a professor of strategic management at Central Florida University (CFU) made national headlines by using the widespread cheating in his course to create a teachable moment. A recording of Richard Quinn's lecture, which has been widely viewed thanks to YouTube, shows an emotional professor reporting to a lecture hall of nearly six hundred students that he possesses "forensic evidence" demonstrating that roughly one-third of those

---

*A phrase coined in 2006 by then Alaska senator Ted Stevens (R), probably intended to demonstrate the elderly public servant's poor understanding of the technology that is the lifeblood of our economy, society, and culture today.

who took the midterm exam cheated by studying an answer key from a publisher's test bank that circulated among the students. Quinn criticizes his students in harsh terms for violating the university's honor code and his personal standards of integrity. He proclaims in the lecture that "the days of being able to find a new way to cheat the system are over. They're over."

Cheating is everywhere, of course. The CFU numbers aren't so surprising, really. But Quinn's lecture also shows a critical misunderstanding of the conditions that have led to so much cheating, both in his classroom and in others like it around the country. In fairness to Professor Quinn, schools are capable of far more insidious things than failing to inspire their students. But if you're trying to improve young minds, that's still a pretty serious shortcoming.

CFU's investigation of the event went on to highlight, among other things, how professors and students think differently about information sharing. Quinn's highly personalized diatribe demonstrates his own understandable frustrations, but he doesn't say much about what all this cheating really means. According to a 2010 article published by the website *Inside Higher Ed*, "the perception of exactly what happened leading up to the midterm has become a point of contention. What is clear is that some students gained access to a bank of tests that was maintained by the publisher of the textbook that Quinn used. They distributed the test to hundreds of their fellow students, some of whom say they thought they were receiving a study guide like any other—not a copy of the actual test."

Not only is cheating everywhere, but the current generation also has a different view of what constitutes it. This is essential to understanding the CFU story. But here's something else to consider: In a six-hundred-person course, and with a school-supplied course textbook, how much opportunity did Quinn really have to design an exam that worked for the needs and goals of his students? This is an issue not just of educational laziness, but of a failure to understand just how accessible information has become. I don't know Quinn personally and I can't speak to his philosophy as a professor, but his behavior in this instance is symbolic of a kind of educator. For our purposes, we will call this educator Dr. Microfiche. Just as the CFU students could not hide their reliance on the modern sharing of information, neither can Dr. Microfiche hide his ignorance. The hope is that incidences such as this might elucidate the error in his way of thinking. He is no longer a gatekeeper of information as he once was.

But one wonders if Dr. Microfiche truly understands the implications of what occurred in Professor Quinn's course. What are his thoughts on the fact that two hundred cheaters in his class of six hundred presumably felt that they could benefit more by passing the class than by learning from it? It seems fair to assert that Quinn and his university sowed the seeds for this type of blatant disregard for the honor system by failing to create "a community devoted to learning."* When at least one-third of all students are proven offenders, it is the environment and not the individual that must explain itself.

Educators are at war with the Internet, whether they know it or not. Traditional educators are at war with the Internet even as they use it, embrace it, and channel their work through it. The Web doesn't just open the door to clever ways of undermining the research process. It isn't just a context in which the student is more comfortable than the professor. It is a capitalist free-for-all where the student has learned to be wholly independent, for better or worse.

The Internet is, as my friend Donovan Root phrases it, putting an end to the "monopoly on knowledge." Donovan spent the ten years following graduation working in the finance industry and offering eerily accurate prophecies about the coming economic apocalypse.

Donovan's position of prestige in the world of finance was achieved on the strength of his burning intelligence and an otherworldly geekiness where the computer is concerned. We're the

---

*William and Mary, often cited as authoring the first formal honor code in the American university system, identifies this as the end goal of any university.

exact same age, but when I was in junior high, I spent my weekends setting fire to things and frantically putting them out for
entertainment. Donovan was building computers from scratch
and creating Web bulletin boards, *then* going outside to set things
on fire. This was in 1992. Back in the days of the dot-com boom,
Donovan was one of the Internet wunderkinds, a computer nerd
version of Doogie Howser, the kind of kid rich adults threw money
at with hopes of striking it even richer.

Donovan has been a witness to the great revolution from the
inside. He explains to me that in his world of finance, as in the
world of professorship and in the professional world in general,
the exclusivity of knowledge has long served to validate the expert and his earning power. Before the Internet, finding information, building it into knowledge, and knowing how to learn and
how to profit from it were all considered to be part of a special
skill set. It would take a doctor to interpret the results of a blood
test. It would take a stockbroker to tell you how your investments
were doing. It would take a lion tamer to show you how to use a
whip.

The Wikipedia entry on lion taming offers a brief definition but
then links to the websites of more than a dozen of the world's
most famous or successful lion tamers. There are tutorials for
how to become a lion tamer on eHow and HowStuffWorks. I also
watched a horrible video on YouTube in which a Ukrainian lion
tamer is mauled by several angry lions, which led me, inevitably,
to a series of articles detailing how Roy of Siegfried and Roy was
dissected by a white tiger with a lot of pent-up aggression. Ultimately, I was dissuaded from becoming a lion tamer, but assured
that I could do it if I wanted to.

Frankly, there's a lot I can do now without paying tuition, kow-
towing to a professor, or sweating grades. The Internet has knocked
over the ivory tower, and all its precious papers are fluttering in
the wind. The cherished notion that knowledge may be obtained
only by those with the time, the dedication, the inquisitiveness,
and, yes, the financial means is no more. Whatever it costs to go
online in your region, that's how much it costs to learn.

It is human to absorb, integrate, and recontextualize. And to-day, it is expedient to do so. As I have sold off my alleged intel-lectual property to be claimed by others, I have become rich in knowledge, stamina, and patience, and without anybody's help.

The powerful discretion of the ivory tower is not what it once was. No wonder academia hates Wikipedia so much. Collective knowledge is a threat to those whose jobs are based on singular knowledge. Students can get what universities are pitching for free. Donovan calls this the "disintermediation of the expert."

The things that we used to need professors for, we can get on our own.

In the era of deregulation, of trade liberalization, of globaliza-tion, in an era when jobs are less about specialization and more about cost-effective commoditization, the deconstruction of claims to intellectual property is as easy as the deconstruction of interna-tional barriers. They're all just ideas, anyway, all social constructs subject to change depending on how you were raised, the nature of your economy, and the ways in which you stand to benefit or be exploited.

Globalization and intellectual property are strange bedfellows.

On the subject of intellectual property, my friend Paulie always liked to quote Ecclesiastes 1:9—not that I would describe Paulie as assertively religious. He would say,

What has been will be again,
What has been done will be done again;
There is nothing new under the sun.

Paulie was an accountant with ten years' experience at one of the Big Four firms. The gig wore him out. When the ax fell on him, it seemed like it was more a relief than anything else. Paulie was one of the most gloriously reckless partyers I've ever met. He was routinely the guy denied entrance into a bar, booted from a strip joint, or asked never to return to a casino. He has always been welcomed in my house.

A master of disguise, a Tasmanian devil in a mustache, and a

Falstaffian character whose abandon struck fear in the hearts of more conservative men, he reminded me often that we have precious little control over our own ideas. To wit, Paulie had a tremendous wealth of intellectual property that he would dispense with seemingly little concern for context, audience, or pertinence. He was great company for a spirited or spirituous exercise in rhetorical combat. He was frequently correct but possibly crazy.

In conversation we have both wondered if such a thing as intellectual property even exists anymore.

We're living in a time of mashups, of sampling, of co-opting, of file sharing. We borrow liberally until information and intellectual property are nothing but bits of quotable human ephemera, connected only loosely to their original contexts or creators.

Ray Charles knew nothing of Kanye West's "Gold Digger" when he sang "I Got a Woman." And I'm pretty certain that the Southern Tones didn't know that their song "It Must Be Jesus" would be adapted (by Charles) into an R&B chart topper about a man-pleasuring sugar mama way across town.

Online piracy, Wikipedia, social networking, and the supposed "knowledge economy" may not be simply new ways of looking at the intellectual property hierarchy; rather, they may be the tools of its destruction.

Historically, selling ideas has not just been a way of profiting from them—it has also served to enforce ideological class division: The person with the idea has something, and if you want it, you need to pay him.

The way Ethan and I viewed it, the Internet and paper writing had given us the chance to create intellectual property of economic value without anybody's approval. Suddenly, for those without expensive credentials, for those possessing only the ability to generate intellectual property at will, the market had produced a great new opportunity.

And evidence suggests that even if my grandmother and Dr. Microfiche do ever come to truly understand the cultural implications of the Internet, they may be surprised to find out that their generations have been disintermediated.

There is indeed a generational divide where the Internet is concerned. But it has less to do with who uses the Internet than with how we are using it. It is deceiving to note that Americans over the age of seventy are the fastest-growing demographic of Web users.

The Pew Internet and American Life Project reports that just 26 percent of Americans between the ages of seventy and seventy-five were online in 2005. As of 2009, that number stood at 45 percent. But the difficulty we're experiencing in harnessing the Internet for the purposes of education is not about access or interest or the fact that your great-aunt Sally knows how to attach photographs to e-mails.

Rather, we're experiencing a paradigm shift in the cultural treatment of intellectual property, and this shift is a direct consequence of how our generations variously use the Web. Sixteen percent of sixty-four- to seventy-two-year-olds download music online; 21 percent of baby boomers (forty-five to sixty-three) do it. For teens, the number is 59 percent; for Gen Yers, 58 percent; and for Gen Xers, 46 percent.

Similar trends emerge in the areas of social networking and blogging. Sixteen percent of baby boomers ages forty-five to fifty-four have created social networking profiles for themselves. Nine percent in the age group of fifty-five to sixty-three have done so. By contrast, 29 percent of thirty-three- to forty-four-year-olds, 60 percent of eighteen- to twenty-three-year-olds, and 55 percent of twelve- to seventeen-year-olds have created social networking profiles. Twenty-eight percent and 20 percent of twelve- to seventeen- and eighteen- to thirty-two-year-olds respectively have created their own blogs, whereas 10 percent of thirty-three- to forty-four-year-olds, 6 percent of forty-five- to fifty-four-year-olds, and 7 percent of fifty-five- to sixty-three-year-olds have done so.

So as much as the older generations are using their e-mail accounts and buying *M*A*S*H* collectibles on eBay, younger users are overwhelmingly contributing to the creation and replication of intellectual property online. And because the Web has become so dominant a force in so many facets of our personal, professional, and educational lives, these patterns suggest a disruption in mankind's long legacy of inherently ageist hierarchical intellectual property gatekeeping.

The ways in which we use the Web for expression and the gathering of information have become inherently more communal, more collective, less accredited, and less consistent with the ways in which older generations have formed cultural bodies of knowledge. Democracy—with all of its wanton, inarticulate, and garbled constituencies—has seized our technology.

Oh, the informality of it all!

Students learn in a way for which many older professors have no frame of reference. Where Dr. Microfiche is concerned, Professor Quinn's students are cheaters and beneath contempt. Where these students are likely concerned, Dr. Microfiche has no concept of the way his role as a professor should have evolved. The information-sharing tactics that Professor Quinn's students employed to "cheat" on their exam are consistent with those they will employ in their future professions and in their pursuit of information in general. That any professor might refuse to accept a role in helping them to do this would be ignorant at best and sociologically regressive at worst.

I can't tell you that the Internet is a trustworthy place. I can't tell you that what intellectual property you'll find there was created fairly and ethically. I can't even tell you that simply using the Internet won't make you a victim of identity theft. However, I would argue that there's not a whole lot that anybody can do to change any of that now.

Professors are not police officers, and it is not their responsibility to make the Internet safe, or to protect students from the enormous wealth of garbage out there, or to protect themselves from it. But if it is the professors' responsibility to help students learn, then every classroom should be equipped with the knowledge and will to help students navigate the evolving virtual space. To date, our educational imagination extends to the ideas of distance education, virtual classrooms, and digitized library catalogs.

The illusion of progress.

These are things that make schools more profitable and make cheating easier but do nothing to enrich the learning process as a function of Web use. The professor, the primary text, and the formal research process remain the main channels through which education is conveyed, and with even less personal attention.

As dinosaurs like Dr. Microfiche slowly go extinct from the profession, it will be incumbent upon the future leaders of higher education to evolve. They should not be gatekeepers or cops or censors but navigators. Professors want to be needed, and for the money we're spending on school, we'd like to need them. The Internet is a pretty scary place, busting at the seams with neo-Nazi militias, cannibal cookbooks, and *American Idol* fan sites. Don't tell us not to look at this stuff. Teach us how to use it. Teach us how to use Facebook responsibly, how to differentiate between sharing and stealing, how to engage openly in a discussion about the blurring of lines between these two acts. Don't tell us not to use Wikipedia. We're going to do it anyway. Show us how to read it, how to verify its claims, how to spot and debunk its errors, even how to correct it and contribute to its improvement.

These things that we perceive as opportunities, schools have treated as threats. If schools had seized these opportunities proactively, perhaps it would have been more difficult for me to exploit them. I never used a professor's intelligence for help in doing the homework assignment for his class—I replaced him with the Internet. And my customers chose my help (that of some anonymous Internet person) over that of their professors. How they came to that decision is up for discussion.

But I presume that at least one factor is that my grandmother and Dr. Microfiche aren't alone out there in their virtual disorientation.

After dinner and a game of Scattergories, my sisters and I left my grandmother's house. I returned home to find Ethan working through an astronomy paper, with *Beavis and Butt-Head* on in the background. Ethan was clever when it came to the cosmos.

He passed me a pipe as I sat down and pulled my laptop from my bag. I opened it, logged on to the wireless network we'd been "borrowing" from one of our neighbors, and popped open the instructions for my current assignment.

"Asshole," I muttered under my breath as I read them.

"What'd I do?"

"No, dude. This professor. Get a load of these instructions: 'Write four-to-five-page explanatory paper that defines a concept or issue for your reader. Need clear and concise thesis statement. Have two outside sources to help define the topic and support assertions. Have two outside sources. NO online sources for this paper. Need copy of resources.'"

The student offered her own addendum to the set of instructions, which I also read aloud for Ethan's amusement. "'Let me know what will the paper going to be about, also dont write about, abortion, euthanasia, clothing or death penalty, yhose were not allowed by my teacher. TTYL.'"

For those who don't communicate in Instant Messaging, that last part means "Talk to you later," like I was one of her girlfriends and we had just made plans to get our nails done tomorrow.

I could forgive that, though. Hell, I probably could have used a manicure.

What I could not forgive was an educator, in this day and age, within the context of an institution of higher learning, denying the evolution of research, defying the logic that was apparent to the student, and preparing the student for a future of conducting research in 1912. "NO online sources," said the professor.

"No online sources, eh?" Ethan observed.

"Yeah," I said. "So what do you suppose is the point of this research exercise? To learn the Dewey decimal system?"

"Maybe it's to justify the grant money for the university's recent library renovations?"

"Maybe this professor hopes to restore the card catalog to its former glory?"

"Yeah, what the fuck is his beef with the Internet? I mean, besides all the misinformation, hearsay, libel, vitriol, and fringe lunacy?"

"Well," I ventured, "I'd say this professor is one hundred seventy-eight years old and thinks the Internet is some type of support undergarment."

Thinking back now, though, I'm sure that wasn't it at all. This professor knew exactly what the Internet was. The Internet was this big, terrifying, spinning vortex that would someday soon swallow him up and swallow up all of his kind. It would swallow up the hierarchy of intellectual property, leaving behind a significant opportunity for the entrepreneurially spirited.

Our little paper-writing company on South Street was a product of pure market science.

CHAPTER 7

Thanksgiving and the Great Depression

I love Thanksgiving. The smell of the cold air coming through the garage as my dad carries folding chairs into the house. The tacky din of the Macy's parade marching from the television to nobody's direct interest. The promise of football, belt loosening, tryptophan, and a general artery-hardening good time.

But it's different when you have to work. By the fourth Thursday of November 2004, I had been doing the job full-time for a little more than a year, and I was already starting to experience the burnout that would become an annual event.

At this time, my commitments were particularly fleeting. I had a girlfriend, but we weren't great together. Besides, my computer and I both suffered frequent separation anxiety. For me it was that sense that, as a self-employed man, I never punched out, that without me out there working, I was making nothing, that there was no limit to how far I could fall.

And yet here I was, a crutch for the unrepentantly lazy. In my self-righteous exhaustion, I hated them, I judged them, I considered their money put to better use in my pockets.

Each of my clients seemed to be a case in underdeveloped ambition and parentally sponsored postadolescent assisted living. I resented them all.

I had a great-grandfather who passed away when I was eight. He left a trust fund for me and one for my older sister. Great-Grandpa Lou lived to be ninety-eight and maintained the clarity and control to sketch eerily accurate penciled likenesses of his attending nurses until just days before his death of natural causes. Even so, he didn't seem to realize that my younger sister existed, so the poor girl was summarily screwed out of any portion of her would-be inheritance. Mine covered a year and a half of tuition and housing. It's a shame to think that the legacy of a man's long and remarkable life could be funneled into eighteen months of low-grade, high-fiber dining hall food and Yankee Stadium–size lecture halls.

When Great-Grandpa Lou's money ran out, it was on to loans. When my Sallie Mae loans topped out, my parents cosigned on a private NJCLASS loan. I was now on the hook for a huge sum of money and the health of my parents' credit rating. I don't wish that kind of pressure on any other stupid kid.

Still, I learned in college what I would need to know as a self-employed writer. There are no handouts for a guy like me. It was probably the greatest gift my parents ever gave to me. My independence was a function of my desperate determination.

I can't say my parents were particularly proud of what I had become. I assume that when people asked my dad what I did for a living, he would brag that I was tops in my prison license-plate-making class. But they were not the types to interfere. I had been raised on the premise that you are free to make your own mess so long as you're willing to clean it up. I had become quite the chambermaid: always tidying up, sweeping dirt under, pushing back this bill, ripping up that one, and hoping the gesture was sufficient to make the debt disappear.

I may not have seemed tough to the World War II vets in my family tree, but neither had I been raised to be fragile. Not compared to my customers, anyway: They were an experiment in twenty-first-century child rearing, more often than not the product of attachment parenting ideology, shortsighted good intentions, and life cycle micromanagement. My parents had many years prior washed their hands of my poor decision making.

Speaking of poor decision making, at the time I was dating Hope, a sweet girl whom I had no business being with. I was doing Thanksgiving dinner with her family this year.

Our relationship was frivolous, temporary, and occasionally miserable. We had been together long enough that her parents already didn't like me. At first, all they really knew was that I was a writer and that I needed a haircut. That was bad enough. As they got to know me better, they just found me confusing.

Her father was a teacher in an affluent suburban elementary school. He was a Republican, an occasional hunter, a frequent fisher, and a man of strong faith. I was none of those things. He looked at me like I was a space alien.

As we pulled up to the house for dinner, I was finishing a paper on the Great Depression. My work, it seemed, always faintly echoed my life.

I folded my laptop into my backpack as Hope parked the car. Dad was standing on the porch with his hands on his hips, wearing a festive holiday scowl.

"Thanks for having me tonight, Mr. Klein." I extended my hand. He shook it.

"That's fine," he said. I could see he was thrilled to have me.

"Hi, Daddy," Hope said.

"Hi, baby. Happy Thanksgiving."

The Klein family never wasted time with predinner chitchat. Nobody was ever there to prolong the event. Getting it over with was an annual family tradition. We sat down right away. Hope's cousin Kevin got there late and found that we were all sitting at the table already, peering impatiently at the door.

They were the kind of family where you could hear forks clinking on plates, people sliding platters over, scooping with slotted spoons, and clearing their throats. Every once in a while, somebody would raise an eyebrow from their plate and look around at everybody else in quiet contempt for conspiring in this awkward showing of thanks. This kind of quiet always made me nervous that I might accidentally cut a fart. So I clenched my butt cheeks, looked down at my plate, and concentrated on my stuffing.

It took two bottles of wine for things to open up, for aunts and uncles to start complaining about their jobs, complimenting the food, and updating one another on friends who were now sick or dead. I kept mostly to myself and, as was often the case, planned out the next day of work in my head.

When the conversation finally fell on me, I longed for those precious minutes of awkward silence now passed.

Hope's dad was a griller. He was a math teacher. He liked to call on you when your hand wasn't raised, when your face was twisted with a perplexed expression, when he could tell you hadn't been paying attention, when he was sure to catch you with your pants down and make you look like a huge asshole.

This guy. I've had lifelong friction with guys like him.

"So, I saw you working on that computer of yours. What's that you're working on right now?" he asked me with an unspoken air of "Something stupid, no doubt."

"Well, I just finished an essay on the Great Depression."

"Oh, yeah?"

"Yeah, very troubling stuff."

"How so?"

"Well, more than anything, just the thought that it could all come crashing down around us and that we'd be powerless to stop it."

"Right . . . so you're back in school, then? Good for you. That should help you find some direction."

"Dad!" Hope said.

"No," I said. "No. I'm not in school. And I'm not really looking for direction right now. I'm hoping to get by on charm."

"What's the depression got to do with it?"

"Well, I'm writing a study guide for a student to use when writing his paper about the depression."

"And somebody is paying you to write about the depression?"

"Yes. Well, not just the depression. About lots of things. I write papers for students."

"Meaning?"

"Well, I write these 'study guides' for students so that they can hand them in at school. I work for a company. I'm an independent contractor, and I get work through this company. They pay me at the end of each month."

"So wait . . . ," said Cousin Kevin, with a sly sort of grin that I've seen a lot during this type of conversation. "So people hire you to do their homework?"

"Mmhmm," I replied through a mouthful of mashed potatoes.

"So what do you write about, then?"

"Anything, really. Almost anything. I don't do, like, computer programming papers or hard math or anything like that. Though other people do that kind of work."

"Other people?" Mr. Klein asked.

"Yeah. I work for a company. That's how I find the work, or how the work finds me or whatever."

"And you make a living doing this?" Kevin asked.

"Well, I don't have prime rib for dinner every night, but y'know . . . I pay the bills . . . mostly."

"Hah! That is awesome!"

Mr. Klein glared at him.

"What?!" said Kevin. "I wish I knew how to do that. Shit. I wish I'd known you when I was in school. That would have saved me some time."

"Kevin!" his mother said.

"So you help people hand in work that they didn't do? You help them cheat?" Mr. Klein asked, his voice rising in anger.

"Well, I don't know what they do with my 'study guides' after I submit them. That's on them, not me."

"Don't give me air quotes. Study guides, my ass. That's just disgraceful."

"Well, sir, please excuse me if I differ. I happen to think American schools are disgraceful."

"Well, you're just a cheater."

"Not me. I don't cheat. I genuinely do all the work."

"Don't be a smart-ass. You know what you're doing. How do you get away with that?"

"Get away with it? This is wide out in the open. I pay taxes. I could give you the company's website. You can read our disclaimers. We just sell study guides. I can't be held responsible if a few bad apples are going to use our research for impure purposes."

"You think it's funny now. But one day your doctor will be some moron who cheated his way through school. So when he botches your operation, you'll have yourself to thank."

"With all due respect, sir, if some incompetent schmuck who doesn't have the qualifications manages to coast his way through life and in spite of all his obvious deficiencies somehow gets to perform surgery on people because he got good grades, there's something terribly wrong with your system, and it's much bigger than cheating."

It was getting heated, which got Hope pretty excited. She was having a great time with it.

"Hope," Mr. Klein said, looking at his daughter like I had just left the room. "Where do you find these assholes?"

"Rick!" Mrs. Klein shouted.

"I should go." I started to get up.

"Sit down," he said calmly. "Everybody eat your turkey."

"It's really delicious, Mrs. Klein. So juicy."

"Thank you, David."

This type of hostility was nothing new to me. I have made no secret of my job, and I've received my fair share of harsh judgments. I've been called evil by complete strangers. I rarely get defensive. I tend to respectfully disagree, and more often I try to avoid being drawn into such confrontations if at all possible.

It was not possible with Hope's father. He always got under my skin, and I let it get the better of me. I enjoyed pissing him off. And I understand where he was coming from, obviously. He was just defending his profession. In the end, the fact that my job even existed was an indictment of what he did and how he did it. Certainly, he could sit in judgment. But he didn't know what I knew. I dealt with a far greater diversity of students than your average educator.

He had no idea. He didn't know the extent of it. He couldn't know how it permeates our schools. He didn't understand why students would take this way out, or why somebody like me would do a job like this. To him, this was a subterranean racket.

It isn't. It's mainstream. It's popular culture. It's taxable income. It's googleable.

Hope's dad was a department head, a sponsor of extracurricular activities, and a joyless prick. In this world, we were cast as ideological and strategic enemies.

"Sorry about my dad," Hope said on the ride home.

"Nah. Don't worry about it. I'm used to that shit. Besides, it's not like he doesn't have a point."

"Fuck him."

"Well, I agree with that, too. But seriously, what can I possibly say to defend myself?"

"You don't have to defend yourself. A lot of people would love to be able to do what you can do."

"Yeah . . . great . . . I've squandered more ability than most people ever get. I should feel really good about that. I'm a real fucking revolutionary."

"Don't let him make you feel that way. You know it's all bullshit. You think he's changing lives? His students hate him."

"It's not him. It has nothing to do with him. It's not even that I feel bad about what I'm doing. I don't. I've had much worse jobs. It's just, I can't take pride in this. I'm doing nothing of value with my life. Even if school is bullshit and what I'm doing isn't wrong, I contribute nothing. Even if I can rationalize what I'm doing, I can't take any pride in it. Your parents are right. My parents are right. I'm trash."

I wasn't feeling sorry for myself. I was just thinking, maybe I really was trash. But I was marketable trash, the kind of trash that sells like crazy as first-semester finals approach.

Let me explain finals.

By the end of Thanksgiving, cheating in school is as pervasive as Charlie Brown specials, Salvation Army bells, and songs about finding love on Christmas Eve. The students come to us in droves with their end-of-semester work, willing to pay a premium for a holiday season uninterrupted by school-related tedium. Holidays are for family-related tedium.

Every year, I have to find a way to fit in both. This is when I turn it on full blast. I am a robot. I am a machine. I am the evil T-1000, Johnny 5, and Max Headroom. I am a cybernetic organism sent from the future to help John Conner ace his Environmental Design elective.

I churn out pages upon pages of academic material for days on end. Twenty-hour days; two-hundred-page weeks; six dozen courses; fifteen majors; ten minutes of stretching here; forty minutes of sleep there, however my face lands on the keyboard. Sometimes I'll stop in between assignments, crack my back, hop around the room, and listen to James Brown. Get Up (I Feel Like Being a) Sex Machine.

Sometimes I don't have the time for funk. I'll just send off one assignment and open the next without pause. It takes me five seconds to breathe out my ten-page reconciliation on the simultaneous existence of God and evil before I start to breathe in a six-page consumer report on the best hybrid cars on the market.

This is finals. These are my darkest moments. When you study and write and defy personal reflection for enough hours over the course of enough days and without rest through the duration of a month . . . well, it can be an almost disembodying sensation. My fingers seem to melt into the keyboard; my eyes have stretched across the void between the monitor and my face; I feel nothing below my shoulders. I am a floating head; a living, breathing Wikipedia; a composite of facts, errors, opinions, and lies, available to the public for use at its own risk. I'm open all night.

But finals pay for my holiday shopping. I rock it out during finals. I admit, it's not exactly working on an offshore oil rig, but sometimes I actually feel like kind of a hard-ass.

Yeah, I've got a thirty-page paper to write tomorrow. No, I don't know what it's about yet. Yawn. Shot of tequila. Bong hit. Late night. Late start. Long day.

Some papers are harder than others. Sometimes I'm in the mood to really give it the old college try. Sometimes I'm in the mood to try less hard. The guy who contacts me two days before the deadline and asks, "Wheres my paper at!"—you'd better believe I'm trying less hard for him. I don't need the aggravation. I can write a five-page paper in thirty minutes if I don't mind producing a piece of donkey excrement.

And I admit, sometimes the sleep deprivation makes me a little moody. My life during finals is a prison sentence: solitary confinement, sensory deprivation, and yard detail. But I do it to myself. I choose my own deadlines.

And I can't get enough. Anything that looks interesting, that looks easy, that pays a good rate, that I've already written about . . . anything. It hardly matters. I just fill my calendar up and deal with it when the day arrives. I have deadlines every minute of every day. Deadlines own me. I write on car rides. I write on airplanes. I write in hotel rooms. I write in restaurants and bars. I write anywhere with an outlet, I write until my battery dies, and I write on other people's computers when I have to. My friends understand. They've seen me during finals before. I work until my neurons are fried.

And I am hopelessly, incurably optimistic. I think I can fit in everything. I never say no to work. A lot of work is scary, but no work is downright terrifying.

So I was buried in work when Hope's mother called me, not more than a week after Thanksgiving dinner.

This was strange. She had never called me. Not once. Panicked thoughts raced through my head. What had I done? Why could she be calling me? Oh god. Hope was pregnant, and her father was coming to kill me with his shotgun.

"Mrs. Klein? What's wrong? Is everything OK?"

"David? Nothing's wrong. Everything is fine. I just . . . I have a funny question for you." She sounded uncomfortable. Nothing new there. She always sounded a little uncomfortable.

"Oh. OK?"

"Umm. Hmm. OK, are you still writing the papers? Do you still do that?"

"Uhhh, yeah. Of course."

"OK. My friend's daughter . . . I'm not sure how to put this . . . but her daughter is a little silly. And she likes to put things off until the last minute. Anyway, now she's overwhelmed with exams and papers, and she's just basically trying to get into colleges now, and that's taking up a ton of her time. So I was telling . . . well, her mother heard about what you do and wanted to know if you could help . . ."

Heard about what I did? Right.

I'm sitting here thinking, You're out there telling your friends about me, I'm sure in the nicest possible terms, and where the hell were you when your husband was ripping me a new one? That's cool, though. It was all just business. Because I cut out the middle man when working directly with the customer, I could charge double my normal rate. I normally earned between fifteen and twenty dollars per page during finals, but without company policy holding me back, I could charge thirty-six dollars a page.

"Sure," I told her. "I can help. Have her e-mail the assignment to me."

The girl's mother—the one who would be paying for the assignment—she meant well. You will rush to judge her. And I don't blame you. My parents wouldn't have tolerated that crap. The way I was raised, you did your own dirty work.

This mom, she just wanted what was best for her kid. But her kid was so far behind. This mom was watching other parents in her affluent suburban development send their kids off to college, and she wanted that so badly for her kid. She was a good kid, she tried hard, and she had genuine learning deficiencies. And the lure of the university was too strong, its sociological importance too pronounced. This mom would do anything to walk her kid right up to the doorstep of the university, maybe even come in with her, hold her hand, and whisper encouraging things to her while she adjusted for the first four years or so.

This kid would soon be eligible to vote, smoke, and be tried as an adult, but the odds that she would be able to live on her own in the years immediately after college were slim.

And she was not alone. Not even a little.

In 2005, the *New York Times* reported that as of 2003, sixteen million American families were living with an individual over the age of eighteen. This was up seven million families from 1995, according to the U.S. Census Bureau's *American Housing Survey*, meaning that the number had nearly doubled in less than a decade.[1]

According to the *Christian Science Monitor*, a 2010 Pew Research Center poll revealed that one in seven households had experienced the return to home of a grown child in the previous year. The *CSM* also reports that according to the AFL-CIO, one in three young workers lives with his or her parents. This does not, of course, account for those from the current generation of recent graduates who are not employed. According to the *CSM*, this is a fairly significant population. The paper reports that "a smaller share of 16- to 24-year-olds are currently employed—46.1 percent—than at any time since the government began collecting data in 1948."[2]

Of course, there are a lot of reasons for this. The economy, the high cost of education, and shifting cultural tendencies all factor in. But it would be remiss of us to overlook the impact made by Mom's crushing embrace.

My customers—years in this business reveal—have been made half brain-dead by the suffocating proximity of their mothers.

Credit cards are the new umbilical cord, and they allow childhood dependencies to stretch grotesquely into college and beyond. It makes for a client base frequently prone to emotional instability. So say the frantic e-mails that have often greeted me after a nice evening out with the boys or an afternoon in the park.

I'll finish a paper, submit it to the customer, and go on with my day, only to learn that something has gone wrong, horribly horribly, wrong.

The citations aren't correct! The pages haven't been numbered!! You failed to hyphenate words that should have been hyphenated!!!

You'd be amazed at how often customers ask for revisions rather than insert the page numbers or hyphens themselves. I understand. My customers are just used to having things done for them. Hope's mother surprised me with her call, but I was hardly shocked by the request. This was something I had seen many times, actually.

I remember the first time I came into contact with a "cockpit mom." A 2011 article on the *Huffington Post* describes the phenomenon of cockpit mothering as the logical parenting model for one who views the "helicopter mom" approach as slightly negligent. The article explains:

Cockpit parents did more than hover. They sat right in the pilot's seat of their child's life, charting the course and navigating all of the twists and turns. And they often remain there well into their child's adulthood. The result is a trend of 20-somethings who are having trouble thriving as independent adults.

Cockpit parenting does come from a place of love. However, this intrusive and often controlling way of child rearing has caused many 20-somethings to be unequipped for life outside of the nest (which is why so many never leave or move back home after college). It is the children of cockpit parents who most often fit the stereotypes of Gen Y: sense of entitlement, consistent need for validation, non-self-starters, mediocre work ethic and a general lack of soft skills.[3]

A customer of mine whom we will refer to as Jub-Jub exhibited exactly that set of symptoms. Jub-Jub ordered a thirteen-page paper on human resource management on a Monday afternoon in late June. Again, contrary to the Thanksgiving rush, work is scarce in the summer, so I take on as much as I can even when the pay is not so great and the deadline is short. Jub-Jub needed his paper the next morning by nine A.M. I was down the shore, staying at a friend's house, but I needed the money, so I took it on. I figured I'd ask for an extension, get up early, and work on it into the afternoon. At thirteen pages for $150, Jub-Jub was getting a good deal; the least he could do was give me a twenty-four-hour lead time.

I grabbed up the assignment and immediately sent an e-mail to the customer requesting an extension to two the next afternoon.

I heard nothing from Jub-Jub. I have a smartphone that I keep on me at all times. I brought it to the beach and awaited the verdict. If Jub-Jub couldn't give me the extension, I could just e-mail the customer service supervisor and ask him to repost the order on the board.

The evening came. We watched the Phillies game. I took Hope out to the casinos. We ate, drank, gambled, and did inappropriate things in public. I didn't make much loot in the summers, but I had my freedom. No word from Jub-Jub. If it was urgent, I figured, I'd have heard from him.

I set my alarm for six-thirty A.M., was up by seven, was show-ered, caffeinated, and writing by eight. I wrote at a shore-town pace. A little sleepy. A little hungover. Under a summer gauze of laziness. I like writing this way. I heard nothing from the customer, and I felt no pressure to speed through the assignment. I took my time. I read sources. I thought out my sentences. I wrote a halfway-decent paper.

I submitted it at two P.M. I heard from the customer less than an hour later.

> I just read over the essay . . . I think the writer is not answering the topic at all . . . my god . . . i have been waiting for this essay for so long, I was expecting an essay at least match the topic. I know there is a rewrite service . . . but how long does it takes? Moreover, I requested Harvard Referencing System, but the writer did not follow this. I'm looking forward your reply. I need this within 24-hours

I responded immediately, "I will review the essay and do my best to address those concerns by this evening."

I had lunch and a Frisbee toss on the beach. Two hours had passed when I received the following message:

> Dear Writer
>
> May I know how is the essay goes?
> May I know when it can be done.(it is already 2 hours after the due time)
> Thank you very much!
>
> Yours Sincerely.

I responded immediately, telling Jub-Jub, "As promised, I will have your revisions completed by this evening. Your patience is very much appreciated."

Jub-Jub responded immediately.

Dear Writer Tomar

Thank you very much for your reply.
I really appreciate your help on my essay.

I'm looking forward to hearing the good news about completion from you.

Thank You!
Regard!

Moments later, I received the following e-mail:

Dear Tomar

After I read all the pages, I found the whole essay is not answer-
ing the topic which I required.

The essay is discussing about "Strategic Human Resource
Management Theory and Practice" from the introduction
to the content then conclusion . . . the topic which i gave is
"Examine the extent to which Strategic Human Resource
Management Theory and Practice is differently applied during
period of significant economic recession from times of rapid
growth"

i can not find anything to talk about "during period of significant
economic recession from times of rapid growth".

moreover, I required "Introduction: not required"
but the essay still have the introduction . . .

besides, i required fully Harvard Referencing System. I think
the referencing is not according to this.

to conclude, there three major area for re-write

1. please emphasis "during period of significant economic re-cession from times of rapid growth", which the main discussion should be this, but not "Strategic Human Resource Management Theory and Practice"

2. please use Harvard Referencing style

3. please do not write introduction

I would hope, before re-write the essay, please take read the topic completely, and also take a look at the requirement which i wrote.

Thank you very much!

Yours Sincerely

Ummm. OK. I had thought we had already settled the matter. Whatever. I sent a message back immediately, indicating that "upon reviewing the essay, it does seem apparent that I have addressed matters relating to economic recession and rapid growth. I think upon a closer review of the essay, you will find that though this exact phrase was not used, the topic was discussed extensively. As agreed upon earlier, I am still more than happy to revise the cita-tions. As I proceed, I will also try to clarify the language where ap-propriate. Thanks so much."

Without a hint of protest, Jub-Jub responded.

sorry, just now forgot to mention, as i said in the requirement/ Instructions before,

"please use: theory+example+further discussion+elaborate in detail."

I responded, "I will take that under advisement." Whatever it meant. I'm no good at math.

Jub-Jub responded, "Thank you Tomar!"

A mere fifteen minutes later, another unprompted message:

Hello Dear writer

Could you do me a faver to meet my essay's topic and finish it before 7pm tonight.
It is the deadline for me!!!!!!!!!!!!

Please understand me!!!!!!!!!!! I am so, so anxiously waiting for it right now!!

Thanks very much

Jub-Jub

What the hell? Was I being punk'd? What the hell was Jub-Jub's problem? All right, I told myself. Stay calm. Be polite.

Jub-Jub,
As I indicated to you in our earlier series of conversations, I will have the assignment revised by this evening. Though we typically avail a 24 hour revision policy, I am making all arrangements to have this work submitted to you by 7PM EST. Your continued patience and understanding are very much appreciated and I am confident you will be pleased with the final product.

Moments later:

Hello Tomar

I have to tell you that I am Jub-Jub's mother, some replies were not from Jub-Jub, but from me, I am sorry that I wrote something looks "funny".

Anyway, I hope you will finish the ordered essay in a good quality and hope Jub-Jub will get it from you as soon.

thanks very much

Mrs Jones

What a relief. I had thought I was writing for somebody with multiple personality disorder. Turned out I was just writing for a kid who would live in his mother's basement until he was forty.

This paper was for a senior in college. So presumably, this was a 22-year-old student. Do you know that the average life expectancy in Swaziland is 39.6 years? This guy would have been a tribal elder there. He would already have been more than half dead. Something told me this guy wasn't ready to lead the tribe.

I felt bad for this kid. I really did. He'd never had a chance. What a life it must be, to have your mother helping you cheat. How long did she plan on holding his hand? How long would she shield him from the wisdom to be imparted by failure? How long would she embrace his baffling impotence?

I didn't know him personally, but I imagined Jub-Jub as a harness kid. His mother had leashed him in public and given him a helmet and a three-foot playing radius. Jub-Jub hadn't been potty trained because his mother had a deathly fear of swimming. She couldn't have Jub-Jub drowning in his own house. Jub-Jub had had a colostomy. It made for less time that he had to be separated from Mom. It just made sense. They had gotten a two-for-one surgery deal by having a LoJack installed as well.

Jub-Jub had always performed well in school. His mother's lawyer was number two on the speed dial, behind the doctor who got Jub-Jub his learning pills. Anytime Jub-Jub got a C, the lawyer got a call. This was usually enough to get Jub-Jub a B or better.

Jub-Jub's mother had raised a sponge. She had raised a loofah. She had raised one of those revolting coconut-marshmallow Peeps. Jub-Jub was soft, squooshy, and destined to be eaten alive.

It's possible I've taken some liberties with Jub-Jub's story. All I really know about him is that he was most likely of a legal age to have died fighting for his country four years earlier, and his mother was still helping him just to correspond with the guy he'd hired to help him cheat through school.

Jub-Jub's mother meant well. She just wanted what was best for Junior. And she would bite the head off a live chicken to make it happen.

Jub-Jub was not a bum for no reason. It had been enabled. It had been encouraged. And it was the only thing he knew.

I remember thinking earnestly about it when pressed by Hope's dad that Thanksgiving Day. Was I to blame for America's future of incompetence? There was no denying it. I was part of a broken system, and one that I despised. But I was just the obvious part, the trash pile in the dumpster out back. Until you've been inside the system the way I have, you don't know that the halls and the classrooms and the administrative offices stink of industrial waste.

CHAPTER 8

Ain't No Love in the Heart of the City

Hope and I broke up. It was a matter of inevitability. I needed to focus on my work . . . is what I told myself as I descended into a sexual drought of epic proportions. So I did exactly that. I threw myself into my assignments, sublimating all of the resentment I had for school, family, and my ex-girlfriends into resentment for my customers . . . not that they didn't deserve it.

I was disconsolate and surly, sarcastic and vindictive, openly condescending and brimming with smart-assery. I hadn't developed the type of thick-skinned stoicism that makes a superior customer service agent. On my darker days, and there were quite a few at this time, I really let the customers get to me. The constant hum of ignorance vibrated in my ears.

Let's get past the idea that there are a lot of students in colleges and graduate schools who are incapable of completing the work assigned to them. This is a fact. Too many students simply arrive at colleges lacking the basic academic skills necessary to conduct empirical research, to write competent essays, or to grasp the complex ideas required to satisfy university-level course objectives. According to the Organisation for Economic Co-operation and Development's Programme for International Student Assessment survey, which ranks the performance of OECD member nations' educational systems, in 2009 the United States ranked twenty-fifth in math, seventeenth in science, and fourteenth among all surveyed nations in reading.[1] On the combined reading scale, therefore, we were outperformed by Korea, Finland, Canada, New Zealand,

Australia, the Netherlands, Belgium, Switzerland, Japan, Norway, and Estonia. We're in a dead heat with Poland and Iceland.

But hey, at least we don't live in East Timor, right?

Well, of course, those struggling students don't just get better or go away. They have become so significant a portion of the student population that we have no choice but to manage them. This is why many of my customers don't simply lack the skills necessary to complete the assigned work. They even lack the skills necessary to competently give the task to someone else. Many of these students just have no idea what they're doing at school. None whatsoever.

Quite a good number of my customers, I learned early, didn't know how to ask for what they needed until they didn't get it. It was just an idiosyncrasy, I suppose, but I've always been a bit volatile. This kind of thing did not sit well with me.

My customers constantly pushed me to the edge of civility with their incessant e-mails, their furious demands, their critical expectations . . . their insults. My writing was subject to a new kind of indignity. I found satisfaction in doing this work—and doing it well when possible—even though I wasn't getting any real credit for it. But that feeling quickly wilted when I had to endure the scholarly scrutiny of a dissatisfied customer who misspelled his own name on the order form.

And the stupidity, the sheer, incalculable, and inconsiderate stupidity, a kind of dumb that bordered on antisocial and made me, frankly, really nervous about this nation's liberal distribution of guns, cars, computers, and other weapons of midrange destruction; this kind of stupidity just flooded into my angry little life and made my stomach churn with hopelessness.

These were my paying customers. I had courted them. Yet faced with a particularly egregious e-mail, I would quake internally with a type of malaise that came from knowing that this person was so stupid and inconsiderate that I had no hope of engaging him in a rational exchange about his assignment. (I recognized that this very incompetence was at least one reason my job existed in the first place. But of course, this was rarely the first thing that came

to mind when my customers berated me.) I would be overcome
with a sort of socially conscious desire to revoke this individual's
right to waste oxygen that somebody else might have used to make
a thought, a desire to reach my hand through the Internet and cram
my fingers right up his nostrils.

I was working through a lot of my own issues at the time,
granted.

Once, I wrote a six-page paper on organizational communication and conflict resolution for a master's-level class. The assignment came with the following instructions:

> comments: there is no topic as such, there are few questions to
> b nswered.

I completed the assignment using the questions forwarded by
the client. I received the following response:

> Hello!
> I recieved paper from David.
> It was absolutely different. he didn't answer those questions that
> I sent him.
> I am suppose to fail for this. It is not those questions that I sent
> him to answer, he just put together my different classe that i sent
> him as an guidelines.
> The paper he sent me is nothing, I can't show it to my teacher.
> My deadline is tomorrow untill 11 pm.
> I hope you will fix it. Or i am lost. You have to do something.
> wating for your reply.
> It is urgent.

"You have to do something," he said.

How about that? What a power trip. This kid thought he was
my boss. As far as I was concerned, I didn't have a boss. As I have
said, I would try to be fair and give revisions where revisions were
due. But I'd be damned if I was going to take this kind of insolence from anybody, let alone one of my half-brain customers. His

stupidity was paying my bills, so I suppose I wasn't really in a position to be self-righteous. But I was anyway.

And so I was always just on the fringe of conflict.

Like any good, healthy passive-aggressive, I turned in assignments with habitual lateness, I ignored customer e-mails, and to those who were impetuously entitled assholes, I displayed contempt in the quality of my work.

Try to guess what kind of paper a repeat customer got after writing the following e-mail to request an assignment about Laurel and Hardy:

Let me tell you that my research paper better get a better grade then my essay because I am not happy with a 70 as a score. I paid a lot of money for that one and this one. I would like a refund on my essay you know I can't even make this one up!

Thinking back now, I can't be sure, but I probably wrote that paper while drinking.

I dedicated half of my emotional energy on any given day just to breathing out the impulse to tell every customer exactly what I was thinking.

"I apologize that this assignment appears not to answer the questions posed in the instructions. Below, please find a link to a dictionary. This contains the definitions of words. These will help you to better understand the English language."

"Thank you so much for your constructive criticism. I will take your notes on 'sentince stricture' and 'gramer' under advisement. I'm getting such good advice here that I almost feel like *I* should be paying *you*. Please provide me with your home address and a self-addressed stamped envelope large enough for a letter bomb and I'll send a check directly."

"I'm sorry that your assignment did not receive the grade that you anticipated. However, if I were in your position, I'd probably be super-polite to the guy who has enough information to destroy you and all your hopes and dreams for the future . . . not that I would, but you should just know that I could."

I never e-mailed any of those clever things, though. I tried to remind myself that this was the business I'd chosen, that this was simply the nature of the clientele, that I should at least be grateful that none of these fools was actually my boss.

How had I gotten myself into such a position, taking orders from morons, absorbing hostile e-mails from losers, enduring wantonly brandished exclamation points from people who wouldn't know a good sentence if it jumped up and expressed all over their faces?

I was working hard, but dispiritedly. And out of the imperative to make money, I continued to take on too many papers, more than I could handle. Leaving aside material exigencies, the more work I did, the less time I would have for personal reflection, which was something I generally avoided at this determinedly single and isolated point in my life.

I had moved through high school and college in a series of melodramatic adolescent relationships with a dozen incompatible girls. That's all right. You're not meant to marry every woman whom you love. And in my experience, you're not even meant to particularly like every woman whom you love. But after a series of these relationships, varying in length from ten minutes to ten years and leading right into the middle of my early adult years, I was suddenly alone in a crowded place.

Fortunately, Philly was a growing scene. At first, it was just me and Ethan there. But after a few years, the city started to become crowded with good company. Country Sam moved into the hood with his bong and his banjo. Damon, a salesman with the industrial cleaning supply company, rehabbed a house with Paulie and moved down from the suburbs. I ran into Gould on the street one day. We had been in the same bunk at camp years back. My oldest friend, big Harmon K., moved back home from school in Boston.

So we started a Thursday-night poker game, with my buddies and I hunched around a coffee table until four in the morning, occasionally standing to stretch, grunt, complain, and muse on how terrible it would be to go to work in just a few hours. Once in a while, the drunk who lived to one side of us or the drug dealer who lived to the other side would join the game.

Then Bree transferred from Rutgers to Temple, up in North Philly. She moved back into her mom's cozy log cabin in the pines of South Jersey, but she spent most of her time in the city. We split pitchers of beer, went out to nice dinners, rented crappy movies, and ate junk food together on Saturday nights.

It was just like old times.

She was my late-night call, the last word of my day, and the reason I sometimes appeared to be elsewhere when I was with whomever I might be dating at the time. We had gotten through college with not too much more than the occasional ill-advised kiss or yet more ill-advised wandering hand; there was never a discussion, very few explicit confrontations with jealousy, but endless dancing around the obvious intensity and intractability of our emotional investment in this relationship. We partied with the same people, behaved with handsy familiarity in public, silently attempted to cock-block one another wherever possible, and, ultimately, went our separate ways when it came time to pair off for the night.

But things were different when she got to Philly. We were both single, and we both did everything in our power not to acknowledge this as an opportunity. Nevertheless, my various incipient love interests vanished anticlimactically, and I became quietly inconsolable about the fact that Bree and I were in all probability meant to be with one another but never would be. After ten years of friendship, even on the blurriest night, the boundaries remained sharply defined.

A customer ordered a love poem, and I swiped it off the board. I was hardly in a position to dispense romantic lyricism, but a job was a job. He wanted a poem that would reveal his true feelings to a beloved ex-girlfriend. According to the customer, the girl already had a new boyfriend, but he was convinced that the right verse would persuade her to break up with her boyfriend, run open-armed toward him, and passionately embrace him in a golden meadow of dandelions.

He asked that the poem be "emotional" and that it "rhyme." The standard two-page paper is about six hundred words, earning me between twenty and thirty dollars in twenty minutes. A rhyming poem would probably be several fewer words, and would therefore earn me a slightly better rate.

Besides, to break up the monotony of research papers and book reports, a sordid love triangle certainly had its appeal. I was in the mood to satirize love. I'd listened to more than enough Journey to know how a bad love poem should sound. I delivered the following completed work:

I hold you in my arms
In dreams that plague my sleep.
I'm taunted by your charms
In daylight's plodding creep.

The minutes spent without you
Drip mercilessly slow
Down time's jagged avenue
But I doubt you even know.

Because I'm idling through my days
Struggling to remember your touch
And I'm thinking of you always
Wondering if you think of me as much.

But I know you're not alone at night
Warmed by memories of me
Instead, I know, he holds you tight.
He's where I want to be.

If you'll give me another chance though
I can be the one
We can start out nice and slow
Like we've only just begun.

I've never gotten over you
And I fear I never will
So I hope that we can start anew
There's a void in my heart you can fill.

What happened in the past,
We'll forever leave behind.
Happily together at last.
Our futures are combined.

I don't know where we're going.
It's inscribed unseen above.
But the horizon's brightly glowing
With the promise of our love.

One hundred and eighty words in ten minutes. Killer.

If this guy had been my friend, I probably would have advised him that writing poetry to a girl who didn't already like you was basically sexual suicide; that she would most likely think it was pretty creepy; that if it did somehow work because she just loved poetry that much, she would wonder why he wasn't as good at rhyming stuff in real life; that if she did ultimately become suspicious and rifled through his old e-mails, she would be horrified to learn that the great testament to his love, the gesture that he would otherwise recount, teary-eyed, for his children with increasing sentimentality at the passing of each year, was little more than a custom-made Hallmark card that had taken me less time to write than a one-page paper on bladder control issues in older adults.

But who knew? Maybe this girl was just waiting for this guy to make a play. Maybe she felt the same way. Maybe she just needed him to make some grand and romantic gesture like charging his mom's credit card to an academic-ghostwriting website for a poem composed by a total stranger in order to see her own true feelings. Maybe.

Maybe not. Two weeks later, the client's situation appeared to have only gotten worse. Being lovelorn myself, I certainly did not intend to minimize whatever it was that the client was going through. I just wondered why he didn't maybe visit a florist or a chocolatier instead. Ours was not one of the businesses that saw a jump in revenue around Valentine's Day.

Whatever the case, he didn't blame the poem. If anything, he was more convinced than ever that this girl just needed to read a really persuasive rhyming poem about his feelings. He came back to me with another set of instructions.

Now he wanted a poem that basically said that he was willing to wait for her. He wanted her to know that he valued her friendship and that he felt that, eventually, their love would prevail. He didn't want to put any pressure on her. He just wanted her to know. He also wanted this one to be emotional and to rhyme.

I guess for this one, I was thinking more Meat Loaf than Journey. Frankly, it may even verge on REO Speedwagon.

I remember when first I met you
How fast my heart did beat
You were tight with my x-girlfriend
But you would make my life complete

You've become my closest friend
The only one who counts
Those times when I had nobody
You gave me every ounce.

I know that you'll be there for me
You know I'm there for you
I'm layin' it on the line to say
I know that you'll be true.

If I could spend my everyday
Looking deep into your eyes
Then maybe I wouldn't need any other girls
And you wouldn't need other guys.

Your beauty is entrancing,
Your grace, your smile, your wit
You bring happiness with your company
And I cherish every bit

I'm sure if I didn't have you
My life would be much worse

My heart is spending money
That you kindly reimburse

Who can say where this will lead
But of this one thing I'm sure
Whatever is between us
It rings down to the core

I'm content today to see you
In any manner fate will allow
But I look ever toward the future
While relishing the now.

The dawning is wide open
To rays of morning anew
So from the dusk of one long day
Will be a sunrise for me and you.

I have no idea how that all turned out. For all I know, they are married by now. They could have three kids, a dog, and a thrice-mortgaged house.

Or maybe she filed a restraining order against him, and my former client is not allowed within one hundred yards of her property. Ah, the mysteries of love.

At the time, anything less than devastating heartbreak would have surprised me. And not just for this guy—for all of my pathetic customers, and for me, too. I had taken to a sort of brooding defensiveness around Bree that intensified with the presence of other men.

For months, really, I had been stricken by her, and everybody seemed to know it but us. I guess that what we were both too dumb to see just struck others as obvious. Over the years of hanging out with her, I had even gotten to be pretty close with her dad. We would hang out and listen to records. One day, as he was leaving my house, he said, "I hope you and my daughter get together. Y'know. She'll figure it out."

This obviously did not help. It got to the point where I could hardly stand to be around her with this feeling pushing its way through me. There was little she could do or say that didn't set me off with jealousy, that didn't touch my insecurities over her passive rejection. One night, as we tried to talk out dinner plans, the reality that we were fake-dating and in all likelihood had been fake-dating for the better part of a decade simply came to a head. And Bree doesn't put up with bullshit. So she called me on it.

"What the fuck is with you?"

"Nothing. What?!"

"Don't give me that shit. Something is up. You're totally weird with me."

"I'm not."

I couldn't even look at her.

"You are. Are you mad at me? What the hell?"

"No. There's nothing. It's fine."

"It's not fine."

Silence without eye contact.

"Yup," she said. "This is definitely weird."

More silence.

"Well? You gonna say something?"

"There's nothing to say. Things are messed up between us, and I think maybe we need to not hang out for a while."

"Well . . . ," she said, thinking about this for a minute, "well, you're simply going to have to get over whatever *this* is because that isn't an option."

"You don't get to just call the shots like that. This whole situation, this whole arrangement between us is fucking me up and . . ."

"And what?"

"And . . . I don't know what. I don't know what to tell you."

"Well, tell me something, because you're not making a whole lot of sense right now."

I supposed I wasn't, but I just figured we both knew what I was talking about here. But she kept pushing, and finally I snapped.

"Fine! Fine! You want to hear it. I'm in love with you . . . and I always have been. And there's nothing I can do to talk myself out of it. And there it is . . ."

Stunned silence.

"I don't know . . . what . . ."

"Yeah, well, I tried to keep it to myself, and now you've forced me to say it."

"Well, no offense, but you weren't exactly doing much to hide it."

"Yeah, well, there it is, and now everything is fucked up . . ."

"It's not that I don't love you. You know I do. I just . . ."

"Yeah, I know all about it. And I'm not trying to have a whole conversation about this with you. I know where you stand. But I want what I want."

"That's not fair! You can't just change everything because you can't handle our friendship. Handle it."

"I can't. I think we need to not see each other for a while."

"Yeah, well, I really think you need to get over that shit."

"Nice. Real nice."

"So then . . . what?"

"I think we need to not see each other for a while. I need to not see you for a while."

And we didn't see each other for a while. A year passed. I went about my business with the passion of a surgically impaired lab rat. The apathy came through loud and clear in my work.

The angry customers ate me alive.

"Oh My God! What is this paper that has been delivered to me?? It has NOTHING to do with what I've asked for—it's not a research proposal, it's not about global marketing, the paper is about globalization in economic perspective with ONE reference in it, and no bibliography included. Bad is not even a word, it's completely irrelevant. In fact, a word marketing is not mentioned ONCE in a paper. Is this a cruel joke?"

I'm thinking back on it now, and I'm pretty sure it wasn't intended as a cruel joke. Maybe it was. I don't remember.

I do remember the assignment that got me fired. It was about Africa during the cold war, and it was only two pages long. I finished the paper late, something about which I had been warned several times by my employer. The customer was pissed about the delay to begin with and even more pissed about the completed assignment itself.

I was a repeat offender by that point, so I hardly had a leg to stand on. But I'm still pretty sure I satisfied the assignment's instructions. Screw the teacher who asked for a two-page assessment of how the different governments of Malawi, Mozambique, Angola, Ethiopia, Zaire, Sudan, and Somalia interacted with the competing superpowers of the cold war. The customer accused me of providing only a superficial assessment of these individual interactions, as though I could be fooled into writing an additional ten pages for free just because you couldn't possibly address the subject in any less space. Customers are always looking for freebies.

And this one time, I slipped up. I was sapped of the emotional energy needed to restrain myself. I was feeling empty and without a whole lot to look forward to, and I wasn't going to be bullied. I'd be damned if I was going to waste an opportunity for satisfaction.

"I apologize that this assignment did not meet your high academic standards," I wrote to the customer. "Perhaps you'd have better luck doing your own work, smart guy."

It was some time coming anyway, but the paper-writing company fired me and was fully justified in doing so. I was unraveling. Ethan was kind enough to let me write papers under his account. I repaid him by taking on too much work, ignoring repeat warnings about my habitual lateness, and, eventually, also getting him fired.

CHAPTER 9

Degree Mill University

How terrifying it is to feel that you have no future. How hopeless it is to feel that *this*—whatever *this* is, the things you have now, and are not satisfied with—is all you will ever have. How devastating it is to feel that the brief time allotted to you by chance on this earth will never get any better and that you will not only not have the things that you want but also, for most of your time here, you will not have the things that you need.

These are the fears that bring panic to my generation.

While I scrambled to find work for myself and Ethan, my buddy Finestone was across town facing the same fears that we were, fears about making an honest living, about making a passable living, and about hopelessness. I went to college with Finestone, and like me, like Ethan, he was wrestling with these fears and exploiting them at the same time.

And his employer, which we will refer to here as Shady Trade University, knew all about them. The university talked about such fears in its training materials. It taught recruiters how to understand and exploit them. They—all the for-profit colleges that fester before our generation—have learned to exploit the terrifying reality of each target's situation. Their admissions processes are driven by cold-calling telemarketers working toward mandatory quotas by using hard-sell tactics and psychological manipulation designed to play on the fears of potential students.

Finestone and I were each raised the same way, and the same way as a lot of middle-class Americans. We were raised to believe that college was everything. You *must go to college!* Your grand-parents didn't go to college, so they labored in the dung mines for the Kaiser. Your parents didn't go to college, so all they could af-ford was a house in the basement of a *Stomp* rehearsal hall. Your brother didn't go to college, and now he sits in a lawn chair at a traffic light selling fabric roses.

If you don't go to college, you will end up a loser. You will have no prospects. You will wander the earth alone like the Incredible Hulk, with nothing to contribute, no viable skills, and nothing to look forward to and possibly wearing shredded purple jean shorts.

And then a chipper-sounding young person calls you on your ten-minute lunch break at the hog-fat-rendering plant and says, "I have a way that you can take control of your life. Education is the key."

You say, "I really can't afford to go to school."

Then he says, "With the job market being what it is today, you can't afford not to go to school."

"But I've never really been good at school. In fact, I recently lost a piece of my brain in an automobile accident."

"It doesn't matter. We have no standards whatsoever. As far as we're concerned, you're already in."

Recruiters are trained to have answers for everything.

It doesn't matter if you can't afford it. We'll get you financial aid. It doesn't matter that you have struggled with long-term learning deficiencies. We'll make you into a better student, and a better hu-man being. It doesn't matter that you can't use a fork without in-juring your eye. We've got classes for that. It doesn't matter if you are sometimes startled and moved to ask "Who's there?" by the sound of your own flatulence. We think you'd probably be a good candidate for distance learning.

It doesn't matter your disposition or deficiencies. There is a school out there that is willing to take your money and give you a degree. And it will tell you anything to make you believe that you can get this degree, nay, that you must get this degree if your life is to be anything greater than a series of random and directionless events.

My buddy Finestone confirmed this for me. While I was looking for another job aiding America's lesser academic specimens, he was helping to create them. In many ways, our two enterprises worked in concert with one another, part of a massive conspiracy to populate the world with morons.

Shady Trade University, according to its website, serves roughly fifty-four thousand students across more than eighty campuses. During his two years of employment there, Finestone was a jack-of-all-trades. He worked in Student Support. He worked in the Business Office. He worked in Admissions. He was shuttled around three departments across three campuses. In a variety of work experiences, Finestone witnessed the ins and outs of this corporation.

Now, before I get into what he learned about them, I must say that I bear no personal grudge against the Shade Trade business or any other like it. Among the larger and more successful institutions that fall under the "for-profit" or "proprietary" label are the University of Phoenix, Kaplan University, DeVry University, Capella University, Strayer University, Walden University, and ITT Technical Institute.

In a way, I kind of loved for-profit colleges. And not just because their students were some of my best clients. Naturally, we would court that type, but no more or less than students at fancy private institutions, state schools, community colleges, or graduate schools.

It's just that the work assigned at such institutions was so easy, the standards so low, and the priorities so far removed from the interests of honest student evaluation that I could pretty much take a laxative, wad up a sheet of paper, wipe my ass with it, fax it over to the student, and collect my pay. I never did, of course. I prefer the gentle caress of a quilted two-ply, thank you very much.

The for-profit school that I encountered most frequently in my work, we will refer to as McLearning University. I treated my McLearning University assignments with all the respect owed to the word jumble in the Sunday funnies. Maybe even less. I'll share a pretty obvious secret of the trade right here. I have been known—at least to myself—to recycle material. I mean, I'm getting paid to churn out content. And it is original, mostly. But look, if I've already written a five-page paper about supply chain management at some fictional industrial conglomerate called Riordan Manufacturing, and I'm asked to write a paper of almost identical details one year later, and again two years later, and again four years later . . . if they don't have any quality control, why should I?

Many a McLearning assignment has been accompanied by the warning that the Turnitin software will be employed to ensure that the assignment has not been copied from the Internet. Turnitin is a kind of plagiarism watchdog, a service that maintains a constantly growing bank of completed classroom assignments and cross-checks all newly submitted assignments for "content overlap" both with this database and with all content available on the Web. But there are easy ways to get around it if you have a mind to. Using an internal thesaurus is a pretty good one: I can change 50 percent of the words in each sentence and create an assignment that won't raise a single red flag.

Still, Turnitin is a great Band-Aid because it fosters the illusion that plagiarism is being deterred, which is tremendous for any for-profit university. Many for-profit schools maintain formal disciplinary procedures in the event of academic dishonesty, but the consequences are highly variant, based on the findings of investigation, hearing, and committee arbitration. In any event, expulsion is a poor tactic in a consumer industry. Meanwhile, my work goes undetected, no matter how many times I resell the same paper to for-profit schools. Replace "argues" with "asserts," "recommendation" with "suggestion," and "conclusion" with "resolution." Give the old paper a new title, slap its bottom, and send it to market.

Even if actual human beings are reading these assignments (and I can't prove that they do or they don't), I presume they don't care either way about cheating. I also presume that they surely know on some level that they need cheating students to survive. Me, Turnitin, McLearning University. We all profit off students turning in clean papers and getting good grades—regardless of how that goal is achieved.

I know I sound cynical, but as a scumbag working in a scumbag racket, I know opportunism when I see it. And Finestone described a world of sleaze that would make Bernie Madoff proud.

So how do these for-profit schools work, exactly? According to a 2011 article in *Bloomberg Businessweek*, the Pell Grant is what keeps the scheme in business. The Pell Grant is awarded by the Department of Education to prospective students who demonstrate financial need and who have not yet earned a bachelor's degree. While most students will require additional private loans to combat the high cost of education, as a grant the Pell does not call for repayment. It is a foundational block in the financial aid pyramid. The *Businessweek* article indicates that though only about 12 percent of U.S. students are enrolled in for-profit colleges, students at for-profit colleges account for a full quarter of all Pell Grants awarded by the Department of Education.[1]

And to what end, exactly? Why, to educate, of course; to help the less fortunate seize opportunity; to give a fighting chance to the disadvantaged among us. Hell, I don't need to tell you. You've driven past the billboards. You've thrown their mailers into your recycling can. You've seen those commercials where the girl with sex appeal says that you can earn a degree while sitting at home in your undergarments.

You can't put a price tag on education and not expect market behavior to take hold. Sure, we'd all love to buy our clothes at Brooks Brothers and Bloomingdale's. But some of us, we're still going to have to shop at T.J. Maxx and Ross Dress for Less. We just hope that our off-brand slacks and irregular T-shirts don't cost us opportunities for popularity and mating. And while I can think of no more important ambition than the perpetuation of the species, this analogy is still more troubling when applied to higher education. Here, the off-brand and the irregular are not simply of a lower quality. They are criminally exploitative.

A 2010 article on the *Huffington Post* reports that one such for-profit institution uses "guerrilla registration" in order to keep its enrollment numbers high. According to its own internal sources, at the end of 2010, the institution had 58,200 students enrolled in online programs and another 7,400 enrolled in classroom-based programs. The *Huffington Post* describes the experience of one such "enrolled" student after she attempted to withdraw from her program. The student recalls:

[An] academic advisor told her she could simply fill out a with-drawal form and incur no additional expenses beyond the reg-istration fees she had already paid. But a year and a half later, in 2006, collections agents began hounding her, she says, demand-ing that she pay some $10,000 in supposedly overdue tuition charges. Despite having attended only two online sessions, [the student] had remained officially enrolled at [the university] for nearly a year after her withdrawal.

Far from an aberration, [this] experience typifies the results of a practice known informally inside [the university] as "guerrilla registration": academic advisors have long enrolled students in classes they never take, without their consent and sometimes even after they have sought to withdraw from the university.[2]

Hmmmmmmm. That's peculiar.

Why on earth would they do that?

In his first days at Shady Trade University, Finestone wondered the same thing.

According to Finestone, Shady Trade University was, at the time, divided into two primary departments: Operations and Academics.

The campus director was the head of Operations, and the dean was the head of Academics. Allegedly, these individuals were equal partners. But in actuality, Finestone assessed, the dean was little more than a scheduler of classes and an occasional tutor. The cam-pus director was the big cheese. Operations, Finestone learned immediately and repeatedly, always came before Academics. In the hierarchy of Shady Trade University, the dean was simply a fore-man on a production line. The real shit happened across the way at Operations, where decisions were made and futures affected.

Operations was divided into three subsidiary departments: Admissions, the Business Office, and Student Support. Finestone began in Student Support.

His title was student support coordinator, and his basic func-tion was to ensure that students who were currently enrolled at Shady Trade were reenrolled for the coming semester. He would call first-semester students from a printout and portray himself as an academic adviser.

But after about a month of calling students, Finestone saw that something was wrong. At a rate of roughly 10 percent, the "students" he was calling were insisting that they had already withdrawn from classes and had no intent of enrolling again. Finestone was confused. Could a pattern this consistent possibly be the result of a clerical error?

Finestone went to the business office manager and explained the situation. The business office manager assured him that the students who "claimed" they had withdrawn had never withdrawn. The students were in fact registered and enrolled.

Finestone wasn't satisfied with this answer. He went to the admissions manager, who said, "Here's what we do. When students submit their withdrawal requests or forms, we don't withdraw them. We ignore their forms."

Before Finestone could protest, the admissions manager looked him in the eye and said, "This is a business decision."

"But why?" Finestone asked.

"So we can hit our recruitment numbers."

"But what good is it having a student that doesn't produce any revenue?"

"You're new with the company. You don't understand. This is a business decision."

This was a shock to Finestone's system. He had come to Shady Trade from a national retail chain with a good reputation. At his old company, if you fudged numbers, you would be summarily dismissed. He contemplated calling an ethics hotline but ultimately decided that he was too new. It was too early to make waves.

There was so much that he didn't know about his employers, or even about his job responsibilities. Finestone told me that, at the time, Shady Trade had no training process for employees working in either Student Support or the Business Office. Only the recruiters working in Admissions were given comprehensive job training.

No job training was required for Student Support. Either you figured it out and went along or you were out on your ass. It was thus that Finestone came to understand many of the business decisions that were made at Shady Trade.

Here was the basic and formal process for dealing with requests for withdrawal from a class. Let's say that a "lead," as they were referred to within the company, was contacted six weeks before the start of a semester, succumbed to high-pressure sales tactics, and, against his better judgment, verbally agreed to enrollment. Then a week passed, and he decided to preemptively drop out.

The lead would contact his admissions officer and explain that he couldn't afford to take time off from work/couldn't be away from the kids long enough to go to school/was serving a stretch of six to ten for knocking over a liquor store/had done some research and realized that community college was a much better deal for the money. Whatever it was, the lead wanted to bail. The admissions officer would be instructed to turn to the internal script, to provide every possible reason why this would be the biggest mistake of the lead's life; why it made sense now more than ever and especially in light of the concerns expressed by the lead for him to invest in his future; why distance learning was a great option for the recently incarcerated and dangerously violent.

No withdrawals were to be granted until after the lead had been given the same hard sell to which previous experience had already proved he was vulnerable. Only after every sales tactic had been exhausted and "un-enrollment" had become imminent was the admissions officer to tell the lead that "as per your request, you will be removed from the class and from our list."

At that point, the admissions officer would hang up the phone and inform the admissions manager that the student in question wanted to un-enroll. Now let's say that this scenario applied to fifteen people during one particular month.

In any given month, the admissions manager might find himself five reenrolled students away from meeting his recruitment quota. Therefore, ten of those fifteen students would be granted their withdrawal. The other five withdrawal requests would be ignored. Those five students would remain registered for classes.

They would accrue fines for failure to attend classes and accumulate debt for the classes from which they had attempted to withdraw. On the bright side, the admissions manager would meet his recruitment quota.

The files for the students who had been secretly denied withdrawal would then be sent to Student Support, where Finestone and his colleagues would call the students to convince them to reenroll for the upcoming semester. Those who believed they had withdrawn from classes in the first place would say stuff like "I thought I told you to stop calling me" or "I don't want anything to do with your bullshit school."

To which Finestone would respond with something like "Well, you do have a three-thousand-dollar balance due from the current semester, so you should really think about following through on your commitment."

Finestone was instructed to do or say anything to compel students to reenroll. He was told to use outstanding balances to leverage withdrawn students back into school. He was instructed to tell resistant students that if they agreed to reenroll, he could see to it that their outstanding balance was eliminated. This was not true, though Finestone didn't know it at the time.

As Finestone said, all the best training material was reserved for the recruiters in Admissions. With regard to said material, in 2011, the Senate Committee on Health, Education, Labor and Pensions completed a yearlong probe and subsequently released internal training documents used by several well-known for-profit universities. These documents revealed a sales premise perfectly harmonious with consumer culture in the post-9/11 era. Indeed, spikes in duct tape and firearm sales suggest that nobody is quite so motivated as the consumer scared crapless.

Enter the most prolific period of growth in the history of the for-profit educational business.

According to a 2011 article on the *Huffington Post*, a document from a for-profit institution that has more than one hundred campuses in the United States advises its recruiters to "remind [potential students] of what things will be like if they don't continue forward and earn their degrees . . . Poke the pain a bit and remind them who else is depending on them and their commitment to a better future."[3]

The Senate committee describes a "Pain Funnel and Pain Puzzle" utilized by the institution in order to freak out potential customers. As you can see in the diagram on page 130, this involves the use of

2. Pain Funnel and Pain Puzzle

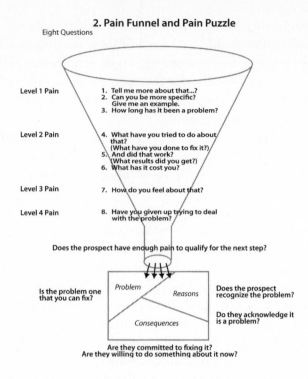

Eight Questions

Level 1 Pain
1. Tell me more about that...?
2. Can you be more specific?
   Give me an example.
3. How long has it been a problem?

Level 2 Pain
4. What have you tried to do about that?
   (What have you done to fix it?)
5. And did that work?
   (What results did you get?)
6. What has it cost you?

Level 3 Pain
7. How do you feel about that?

Level 4 Pain
8. Have you given up trying to deal with the problem?

Does the prospect have enough pain to qualify for the next step?

Is the problem one that you can fix?

Problem

Reasons

Consequences

Does the prospect recognize the problem?

Do they acknowledge it is a problem?

Are they committed to fixing it?
Are they willing to do something about it now?

four "Levels of Pain," all to be poked and prodded until the lead is so miserable and despondent that your crappy school seems as if it must be the answer. As the figure shows, the Pain Funnel cloaks the lead in all the misery, self-doubt, and regret that have marked his life to this point. Then, when the lead reaches the point at which only suicide seems like an appropriate resolution, the Pain Funnel spits him out into a discussion about enrollment like a giant sphincter firing one out into a toilet bowl.

Another prominent proprietary school named by the Senate committee uses a slight variation on the sphincter-and-toilet-bowl model, but it has very similar ideas about how to stimulate enrollment. Its training material reports that "it is all about uncovering their Pain and Fears. Once they are reminded of how bad things are, this will create a sense of urgency to make this change."[4]

The idea that a sense of urgency is something that must be "created" is particularly compelling and feeds into the modern debate

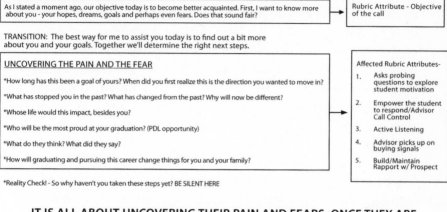

Reiterating the Objective of the Call:

| As I stated a moment ago, our objective today is to become better acquainted. First, I want to know more about you - your hopes, dreams, goals and perhaps even fears. Does that sound fair? | → | Rubric Attribute - Objective of the call |

TRANSITION: The best way for me to assist you today is to find out a bit more about you and your goals. Together we'll determine the right next steps.

UNCOVERING THE PAIN AND THE FEAR

*How long has this been a goal of yours? When did you first realize this is the direction you wanted to move in?

*What has stopped you in the past? What has changed from the past? Why will now be different?

*Whose life would this impact, besides you?

*Who will be the most proud at your graduation? (PDL opportunity)

*What do they think? What did they say?

*How will graduating and pursuing this career change things for you and your family?

Affected Rubric Attributes-

1. Asks probing questions to explore student motivation
2. Empower the student to respond/Advisor Call Control
3. Active Listening
4. Advisor picks up on buying signals
5. Build/Maintain Rapport w/ Prospect

*Reality Check! - So why haven't you taken these steps yet? BE SILENT HERE

IT IS ALL ABOUT UNCOVERING THEIR <u>PAIN AND FEARS.</u> ONCE THEY ARE REMINDED OF HOW BAD THINGS ARE, THIS WILL CREATE A SENSE OF URGENCY TO MAKE THIS CHANGE.

about whether or not we are teetering on the top of an education bubble, wherein a universal "need" for college has created a rampant and saturated marketplace that is bound for bursting.

According to Claudia Shapiro, who spoke to me about her role as an administrator of academic affairs at a highly competitive for-profit institution that we will refer to as Krap-Wiesel University, this recruitment strategy produces a student body that is inherently deficient and necessarily held up to inferior standards. Shapiro remarked that in addition to lacking academic proficiency, most students present disciplinary challenges that for-profit schools have no capacity to prevent.

Shapiro reported that

the students presented a bevy of behavior and personal problems that led one to believe they were pushed through the public school system without the benefit of an actual education. The average student was single, aged mid-low twenties, and had more children than an Orthodox Jewish family. Accommodations were made for students with learning disabilities, but most of the students just plain weren't smart enough to handle the material. And that is saying something, as the material was insanely easy in many of the classes I observed. Instructors were encouraged to employ progressive discipline, but they often were not backed by the higher-ups, and rude students were allowed to return to class if they cried foul loud enough.

It was Shapiro's responsibility during her year of employment with Krap-Wiesel to conduct teacher evaluations. She observed between five and ten sessions a week and served in a supervisory role for the instructors. It was also her responsibility to organize and plan "for several hundred students to take a corporate survey at the end of each class" (each month).

Her observations revealed a faculty whose deficiencies mirrored the students':

> I evaluated the instructors with a corporate-approved checklist. They were judged more on specific facilitative techniques than actual teaching or knowledge, both of which most instructors lacked. Some of the most important standards I was expected to watch for were: movement around the classroom, facilitation— games, activities, etc.—removing students who didn't fit the dress code, and putting the day's objectives on the board. Though there were plenty of other benchmarks on the evaluations, those were considered most important to corporate.

Shapiro balked at using the word "teacher" to describe the instructors she evaluated, particularly because no teaching certificate was required. It was only necessary that the instructor had completed three years of schooling in the subject to which he or she was assigned. Shapiro pointed out that a vast majority of the instructors had obtained such experience from similar so-called proprietary schools.

When I asked Shapiro if there was a considerable difference

between what she considered competent instruction and what Krap-Wiesel looked for in its instructors, she responded emphatically, "Oh, absolutely."

She told me that many of the instructors habitually misspelled words on the blackboard. She had an instructor in a medical assistance class who called the larynx a "larnyx." She once observed an instructor who explained to her class that AIDS was now curable, "but only for rich people like Magic Johnson."

But Shapiro was under strict orders never to correct an instructor in front of the students.

As to whether or not Krap-Wiesel University fulfilled its promise of a higher education, a better life, and a remedy for one's innermost pains and fears, Shapiro reported that

> a lot of what went wrong could be blamed on students who didn't show up to class or screwed up their externship, but you can still fault the school for admitting and keeping students who don't belong. In general, though, no, the school does not fulfill promises. If you ever see the commercials, the students are led to believe that a six- to twelve-month program will net them a profitable job. Truthfully, only the electricians really have that opportunity, and employers are still going to pick community college and university students over proprietary students. Medical assistant, dental assistant, and medical office assistant jobs are low paying and hard to find. I recently saw an M.A. graduate working at ShopRite. Really, it's hard enough to find a job with just a bachelor's from a highly regarded institution. What hope do these graduates have?

It is easy to understand, then, why it has become fashionable to employ the phrase "education bubble." For-profit schools are part of a market so saturated with product that it has lost all quality control. Schools are producing a mountain of debt and a flock of graduates without any prospect of paying for their investment.

U.S. Department of Education publicity flack Jane Glickman made the following statement in September 2010: "U.S. Secretary of Education Arne Duncan today announced that the FY 2008 national cohort default rate is 7.0 percent, up from the FY 2007 rate of 6.7 percent. The default rates increased from 5.9 to 6 percent for public institutions, from 3.7 to 4 percent for private institutions, and from 11 to 11.6 percent for for-profit schools."[5]

Glickman continued, "In award year 2008–09, students at for-profit schools represented 26 percent of the borrower population and 43 percent of all defaulters. The median federal student loan debt carried by students earning associate degrees at for-profit institutions was $14,000."[6]

Eventually, Finestone came to work in the Financial Aid Department at Shady Trade. Here, he reiterated, it was all about meeting recruitment quotas. It did not matter how the student's name and financial information came to be in the university's hands. Once this was accomplished, Finestone said, the lead was just another busted ATM, dispensing cash without discretion.

Finestone worked in all three departments and on three separate campuses in one region. On all three campuses and on multiple occasions, he was approached by students who had been enrolled in the university without their knowledge. After some debt had been incurred and the collections process had begun, students who had never applied to the school would find that they were on the hook for a year's worth of university bills.

We may deduce, Finestone said, that in many cases an admissions officer had cold-called a lead and used the typical coercion tactics. One popular tagline used by admissions officers was "Come to school. I'll put money in your pocket."

Now, during this lengthy discussion, the officer may have said, "Let's just see if you're eligible for financial aid. Give me your Social Security number and we'll take it from there."

The lead may have naively handed over this information before ultimately deciding not to enroll and ending the conversation. And a year later, thanks to a friendly correspondence from a collection agency, he would learn that he was just one of thousands of students taking control of their lives by having enrolled in Shady Trade University.

A cocktail of Pell Grants and private loans is used to keep students filing through a revolving door, pass or fail. Low graduation rates are not a problem. On the contrary, low graduation rates help to create what Finestone called the "career student." Because the threshold to qualify for a Pell Grant is so low, it is a very compelling way for some students to "make money," as it were.

Finestone recalled that during his stint in Financial Aid one student called him and candidly informed him, "I need my grant money today because I have to go Christmas shopping." Others used loans for trips to Paris and big-screen TVs.

Not that it was just Shady Trade. Finestone described the career student as one who careens from one grant or loan to the next, bouncing from Shady Trade to McLearning to Krap-Wiesel, and so on. The career student remains sheltered from the storm of unemployment out there in the world, staying in one school until he fails out and subsequently borrowing more money to jump to the next one. When one debt catches up with him, he'll use a new loan to pay it down.

And no for-profit university will ever reject him. On the contrary, this guy is a boon to Shady Trade University and its kind. Their admissions officers meet their quotas. Their campuses meet their recruitment targets. And ultimately, the institutions meet their projected earnings.

Finestone did have some friends at Shady Trade. He worked on one campus with a buddy who shared his integrity and his sense of humor. They were close allies who could count on each other for a dirty joke, a commiserating soul, and the psychological support necessary for survival. They would meet to blow off steam on bad days, which were more common than good ones.

Finestone's buddy was transferred to another campus, one where Finestone himself had previously worked. One day, his buddy reported during a phone conversation that the campus director had rented a van, taken it to a local shelter, filled it with homeless people, and carted them to the Financial Aid office for processing.

From his new position in the Financial Aid Department, within the Business Office, it was Finestone's job to help reluctant students process financial aid forms. Once a person has set foot in an administrative office at Shady Trade, all personnel are under strict instructions to keep him from leaving until he has signed away his personal information. If a lead demonstrated any hesitancy about providing this information, Finestone was instructed to call in an admissions officer. Between them they were not to let the student leave without consenting to have his personal information processed for financial aid eligibility.

The admissions officer would then proceed to hound and harass the student in front of Finestone. He would prod Finestone to "assist" the student in completing the financial aid forms. Using uncomfortable, high-pressure sales tactics, the admissions officer would coerce the lead into signing forms that required sensitive personal and financial information.

In some instances, students' applications for financial aid were rejected. Some continuing students had used up all the financial aid for which they were eligible. Other students were naturalized citizens without the selective service information or proper citizenship documentation to be eligible. Others still were simply waylaid by bureaucratic discrepancy. In these instances, and using forcibly obtained personal information, the campus director would register the students anyway. They would accrue personal debts that ranged between five hundred and twelve thousand dollars, with accounts assigned to collection agencies before many of them knew it.

It was policy in the Financial Aid Department to aggressively reenroll students who lacked this basic eligibility. And Finestone was learning firsthand during his interactions with students that lives were indeed being ruined. He began to resist. He made it clear to his campus director that he would no longer recruit students who were in tremendous debt and who had no ability to get financial aid. He argued that it was bad for the student, that it was bad for the school, that it was just bad business altogether.

After that conversation, Finestone was moved to a new campus. Then he was moved again. And again. He was forced to come in seven days a week. Eventually, his campus director said to him, "If you can't comply, I can't use you."

Finestone stopped asking questions and began to follow his protocols. And suddenly, through what he believed to be a glitch in the system, his employee account gave him access to any and all student information. As an officer in Financial Aid, he never should have been able to see the information used by recruiters, and vice versa. He informed his campus director of the glitch. The director instructed him to use this information in any way possible to complete student enrollments. So Finestone would open up a student's recruiting file and use the information to process uncompleted financial aid forms. He would locate student PINs and use these to electronically forge signatures in order to complete financial aid forms.

This was a time when banks were collapsing and, therefore, evacuating the student loan market. So one thing that Finestone did frequently was use financial aid documents to find a valid lender amid the many who were pulling out. Under instructions from his superiors, Finestone would sign students not eligible for Pell Grants up for private loans without their knowledge.

Eventually, Finestone told me, the system in his region fell in on itself. An internal whistle-blower ratted out the regional director, his immediate campus director, and his business office manager. The anonymous individual called HR and said that these three officers had all physically forged students' signatures on financial aid and enrollment forms. The sweep was internal. There was no public statement. No press. No legal recourse. Just quiet terminations and official policy reforms.

Finestone soon had a new boss, who also pressured him to recruit and enroll students. Company-wide, Finestone reported, it was difficult even after the reforms to really know the difference between right and wrong.

In the shakeout following the reforms, the new regional director decided to fast-track Finestone on the road to management. He was moved to the Admissions Office with the idea that he should know the internal workings of each of the three Operations departments.

A student called and told him that he wished to withdraw and that he wanted to know how to fill out the proper paperwork. Finestone told him that he didn't need to fill out any paperwork, that he could simply withdraw right then and there. He needed only to give the word over the phone. But, he suggested, the student should really reconsider. He asked the student why he wanted to withdraw, went through the training-manual script, and did his best to "save the student," as the new corporate lingo phrased it.

The student demanded to be allowed to withdraw, and Finestone conceded. Shortly thereafter, he was called into the office of the new campus director. The new director was upset that Finestone had allowed the student to withdraw.

Finestone insisted that the company was now operating honestly and with greater transparency. The director told him that if he wanted to succeed at Shady Trade, he needed to let her help him "better understand how to save students." He tendered his two-week notice the next morning.

As for his superiors who had left Shady Trade during the internal sweep, two of the three now work for McLearning University.

And until my termination, I had also worked for Shady Trade, for McLearning, for Krap-Wiesel, and for a host of other for-profit schools. I worked for all of them. I was a part of this system. I was helping to make all this possible.

CHAPTER 10

The Bends

In spite of my dishonorable discharge, I was back on duty in no time. I googled for companies until I came across a website hosted by the Coastal Carolina University. The university's Kimbel Library has a page called Cheating 101: Internet Paper Mills, which provides links to roughly two hundred paper-mill companies and dozens of additional links breaking down the various subsidiary companies that are syndicated under a single name. If you want to know the names of the companies I have worked for, I can't tell you. But most of them are on that webpage.

Originally created as supplemental material for a 1999 presentation on cheating prevention, the page was designed to function as an instrument for identifying, hindering, and punishing academic dishonesty. I have used it as my own personal Monster.com. Can you imagine? Can you imagine that in this economy, where we pretend not to be insulted by the verbal pretense of begging for work on a site called Flipdog, where we risk unsolicited sexual assault every time we scan Craigslist's Gigs category, where we throw our names into a pool so large that there's always a risk that our application could get mixed up with the application of another guy who has the exact same name . . . Can you imagine that just a week after being fired, I was copying and pasting one cover letter and writing sample and sending them out to every company in my field without even a hint of competition?

It was September 2004, and I had my very own classifieds.

Good thing, really, since I was applying for two. I could work for no company that would not also have Ethan as its employee. I owed him that at the very least. At the very least.

I received ten responses, and after reading my sample work and Ethan's sample work, the most promising of the companies agreed to hire us both.

And we were off and writing once again.

Ultimately, we took the bulk of our work from the one company that paid best. This company's model was different from that employed by my old company. The new company brought in almost as much work, but its system was slightly less automated. Every minute of every day, my in-box would flood with e-mails detailing available assignments: for example, "plant species of the Paleolithic era: 10 pages, Due 2/14, 6 sources, APA format, College (4th year)."

I would respond with a quote: "I can write this for $130."

I would receive a "Go Ahead" e-mail from the company anytime one of my bids was accepted. Then the paper was my responsibility. Once it was completed, I would forward it to the customer using an e-mail service provided by the company. At the end of each week, I would calculate my total earnings and invoice the company using PayPal. This company didn't have the handy calendar system maintained by my previous employer. I had to keep track of my own finances, so I created an assignment book. The assignment book became a constant companion, a predictor of fortunes and miseries ahead.

Ethan and I were taking some regular work from a hodgepodge of paper-writing websites. None were quite as prolific or profitable as our primary employer, and some were downright shady Eastern European websites without phone numbers or direct e-mail addresses. But I was taking work anywhere I could get it. Unless otherwise noted, my assignments were almost always due by eleven fifty-nine P.M. eastern standard time.

At the main company I worked for, we submitted assignments and e-mailed customers through a company-assigned e-mail box, but the bulk of the correspondence was mediated by Melissa, the customer service representative.

These were the years when I really sharpened my tools. Because the company's system was not as automated, and because I developed a reputation with my employer for efficiency and a willingness to take on unpleasant assignments, I would receive daily e-mails from Melissa. The details of a particular assignment would be forwarded to me with an inquiry such as "this one?," "can you complete something like this?," or "pretty please?"

It was the beginning of a whole new training regimen. If I'd been a fastball pitcher who occasionally used a changeup to throw off the batter, I was now being asked to develop a curveball, a slider, and a knuckleball while spending considerable time working at the batting cages, too. I was becoming a multidimensional player. I said I would write anything, and they held me to it. Even if I preferred the rhetorical fluffiness of history and sociology, I was being asked to report on tax law, to explore the epidemiology of kidney failure, to dissect competing economic theories, to explain American monetary policy, to outline the changes in data management trends. In short, I was being asked to write things that nobody would ever volunteer for. And I never said no.

At a certain point, with business cranking, Ethan and I even created our very own paper-writing company and website with the intention of cutting out the middleman. Almost universally, wherever I have worked, you collect half the money and the company collects the other half. We figured we could charge a little less overall and still make more. We enlisted Donovan Root and Bobby, another of our computer-prodigy friends, and we collectively designed a fully functional e-commerce website.

We called it Paper911. It was a flop.

We got a couple of regular clients. One guy from Saudi Arabia ordered three papers a week from us for a year. But ultimately, it was tough to compete with the type of work we were getting from the other companies combined. There was also a growing sense for both Ethan and I, as the intensity of this way of making a living became ever more apparent, that one could not realistically attach oneself to this kind of profession and hope to ever be a normally functioning human being. The body simply wouldn't stand for it, to say nothing of the psyche. Paper911 folded from disinterest as the workload from the other companies increased.

Then, in 2005, Ethan bailed. He was burned out and tired of working his ass off for pennies. I couldn't say I blamed him. He got a job at a big-time *Fortune* 500 company writing project proposals. He told them exactly what he'd been doing for a living all these years, and they found the experience fascinating. I was most officially on my own now. Just me and the assignment book.

My constant bedside partner was the sleepless night. Greeting me in the morning was the cycloptic stare of my computer. And my assignments were getting bigger, too.

I wrote an eighty-page paper on kava, which is a mildly hallucinogenic substance ingested ceremonially by the tribal people of Fiji. I loved that paper. Did you know that at low tide you can literally wade from one Fijian island to the next?

I also wrote fifty pages on the plays of Tennessee Williams in two parts. A little melodramatic at times but compelling nonetheless. Dude choked to death on the cap from his over-the-counter eyedrops. The longest papers weren't always the worst ones.

It was usually the customer who made it terrible.

The following exchange concerns the completion of several admissions essays for a student with big dreams.

The standard prospective-assignment e-mail contains the following prompt to the customer, along with additional disclaimers:

To ensure that your writer completes this paper to your satisfaction, we encourage you to send the name and level of your class as well as any other information you feel is important—including any faxed materials—as soon as possible.

If you do not inform the writer ahead of time concerning any special requirements, we cannot be responsible if we do not follow them!

I received an e-mail from Melissa.

Interested in this one? Due in five days . . . If so, bid?

http://www.psu.edu/admissions/intlapply/pdf/IntlSupplement
.pdf
How much would it cost me to get those essay questions answered?

I responded.

I can write this for $25. I can answer each of these two ques-
tions in the space of a page, using information provided by the
client to highlight academic achievements and other personal
accomplishments entitling admission to Penn State.

Melissa gave me the go-ahead with the following instructions:

Please do these, and thanks! And please do the OPPOSITE of the
bilingual dictionary assignment with him—he was VERY CLEAR
that he wants an "ivy league" writer (his words) . . .
Thanks!

Very shortly thereafter, she sent me the following request:

These would be for the same client as the PSU ones (which I am
about to assign to you) . . .
Can you do as well? If so, bid? (total 2600 words)

I need my Brown essays: italics are my comments

Question #1:
Tell us about the academic areas which interest you most and
your reasons for applying to Brown.

*I want this to be about 750 words. What interested me most was
Brown's location and it's student body. I need the writer to elab-
orate and find other things about brown that make it interesting*

Question #2:

Who interested you in Brown (e.g., college counselor, Brown alumnus/a, admission officer, undergraduate, relative)?

No one interested me in Brown. I have searched through many Ivy League schools and I foun that brown is

The top choice for me due to it's great collegiate sports for entertainment, and it's great professors. About 350 words would do it.

Question #3:

In reading your application, we want to get to know you as well as we can. We ask that you use this opportunity to tell us something more about yourself that would help us toward a sense of who you are, how you think, and what issues and ideas interest you most.

This is where I need the writer to throw some sort of hook that will make them really look at me. I need about 1500 words that will really blow the wall open with explosiveness.

As you will have noticed above, the customer did not provide me with any information regarding his chosen area of study, his academic strengths, or his professional aspirations. So I simply did my best to blow the wall open with explosiveness.

And I can do this because I've written a lot of admissions essays. According to a U.S. Census Bureau report, in 2009 there were more than nineteen million students enrolled in two-year colleges, four-year colleges, and graduate schools. And of course, most of them probably applied to multiple schools. And that was just the people who got in. So if my calculations are correct, that amounts to a metric fuckload of admissions essays.

God help the poor souls who have been charged with the responsibility of reading them, of wading through claims of personal excellence, of challenges met and bested, of spin-doctored triumph, of tragedy terrible enough to distinguish the individual as having depth and experience, all to find that perfectly singular little snowflake in a blizzard of poorly obscured mediocrity.

I wonder how frequently this is actually a rewarding job. How often can millions of people asking for the same exact thing every single year find a unique way to ask for it? So I do my best to make the admissions-essay readers' job a little more interesting. I indulge in the generic and craft sentences that seem to view their own content as remarkable in spite of its mundane obviousness.

The student wants you to know that he has overcome a great deal of personal anguish brought on by the death of his great-grandparent, and that watching a man die in his late nineties really makes you think.

So I say, "I have stared unblinking into the eyes of the grim specter of death. Perhaps more than most students, I have come face-to-face with the fragility of human life. That a man could be snuffed out so easily and senselessly would fill me, though, not with a sense of dread but instead with a sense of determination. Life is short and precious. I am determined to make every second count, beginning with my selection of a university such as yours. No doubt, my time on earth will have been well spent should the next four years of it be in the company of your brilliant professors, your diverse student body, and your state-of-the-art facilities."

Or the student says that he wants his hoped-for university to know that he learned a sense of personal responsibility in high school during his fifteen hours a week stocking shelves at the Safeway for minimum wage.

So I say, "As a young man, I had a distinctly tragic upbringing. I toiled in a Dickensian sweatshop without proper fire safety regulations. I learned in my early teens that survival is largely a consequence of determination, willpower, and optimism. Every time I tasted the lash of my supervisor's whip, I closed my eyes and dreamed of a brighter day when I might sit beside my peers at a university and learn how to make a better life for myself, and in turn, for the world."

Or the student wants me to make some explanation for why his performance in high school was relatively subpar and why his college performance will be considerably better.

So I say that "I boldly faced the challenge of balancing my studies with a full extracurricular schedule. In addition to my participation in after-school sports and my active role in student government, I spent the better part of my time outside of the classroom battling the unending scourge that is the walking undead. In my junior year, I succeeded in fighting off a zombie apocalypse while maintaining a 2.8 GPA. While my dedication to my studies may not be reflected in my class rank, the fact that the world has not yet been overrun with pus-spitting, brain-eating corpses is a testament to the work ethic that I will bring to your campus if granted admission."

Well, anyway, this was my general take on how best to approach my Penn State and Brown essays. This guy seemed like a sport. And he seemed like a business major. And since he didn't give me any information at all on the Penn State essay, not even so much as the suggestion that I blow the wall open with explosiveness, I used what I could glean from the Brown notes. And I wrote an explosive, wall-blowing-open essay for Penn State about my business acumen and ambitions.

I guess I had misjudged him.

A day after completion, Melissa forwarded the following e-mail, straight from the customer:

See, He didn't ask me.
I wanted to go into the Premedicine/Medical 6 year program.
This needs to be done, and quick.

Melissa followed this up with her own message.

Hey Dave,
Can you please either revise, or explain to him why what you did will work?
I also told him that it was HIS responsibility to send you information, not yours to ask . . .
Thanks,
Melissa.

Now the timing was pretty bad. I was on a train heading up to New York with Harmon. Harmon and I have been friends our whole lives, going back to diapers, nursery school, and row homes in Northeast Philly. We were on our way to see Tom W. play a show in the city.

We had also grown up with Tom W., a rock singer now verging on mainstream recognition. At the time of the show, he was an unknown singer-songwriter zigzagging desperately across North America and Europe for gigs while living in Queens.

He was doing a homecoming show after his most recent road wars. So I got this bitchy little customer e-mail while I was trying to enjoy the uniquely scorched and devastated stretch of the Northeast Corridor from New Jersey's Metropark onward.

I pried my eyes away from the view and an unconscious fantasy about survival in the *Mad Max Beyond Thunderdome* world streaking by us.

I opened my laptop and composed the following message:

Naturally, having never received any details from the customer on personal preference, aside from the italicized information accompanying the Brown essay request, I made some assumptions. I don't mind fixing the essay up, but it's up to the customer to provide me with any information he'd like to highlight. Otherwise, I'm left to my own resources and I tend to be creative. I can fix this by tomorrow morning but I would advise the customer to provide me with as much detail as he'd like. Likewise for the Brown essays, which I will confirm as well, the more detail, the better.

Dave,
I hear you, completely, and I told him this. Between you and me, he can be really obnoxious. Anyway—like I said, I did tell him this, but for the Brown essays, can you please also tell him this, and BCC me? That way, there will be no misunderstandings, and there will be a record that you told him to send whatever he wanted you to know . . .
Thanks, and I appreciate this,
Melissa

Melissa,

I could theoretically have the PSU revision completed tonight if the customer were to forward some basic details. For some strange reason, though, he has not sent any such information. Also, regarding the Brown material, if he should confirm these essays, I would need additional information.

Let me know if you hear from him. Thanks.
Dave

Dave,

I have told him now twice that he needs to send you more information. So, since he has been well-informed, all you can do is your best, and if he's still not happy, he will have to live with that. :-)
Thanks!
Melissa

Ok. That sounds fine by me. Let me know if you hear from him.

Thank you, I will!

I closed my laptop as we pulled into Penn Station. We had to grab a taxi and get to the venue. We got to a mildewy dive on Avenue B at eight, and Tom W. wouldn't go on until eleven. Plenty of time to get started on my Brown essays with a new focus on my premed studies. If I could knock those out now, I could hope to get enough information from the student to complete the PSU revisions before morning.

Harmon and I walked outside and smoked a joint in an empty basketball court. I humped a computer pack on my back like the dork in my army platoon. Then we returned to the bar, jammed a bunch of dollars into the jukebox, and ordered dinner, which was a Guinness and a shot of tequila. As I wrote, we repeated this order every thirty minutes until Tom W. went on. I finished up my Brown essays and sent them to the customer.

By the time Tom W. got up there, his solo performance looked like a power trio to me. My vision was sliding in and out of focus like a windshield with slow-moving wipers.

It was around midnight, right in the middle of Tom's set, when I got yet another e-mail.

Dave,
Here is the latest correction from [the customer] re: *Brown revisions . . . I've been assuming 4 characters per word . . .*
Thanks, and please let me know when you can do them and if you need more money . . . Thanks! :-)
Melissa

Melissa,
I have no idea what this guy is asking for. When I mentioned to him that I would revise the PSU paper, he failed to provide me with additional information in the due time so I assumed he didn't need the edit. For $15, I can go through it and suit it to a premed. course of study. As for the Brown essay, I have no idea what he's talking about. I'm not sure how to help him.

Dave,
That's OK.
I think he didn't realize you needed more information for the PSU paper. Can you please ask him for more, and explain to him what you told me?

Also, what he wants, basically, is for you to edit the Brown essays down from whatever the word counts are now to 1500 characters (or, probably about 500 words) for the first essay, 500 characters (or probably about 100 words) for the second essay, and 3500 characters (or about 700 words) for the third one . . .
Melissa

As we sorted through this, the customer sent another message, which Melissa forwarded my way.

Have not gotten my penn state revision
Can you resend the link I gavey ou for the supplement and the
essay?

Now it should bear noting that I was hammered at this point,
when I composed the following message in an attempt to recount
the series of events that had led us to this impasse:

Melissa,
I have to tell you, I am intensely confused over the dealings with
this customer. I am prepared to make an edit to the PSU essay
for $15 as stated, though the customer still has not responded
with additional information. I decided to charge for this edit due
both to the fact that the revisions differ from the initial assignment instructions and that the customer has been so difficult to
communicate with. Either way, the information that i have been
given constitutes a completely restructured essay that is entirely
different than the first one requested.

After reviewing the customer's error regarding the Brown essay,
I would say that the same is necessary. In order to conduct a revision, I will need to ask for an additional $35.

Just between the two of us, this customer is very difficult to deal
with. I don't mind doing all the work but this person doesn't
seem to know what he's asking for until it has already been completed incorrectly.

Give me the go-ahead at these rates above, and I will have all
of these editorial changes ready by tomorrow morning. Let me
know. Thanks.
Dave

Dave,
He really is difficult, I totally agree. I have had to tell him to stop
swearing at me several times (and frankly, I swear all the time,

but NOT online to people with whom I am conducting business. I mean, really).

Anyway—please do the PSU revisions for $15 and the Brown revisions for $35.
Thanks!!!
Melissa

Melissa,
I'll take care of these revisions by morning.
Maybe I'll throw some obscenities into the revisions. He may like them better that way.
Dave

Dave,
Well, if you do, let me know and I will send you a list of his favorites. ;-)
Melissa

When Tom W. finished his set, he came down and had a round with us, then we hopped a train for his Queens apartment. On the train, my "conscience" kicked in. My conscience lives in my stomach and is particularly sensitive to the evils of alcohol.

I sat in a sweaty pallor on the train, with my head dipping crane-like between my knees, closing my eyes to fight off the stroboscopic motion of the car windows, then swiftly opening them to fight off the vertiginous brain-eclipse spins.

We had boarded a full train, but people shuffled off at every station. With each pulsing stop, my head became more jumbled and my innards more stewed.

I did my best to wait until the car was mostly empty.

Harmon looked at me and asked, "Dude, you gonna make it?"

Nope. Couldn't even shake my head to tell him. I jumped up, went to the far end of the car, where the handicapped benches were, and painted the empty space with stomach chowder.

The train was pulling to a stop as I finished up.

I returned to my friends.

Tom said, "Um . . . let's . . . move to another car." As we walked through the door, the one poor bastard left in the car was holding his nose and grimacing in disgust.

I mumbled a meek apology at him, which (so far as I can remember) he did not accept. A few stops later, we were at Tom's house. I had a big glass of water and sat down to write about why I thought that I would make a perfect addition to the student body at PSU and why I felt that my premedical major would best be pursued at the storied Ivy League institution of Brown University.

With my eyes squinted, with my brain rotating slowly one way, then forcing itself back to center like an oversized microwave casserole, with my back pressed firmly up against the wall to keep me from falling off the floor, I punched out my revisions, then collapsed in a drunken heap over my laptop. I never heard from the customer again, so I guess he was happy.

But me, I was a disaster.

I was a bum.

I was an empty husk.

I was a guy who had vomited somewhere in New York's public transit matrix. And I knew I wasn't the first. I was, more likely, now part of some grand Gotham tradition that dated to the earliest days of drunken, debauched, and vomitous trolley-dodging. But still, it didn't feel right. Somebody had to clean that up.

I went back home and thought about how this asshole whose admissions essays I had just written was about to go to a big bright university while I sat in my dark little office with its exhaust-frosted windows and its stolen now-you-see-me-now-you-don't, high-speed-my-ass wireless Internet. Working from home is great a lot of the time. I don't envy the world its cubicles and Dilbert comics and traffic snarls and lunches at Applebee's. But a normal human being could really lose some marbles working in isolation. I never painted a face on a volleyball with my own blood, but I definitely had the occasional conversation with Oscar Peterson or Sam Cooke or whichever other dead man happened to be coming through my stereo.

"What's that, Sam?"

"Shake!"

"But Sam . . . somebody could be watching."

"Shake!"

"Sam. I really shouldn't."

"Shake!"

"Well, jeez. There's no need to yell."

"Shake!"

"All right, all right. I'm doing it. I'm shaking."

Now that Ethan was working outside the house and Bree wasn't dropping by to visit me, I was cracking up.

And I was burning out . . . again.

But again, I was making loot. A pretty decent amount, really, and for the first time.

To be clear, this was not the kind of money that made my college education seem financially justified. But it was enough that I no longer felt absolutely certain that I'd have to sell a kidney to stay under a roof into the foreseeable future.

But in order to do something better than just stay afloat, I had to put in an amount of work that simply isn't healthy. And I did this without end, without retreat, and without discretion. At times, my exhaustion teetered and toppled over into illness, my insomnia into somnambulant half consciousness, my ingenuity into automation. I pushed my body until the veins in my wrists palpitated visibly, until the lump on my neck bulged like a softball, until my lower back kinked like a tangled Slinky. I missed deadlines, I bargained for extensions, I promised to get my act together. Then I scarfed up more assignments, bigger, longer, more boring than ever, and did everything in my power to turn them into the money that would pay back my repeatedly defaulted student loans, that would keep the electricity on, that would get me questionable Mexican food for dinner.

But I was toast. My brain wanted to work, but my body was filled with bitter, rubbery resentment. It sagged and knotted and wished that my brain would just die and leave it alone. Eventually, my body would utterly refuse to go on and I would sleep. But every time I slept, I did it in guilt, with a deadline hanging over my head, an assignment passing its due time, frantic customer e-mails silently pelting my in-box while I cuddled with apnea and perspiration. And I'd wake up in mid-gallop, quaking with arrhythmia, confirming two more new assignments before my first cup of coffee was done brewing.

I was in a bad state. In what was becoming an annual tradition, I crashed. And in this year and all the years thereafter, when I crashed, I crashed hard, with fatigue and snotty colds and influenza and a seasonal hay fever death rattle.

I knew it was coming when I got fired one morning.

I don't make any excuses for this stuff. I have always overbooked myself. I take on as much work as one human being possibly can. I don't schedule carefully. I don't look to see if I already have twenty pages due on a given date before taking on another fifteen-page paper. I just figure, we'll cross that bridge when we get to it. And cross it we do, half asleep at the wheel, a dozen weigh stations and twenty-five county lines till we can drop off the last load for the night.

In my time, I have missed many a deadline. I would have four, five, six, maybe seven deadlines a day during peak season, and I didn't take the weekends off. I would've planned ahead, but ultimately I found it much more palatable simply to think about what was on tap for the next day. Had I tallied all of my deadlines for a month and counted the number of pages I had to write, I might've thrown myself from a tall building.

It served my psyche far better simply to take each day as its own distinct challenge. But of course it all blended together, so much so that on any given night, I might finish writing a five-page paper about the early history of the quadruple bypass and then immediately forget what it was about. When I prepared to upload the file for the customer, I would find myself racking my cloudy brain. Was he expecting a paper about setting personal goals for his future as a social worker, or one about McCarthyism and the Hollywood blacklists? Whatever, let's give him this one about Martin Luther. He's probably not going to read it anyway.

And into this blurring spin cycle were always thrown I-forgot-to-add-the-fabric-softener-type moments: revision requests, requests for additional pages, last-minute rush assignments with rates simply too good to pass up. The schedule ahead always got thicker, the completion of my work in accordance with the dense cluster of deadlines ahead always seemingly less plausible.

And I had zero patience for the customers. I was curt, rude, and dismissive in e-mail correspondence. And eventually, I just started ignoring them altogether.

If a customer really annoyed me with impetuousness, with bratty rudeness, with brazen hostility, or even just with too many e-mails, I became as quiet as a tombstone.

I would just stop responding to e-mails. I'd complete the paper and submit it, but it would come with a cold shoulder. No polite customer service repartee and no apologies. When a client burned over the smoldering embers of panic, I fanned them with my silence.

It became a real hassle for Melissa, who was good-natured but had limits to how much crap she would take. It was her job to take orders, interact directly with customers, and function as a liaison to a team of writers. She was also responsible for mediating any conflicts between a writer and a client, determining whether a refund should be issued to a customer, and, eventually, firing me.

This time around, my termination came with a fantastic letter of condemnation. My employer said that at one time I had been an excellent writer, perhaps even "the best in the business." But over the course of my employment, the quality of my work had declined significantly. I was turning in assignments later, receiving more revision requests, and generally failing to adhere to the high standards that the company maintained, indeed, the high standards that I had set for myself.

In my defense, the nature of the work itself is positively draining. After a couple of years solid, it can be difficult to stay on your game. Or maybe more accurately, I couldn't manage my time well enough to stay on it. I had an obsessive-compulsive instinct. It told me that I always needed to have my next dozen or so paychecks lined up. Even in my sleep, the clock was ticking. I never punched out. The fear that there was no bottom, that everything could drop out from beneath me and I'd have nothing to stop my fall—that kept me in deadlines. And it pushed me to take on more than I could realistically handle in the time allotted. It was never for lack of trying. I would just pile it on. It was the only way to go from making some money to making more money. It was all a matter of volume. I had to find ways to cheat the number of hours in a day. So I did. I tricked the day into being twenty-four hours long.

I could always fool it for a while. But eventually, the day would catch up to me. It would strip me of my false credentials and cast me into sickness. I was almost relieved when I finally got fired. I had been with this company for a couple of years, but this had been coming for months now.

After no shortage of warnings that I had better straighten up and fly right, they told me that they regretted that it had come to this, but felt that it was probably for the best. They observed that I had burned out. I agreed with them. I asked for another chance. They declined and said that I probably needed a fresh start elsewhere.

They were right. I don't take a lot of vacations. And even when I do, I usually carry my laptop with me. If I didn't get fired once in a while, I'd never take any time off. I still had work with a few of the smaller, crappier, and less trustworthy companies, but nothing I could live on, really.

During this stretch of underemployment, I was struck by the disconcerting idea that perhaps it was time to look for a "real job." And so I went on a few "real job" interviews. I interviewed for work as a copywriter for a nonprofit agency. I interviewed with a company that made juvenile reading-education software.

Ethan even scored me an interview with his *Fortune* 500 company. They were looking for another proposal writer. So I donned my cousin Marty's secondhand suit and took a cab to the shiny glass towers downtown. I looked like a grifter wearing something he had won in a game of three-card monte.

I was more than qualified to do any of the jobs for which I interviewed. But I suspect that they could see through my feigned enthusiasm, through my threadbare suit, through my charade of acquiescence. I didn't feel fit for this part of the world. Most of these people were actually impressed by my résumé, but none so much as the next paper-writing company down the line. I returned to the Coastal Carolina website that I had visited some years prior to procure the job I was now hoping to replace.

And, without formally identifying myself as a prior employee, I reached out to the same company that had fired me and, subsequently, Ethan just a few years back. They hired me back instantly. Either they never knew it was me, or they figured that even with my various faults, I was an asset to them. I completed a two-page test paper on constitutional law and I was back in the saddle. To this day, I have no idea if they remembered me from the first time around or not.

Fortunately, nobody checks references in this business. Chances are, if you approach a custom-paper-writing company and tell them you want to spend your days and nights writing academic essays for something between ten and twenty dollars a page, you have the ability to do the job. Nobody who couldn't churn out pages by instinct would volunteer for this kind of personal hell. If you couldn't do it, you wouldn't even try.

And even if you did fake your way into the job, it wouldn't be long before your limitations revealed themselves. It's not like working in a corporation or going to school. There's nothing to hide behind. Either the work gets done or it doesn't.

I had one month off. A week after I returned to work, my schedule was as densely packed as ever. I had lost time to make up for. And I was feeling confident. I knew I had just been fired, but I felt like an NFL coach. This kind of thing just had to happen every couple of years. It was a necessary way of purging my fatigue, of gaining a new outlook, of starting out fresh.

And I needed that. And I needed a couple of interviews, too, just to look around at the kinds of places in which I might have found myself in an alternate dimension, to see the file cabinets and secretarial desks and people bustling around or hovering over one another and snorting about what had happened on *Dancing with the Stars* and *Real Housewives of Wilmington, Delaware* last night. That kind of stuff made me grateful that I at least had a choice.

And gratitude can be a tremendous motivator. This time, I was all in. No more screwing around.

A four-page paper on Transportation Security Administration regulations? Check.

A ten-pager on Turkey's fight for independence? Sure.

A seven-page report on *The Bridges of Madison County*? Hmmmmm. Shit. I really didn't want to know what that book was about. Oh well. Click.

Isaac Newton, Jesus Christ, J. M. Coetzee. Darwin's theory of evolution, Erikson's theory of stages, Piaget's theory of genetic epistemology. Moses, Mohammed, Ming, and Marx. Machiavelli, Nietzsche, Kant, and Wundt. The British, the Ottoman, the Holy Roman, and the Mughal. The Crimean, the Trojan, the Peloponnesian, and the Hundred Years'. Cold wars, Star Wars, drug wars, terror wars. Nurse leadership, business leadership, military leadership. Group dynamics, independent learning styles, and the knowledge economy. Corporate ethics, corporate citizenship, corporate social responsibility. Scorsese, DeMille, Godard, and Coppola. Mozart, Dylan, Lennon, and Armstrong. Policy, legislation, constitution, scripture.

It got to where nobody would play Trivial Pursuit with me anymore.

CHAPTER 11

Tunneling Out

If I were on a desert island, this is about the point at which the scene would fade out, a number of years would lapse, and I would have gone from the Silly Putty–bodied city slicker who couldn't catch a tankful of fish with a grenade to a loincloth-wearing, tan-hided savage who could start a fire by refracting the sun off his eyeball.

Did I crave isolation, or was I simply allowing it to control me? Why was I compelled to write endlessly, to create constantly, but with no real compulsion to be seen, no drive to broadcast my work and stand beside it? It was no longer cool to be a hermit writer. The private martyrdoms of Ernest Hemingway and Kurt Cobain seem almost quaint as we watch Charlie Sheen's slow, tweeting death.

Today, if you are tortured, lonely, and imprisoned by your own psychic inner turmoil, you're supposed to complain about it in your Facebook status and eHarmony profile so that other people can know that you're lonely and drape you in their virtual sympathies.

And if you're super-lonely and you have some disposable income and you can make neither head nor tail of the modern dating scene, you might even consider employing a compositional expert to help you express this deep sense of loneliness.

The following instructions came with an assignment ordered by one such super-lonely soul:

> i want write a short message through an online dating site if
> you could give six short message i think of . . . not sounding as

a plead or a nag. in the hopes of him to respond and ask me out.

i went out on a first date and i was not very comfortable at all and came off like i was in a rush to get away from him, which killed the attraction. the handshake is a good indicator that the attraction was burned out.

four days later after first date . . . i texted on a thursday at eleven thirty at night saying maybe we can chat over the phone this week or go out this weekend . . . again the text was arkward and i've should have called since im not a teenager im in my mid thirties.

I have to stop there and tell you that it went on like this for another page or so.

Basically, she needed somebody to help her fix her Match.com profile and write her correspondences with a potential love interest. It was the first time I realized I was losing my stomach for this line of work.

I couldn't bring myself to take on the assignment. At that particular time in my life, I had a very profound respect for the concept of loneliness, far greater than my respect for school. Loneliness, love, and desperation of this magnitude are universal.

A few years back, and specifically before Bree forced the true nature of our friendship out into the open, I would have laughed at this customer. But it isn't funny. I won't judge you for laughing, but I was creeped out. To me, writing this shit seemed like a greater act of fraud than writing a college application or a dissertation. I guess I hadn't felt that way even a few months prior.

Work was work, and business was business. But with a few bucks more in my pocket and a little more self-assuredness, I could afford maybe just the smallest shred of principle and maybe even a few weeks off. I was struck by the idea that perhaps I could head my exhaustion sickness off at the pass this time.

So as another year's finals came to an end, I emerged from my cave, cracked my arthritic fingers, and soaked in the warmth of summer.

I took three weeks without my laptop, enlisting for a free pilgrimage with Birthright Israel. This is a remarkable program through which young Jews from all over the world can apply to go on charity-funded guided tours through the Holy Land, with flight, lodging, and food covered. We had to pay for our own liquor and cigarettes, but other than that, it was pennies from heaven.

Not that this was a religious pilgrimage for me. I was there to cleanse myself of the toxins that generally swirl about the Northeast Corridor and cling to our pulmonary walls. Plus, my job made me feel dirty, and not in a good way.

I met fascinating people in Israel. And I met people who were fascinated with me, with my job, with the very notion that one could make a living in so flagrantly subversive a manner. I hiked, rode on camels, and ate in Arab restaurants. I drank heavily, pitched my best woo, got a desert tan, and came up just a few cans short of a six-pack from eating nothing but cabbage and chickpeas.

I even managed to fit in a paper. I sat in the lobby of a hotel in Eilat, stuffing coins into the pay computer shared among its several dozen guests. With a battalion of irritated Israeli soldiers gathering in a line behind me, I tore out a five-page paper on the global public equities market.

I wrote the entire paper in the body of an e-mail to myself, since Gmail was the only function I could use in English. When several of the young, armed, and combat-trained individuals suggested I step aside to allow for others to use the computer, I calmly explained that I was on a tight deadline several continents away . . . while dropping a huge terrified load in my pants. They said something derisive about me in an ancient tongue and waited for me to finish.

But really, only two things of great incident occurred on my trip, and both I experienced in relative solitude. One night, when all the formal activities were finished for the day and we had taken up lodging in a comically unpleasant, scum-ridden, and tiny hotel on the coast, a small group of us wandered out to a bar with a platform leading to the beach. Among us were five from the tour group of forty or so, as well as our tour guide, Sergei. Sergei was Israeli by way of Russia and still spoke with a thick, friendly Yakov Smirnoff accent.

We sat by the Mediterranean Sea sipping vodka. After a few drinks, I quietly wandered off the platform and toward the water.

As I approached the water, the burbling conversation on the platform grew quieter until it was washed away altogether. I stopped at the edge and looked out into the swaying darkness, unaware that anybody was watching me.

I kicked off my sandals and heard Sergei calling from the platform: "If this is first time you are going into Mediterranean, you have to make eh wish!"

A week later, with the final night of the trip upon us, we gathered in a grove of trees on our kibbutz just outside of Jerusalem with junk food and music and booze. Hours into the festivities, I was struck by the obvious reality that all of our affections here, however genuine, were temporary. I was truly among strangers, and the loneliness filled me once again. I excused myself rather suddenly from the party and went back to my room.

I got into bed and closed my eyes. I hadn't smoked weed in weeks, so in addition to having a lot of trouble sleeping, I was having the most intense, surreal, and tangible waking dreams. This time, I could see myself in the cabin. I could see that it was all dark around me, and I could feel that I was sleeping. It was like I was asleep but totally conscious, at rest but fully aware. And there was Sergei, standing in the doorway, urging me like Yakov Smirnoff, "You can do this, man! Just do it!"

I forced myself to wake up fully, to redraw the line between reality and imagination. I shook my body awake and waved my arms at the room like I was swatting through a horde of gnats. I was alone . . . and I had just dreamed a Nike commercial.

Twenty-four hours of planes, trains, and automobiles later, and I was back at the station in Philly. I dragged my army duffel back to South Street, all at once grateful to be back but immediately reacquainted with that old desperation. It was only a twelve-block walk but long enough to make me feel like I had no home, not a million miles away and not here. Ethan was sort of happy to see me, but he'd also been happy to have the place to himself for a few weeks. We were beginning to reach that age when two grown heterosexual men can no longer successfully live as roommates. We were still buds but also increasingly short-tempered with, cramped by, and resentful toward each other.

So this wasn't home, and my parents' house wasn't home, and the Jewish national homeland wasn't home, and Rutgers wasn't home, and my job wasn't home. I was existentially homeless and, once again, broke to boot. When Bree called and offered to buy me dinner on the Fourth of July, I really had no choice but to go. We had barely spoken in more than a year.

But I had reached a place of new resolve while I was away. I could handle this girl. I could be cool. I could keep it together. I could live with whatever it was that we had built as friends over ten years.

And the minute I saw her, I knew that all of that was bullshit. I did my best to play it cool, as if it was possible that we'd both forgotten everything that we'd said to each other. We had a seafood dinner, then we grabbed a bottle of white from the Liquor Ranch and threw a blanket down by the river. We were surrounded by thousands of South Jersey's Bud Light cultural elite, gathered here "deown by the wooder" to see fireworks. The stalwart hit-making seventies and eighties band Foreigner was the opening act, and would be far outdone by the sparkly, colorful pyrotechnics set to a prerecorded *William Tell* Overture.

The aromas of patriotism and Winston Menthols were in the air.

"You look good," Bree said. "All kinds of tan."

"Yeah, well, they call you a pussy over there if you use sunblock."

"Was it crazy hot?"

"It really was. There were points at which I thought I might literally spontaneously combust. And who knew the desert was so dry?"

"Right. So the people were cool?"

"Y'know? They really were. It was a sharp bunch of people in my group, people studying to be oncologists and social workers and one chick who does voices for cartoons."

"Cool. So you made some friends?"

"Sure."

"Get any action?"

"Dude. Come on."

"What? Can't a friend ask?"

"Don't be a bitch."

"So . . . no?"

"Well, I didn't say that, did I?"

"So, yes?"

"Sure. Maybe a little."

"Really?"

"Well, you could try to sound a little less surprised about it."

"No, it's not that. It's not that at all. I just . . ."

"Forget it. Listen. They're about to play 'Juke Box Hero.' If we miss that, what's even really the point of being here?" I lay back on the blanket.

"You're right. I'd never forgive myself." She tucked herself under my arm, and we were a slice of pure Jack & Diane Americana.

After the fireworks, she drove me back to Philly.

Standing there under the halogen glow of the motion sensors behind the garage, we embraced, then separated and felt a momentous shift.

"Sooo? You have, like, papers to write now or something?"

"Baby, I don't have to do a thing. I'm my own boss."

"Ooooh. Tough guy."

"Yeah . . . so . . . you wanna come in?"

She nodded. We went in.

I was home.

We basked in warmth all that summer. We drove to the beach at night and played mini golf and talked baby talk to each other and unleashed ten years' worth of waiting on each other.

With the approach of autumn came the start of another school year. When I was a kid, commercials for back-to-school sales on clothes and book bags and Trapper Keepers filled me with dread.

But in this line of work, summer had become a time of austerity. I was often forced to supplement paper writing with the occasional side job. I would pick up a few bucks putting together local parties and concerts with Damon and Tom W. Donovan Root could always score me a short-term gig editing or writing for one of his mega-companies. I even spent one summer working as an extra on the set of a terrible Mark Wahlberg movie about the Philadelphia Eagles called *Invincible*. If you pause it, you can actually see me right over Greg Kinnear's shoulder at one point.

Sometimes, I had to piece it together however I could. So now, I greeted all those back-to-school commercials with excitement. Work would be plentiful again. There would be much to choose from. The leaves of the mighty oak would soon be gently aflutter across the sun-dappled golden campuses of America as students scurried about in mad pursuit of their various ambitions or obligations.

Bree and I moved in together, and she soon became witness to my daily grind. We were living on a charming little side street in the Irish part of town. It was a lot quieter than South Street, and now I had my own office in a spare bedroom upstairs. Ethan and I parted ways as good buddies, like two soldiers who had been through the shit together. We would reunite often to share war stories.

Bree was serving drinks a block away at For Pete's Sake, a brick-faced pub with a loyal clientele and a *Cheers*-y familiarity, as if George Wendt could stagger through the door at any moment. She worked until closing on a lot of nights and would return home at two thirty in the morning to find me wired and running low on words.

I was back on the bulletin board system. But this time around, my prejudices were fewer, my resentment less, and my resolve greater. I was going to do this job with all of my faculties intact. College was a faraway thing to me now. Even the industrial cleaning supply company was far away. It was just me, my computer— now upgraded from a Dell to a MacBook Pro—and the sad hapless saps who piled into colleges without a fuck's clue what to do there.

The poor bastards. I was actually starting to feel a twinge of something for my customers. Not quite pity. Not quite sympathy. Something more personal. Relatability. I could relate. I really could.

I could relate to the sense of desperation. I could relate to the feeling of gasping for air as cinder blocks of debt tugged one below the surf. I could relate to the fear that no greater thing existed ahead than a lifetime of indentured servitude. I could relate to the mounting sense of reality, the eroding cocksureness, and the diminishing right to dreamy illusion that all constituted growing up.

And my greatest handicap was nothing too much more than a bad attitude. Unlike many of my customers, I experienced all of this without a major learning deficiency or a language barrier to overcome.

My heart really does go out to all those immigrant students who are rubber-stamped through our schools. It seems that they are, so many of them, desperately alone.

Now that I was back with my old company, I was picking up all kinds of everything. I was even taking on some legitimate editing assignments, a far less popular service than custom writing but one offered by our company and most online paper-writing companies nonetheless. Editing assignments paid less, and you wound up having to rewrite the whole thing most of the time anyway. Despite my promises to myself not to do it, I couldn't let those confusing, inarticulate sentences stand.

One Thursday night, I was working on a most infuriating assignment. It was also poker night.

As more and more of my buddies had settled in the area, our little Texas Hold'em game had grown. While life gradually pushed each of us toward things like marriage and procreation, this was a stable context in which to make disturbing off-color jokes and wax angry-poetic about baseball.

Mickey and Damon usually showed up early together so we could listen to tunes, trade sports trivia, and toss the Frisbee.

After that, there was Paulie and Gould and Damon's brother Jackie. And Harmon never missed a game, even after he had two kids. Our game grew with each arrival of an old friend in the city. There was Boone, the attorney, whom I'd known since I was six, from Hebrew school. And there was Levi, the engineer, whom I knew from camp.

There was Gordon, the banker, and Dweezil, who owned a dog-walking company, and Barney, who didn't seem to do much of anything for a living but always had loot anyway.

And after just a few years, the poker game had grown into more than just a poker game. While we cursed and stank and spoke with great importance about things that mattered not in the least downstairs, Bree hung out upstairs with the ladies. Gordon's wife, Courtney; Jackie's girlfriend, Sugar Magnolia; Minnie the real estate agent; Donovan's little sister Cass. Poker night was also girls' night now. On any given Thursday, we might have fifteen of our dearest friends under our roof. One big happy family.

This particular Thursday, the guys were hollering back and forth about this running back's shredded knees and that umpire's alleged blindness and this chick's enormous rack and about getting sucked out on that last hand. It was all a din of sweat sock testosterone in the background as I tried, between hands, to make sense of a foreign accent so dense that it garbled even my client's typing. My job has put me on the front lines of the global economy. I have gained a sense of how a great many newcomers are faring in America's educational system.

And I tell you, there are innocent, well-meaning immigrant students who are floundering out there. The passage below is from an assignment that I foolishly attempted to edit while also playing cards. I probably lost as much money as I made that night. The paper's subject was typography.

That is a most advance of all human's most developed sense is touching by hand and remember what I told you before, stand point, vanishing point, and vertical lines . . . In fact the subject is involving a group of relations with management and private organizations large and small. This is why I love this topic, because it was my first when treating me with the people. For these discoveries, which I discovered in my career, scientific and grandmother in this article, of course, in the beginning, I was genuinely fearful of the difficulty so far, but with reading some topics and some of the problems specific to management, Ive found a very simple, some of which we can grasp in our daily lives.

This student's intentions were genuine and totally honest. He was paying for help with work he had already completed on his own. He had conducted the research. He had written the paper. He had followed all of the instructions provided to him. But this student had completed something that didn't come anywhere near approximating even a coherent high-school-level paper. He was studying a subject about which he understood not a single thing. I don't know if it was his major or just an elective. Neither would surprise me, but I do know that this guy was not a cheater. He was not dishonest. He was writing in his second language—and, frankly, about ten times better than I could have in spite of four years of high school French classes. The school he attended had presumably seen his written work before, and should have known that it wasn't reasonable to expect better from him.

He was also ruining my poker game. But this was how I worked at this point. At all times, I was typing. If I was going to make a living at this, and even eventually have worked enough that I might somehow be done with it (though I couldn't possibly conceive of how such a thing might happen), I had to know how to write while doing other things; I had to always have one foot in this absurd underworld and the other foot in the world of the sane, honest, and hardworking people in my life.

My work crisscrossed my personal life like Band-Aids across a cutter's scars. My friends pushed through various stages of employment, unemployment, underemployment, and self-employment, and my customers pushed through various stages of composition, dissertation, and graduation. For every stimulating moment shared with a brilliant friend, there was a deadening moment shared with a disadvantaged client.

The request below was for a fifty-page paper, meaning that this guy had advanced pretty far in the educational system with the linguistic deficiencies demonstrated here.

if you do not understand anything that i try to tell you you can
ask me because i don't want you waste your time by rewrite
and rewrite
i know my english is hard to understand but i don't know how
to explain to you if you don't ask me i hope you understand
what i need in this report
thank you

This guy above, this guy is a cheater. That's for sure. But he's also
a net loser in the broken system. It's globalization, baby! The world
is getting smaller. We're erasing the imaginary borders that separate nations, cultures, and peoples. And that's awesome if you're
Walmart, McDonald's, or Lockheed Martin. They can afford trans-
lators, cultural-sensitivity training, and . . . well, they can afford to
not give a shit if a bunch of non–English speakers are struggling in
their factories and customer service call centers.

We've opened our doors to all the ambitious young men and
women of the world. And that's a good thing. But we've done nothing to prepare them for the realities facing them. Even if we want
to bandy about the old and fading notion that America is *the* land
of opportunity, we must admit that the new arrivals are struggling
to seize it.

Ultimately, it makes the product that our schools are manufacturing a lesser one. Cultural diversity should be a boon to our society and our shared body of knowledge. Too many educators treat
diversity as an obstacle to be ignored, or perhaps even overcome.

Here's a typical revision request from a student who hasn't been
given the tools to adapt to globalized education. He's also kind of a
jerk.

I dont like the paper, can yiy do it over again, because my subject is Diversity in Criminal Justice. I want the paper to base on
CORRECTION/INCARCERATION/PAROLE/PROBATION."
in simple english
"not Big grammar.

Not Big grammar.

Indeed. This guy here, this guy is going to struggle. He will never achieve a level of proficiency in English sufficient to create a passable résumé, compose a usable cover letter, reach out to a public official, or write to request a refund for his defective blender. And even if he does, he still may not have developed the cultural etiquette to say please, thank you, and so on and so forth. In short, people will treat him like he's stupid even if he's not, and people will assume he's a jerk even if he's not. Not that I'm discounting either possibility. But according to a study produced by Princeton University in collaboration with the Brookings Institution, as of 2006, half of all surveyed foreign-born adults aged twenty-five or older lacked proficiency in English. One consequence, the study notes, is that as of 2005, the median income of U.S. immigrants was 25 percent lower than that of native-born workers.

Of all the people who we push through our schools, perhaps immigrants are pushed with the least care. And when one considers the portion of the student population comprised by immigrants, this is no marginal oversight. According to a table in the U.S. Census Bureau's *Statistical Abstract* titled "Students Who Are Foreign Born or Who Have Foreign-Born Parents," as of 2009, 9.6 percent of college students and 17 percent of graduate students were foreign born. The census also reports that 22.6 percent of college students and 28.5 percent of graduate students, had at least one foreign-born parent.[1] A study published in the journal *Developmental Psychology* in 2010 reports that because of the dearth of effective support mechanisms for immigrant students' transition into the American education system, the cultural barriers and language barriers that they face are compounded by the inherent challenges of American formal education and by the relatively limited ability of their parents to assist them in navigating the system. The study authors argue that this produces an "inferior educational experience" for the immigrant student. To support this claim, they report on a five-year longitudinal study examining academic trends among immigrant "newcomers." The study found that "two-thirds of the participants demonstrated a decline in their academic performance over the 5-year study period."[2]

I suspect this describes some of my clients: no longer newcomers but now part of a loud multilingual buzz of unmet expectations. Maybe they're just trying to finish school and retreat to a country where an American degree is far more valuable.

According to a 2011 article in the *Chronicle of Higher Education*, there is a fast-growing trend among immigrant students toward using the diversity quotas in our universities as a means of literally transferring knowledge out of the American economy. The *Chronicle* reports that the average age of Indian immigrants returning from the United States to their home country is thirty. For Chinese immigrants, the age is thirty-three. The article adds that in a Facebook survey conducted by *Bloomberg Businessweek*, less than 10 percent of Chinese students and 6 percent of Indian students planned to remain in the United States permanently following the completion of their studies.

America is facing a brain drain as the best and brightest immigrant students return home to frame their American degrees and build their developing economies; meanwhile, the lowest-performing and most desperate of them take up residence in our urban slums and attempt simply to read the words on their American degrees.

Give us your tired, your poor, your huddled masses, yearning to game the system.

These people, every bit as much as my friends, were my constant companions, my daily relations, the prism through which I saw the world.

And the more time I spent trying to work my way through this one typography paper, the angrier I got. I guess I felt I'd been duped. This was just supposed to be an edit. But in twenty-five pages, I couldn't find a single sentence that would actually qualify as a sentence.

"Motherfucker," I said out loud.

"Is that a tell?" Jackie asked.

"Huh? Oh. No. I didn't even realize I had cards in front of me."

"Yeah, well, it's your turn," said Gordon.

"Right." I looked at the two cards in front of me. Seven-two off-suit all night long. "I fold."

"Dude, you haven't played a hand in forty-five minutes," Dweezil observed.

"Yeah . . . well, I forgot I was even here. My brain hurts. This paper is making me dumber."

"What's so bad about it?" asked Barney.

"OK. Ready? Here's the paragraph I'm editing right now: 'Paper is usually square. When designer die cut the paper, it might not be the square. But we assume that paper is the square, which is a flat square.'"

Disturbed commentary ensued.

"What the fuck does that mean?" Gordon asked.

"What paper is square? Is this an essay about napkins?" said Jackie.

"That's fucked-up, man," said Dweezil. "How did that kid get into college?"

"Oh, don't worry," I said. "He's not in college. According to his order form, this paper is for a master's."

Shit. As I said it, I realized, this kid was well on his way to having more academic credentials than I did.

CHAPTER 12

Death and Taxes

There was a point, many years into this profession, when I had become fairly convinced that I would die in front of my computer: that as a young man, I would feel that bolt of numbness in my fingertips, I would clutch my chest and gnash my teeth, and they would find me mashed facedown into my keyboard, my last recorded words on earth something like "asdklihujjjjjjjjjjjjjjjjjjjddddddd ddddddddddddddddddddddddddddddddddddd."

But as my aspiration to be done with the profession grew stronger, so too did my work ethic and my resolve to make it pay. I do not exaggerate in the least when I tell you that I was reaching a breaking point and verging on a moment of physical collapse. I really and truly thought I might stroke out and go all droopy on my desk.

But I was past burning out. I had outgrown it. Bree would glance into my office worriedly. She had known me forever, but she was only now coming to understand how constantly I felt I had to work for survival. And now I actually had a motive for survival, which was a new feeling.

There was only one way to make this job work, though. When it came time for finals, I was prepared to descend the seven circles of hell without flinching. In the springtime, fresh assignments crowded each other out for attention on the writers' board, leaving the more complex and time-consuming works twisting in the wind. I gobbled up assignments about the U.S. Constitution, the French Revolution, the Cold War, abortion, nursing leadership, global warming, affirmative action, business ethics, and *The Great Gatsby*. On any one of those subjects, I pretty much wrote the same paper twenty or thirty times a year with modest variations and recycled sources. Now was when I really got cranking.

An abortion paper of about eight pages in length would pay between $96 and $120 during seasons of heavy demand. That may not sound like a lot, but I could turn this assignment out in two hours flat. And I could do that all day long, and well into the evening hours, too. And it wasn't that difficult.

But natural market demands always had a different plan. Let's say that a customer needed a twenty-page comparative essay on public equity investment in China versus India and that it was due in six days. And let's say the paper was posted on the writers' board at a rate of $220. Nobody would touch it for days. Particularly if the three pages of directions requesting the use of specific sources, outlining a format, and calling for the delineation of numerous international trade agreements suggested that this assignment would take something like seven or eight hours. At $220, I wouldn't touch it with a ten-foot pole during busy season. Remember, I could make that writing two abortion papers over the course of four hours.

The assignment would continue to hang out on the board while papers about Freud and Faulkner flew off the racks. Then suddenly, desperation would set in, and the customer would contact our service department.

"Why isn't anybody taking my paper?" he would ask.

"This is a very busy time of year, and most of our writers carry extremely full schedules. Perhaps if you raised your offer, one of our writers would be in a better position to take on your work," the customer service rep would say.

Bingo, bango, $300 for the paper about equity in India and China. I'd be all in. I would grab up the paper, and it would go on top of the huge, miserable pile of shit that I had to shovel through. Looking at my schedule now, with this twenty-page bastard stuffed right in the middle, I wouldn't see a day when I could sleep for more than three hours coming for at least a week. As soon as I finished one paper, I started another. As soon as I submitted an assignment, I went to the writers' board and picked up another one to take its place. This was standard operating procedure. In the midst of such stretches, even the sleep that I did get was riddled with tension. Deadlines, deadlines, deadlines. Always on the clock. Tick, tick, tick, tick, tick . . .

During finals, I would have two recurring dreams, sometimes interwoven with each other. In one, I was driving along the New Jersey Turnpike and struggling to keep my eyes open. Then I couldn't fight the sensation any longer, and I was sleeping behind the wheel. I would wake up suddenly, expecting my bed to veer off into a guardrail.

In the other dream, I could see myself in bed sleeping through a deadline. I could see the clock flashing nine A.M. even though it was still pitch-dark outside. I could feel those jerky little e-mails from the customer: "I'm wating." "What happens to my papper. It was suppose to be for today." "Hurry with the paper please. I'm running out of tim."

Shit. This job was making me dream in developmental delay.

And I was getting night sweats. I would get up in the middle of the night and get a towel to sleep on. I would soak through that. I was constantly awake, even when I was sleeping, fully aware of myself, my restlessness, and the deadlines on my head. I was drowning in pools of perspiration, the sheets were getting drenched, and Bree was having dreams about fishing and water parks.

It was the early spring of 2009, and I was at both the height of my exhaustion and the peak of my powers, when I took on my biggest assignment ever, a 160-page paper about international financial reporting standards. Posted to the board at an initial rate of sixteen hundred dollars, it went untouched. Eventually, the motivated buyer called customer service in desperation. The paper got bumped to two thousand bucks. Say what you want about the rate and the obvious horribleness of the assignment. It would be the biggest commission I'd ever had. The assignment was due in two months, and knowing myself as I did, I suspected that if I accepted it, I wouldn't even think about starting it until the week of the deadline.

My schedule was full but manageable in early March. By the paper's May deadline, I would envy the dead their rest. My finger hovered over the "Write It" button for a good two minutes while I tried to talk myself out of this thing. This paper will be the end of you, I told me.

Nuts to that, I figured. I had to know if I could pull it off. At this point in my career, I was working aggressively to find my own limits. Where was the line of exhaustion past which I could not go? What was the threshold of boredom beyond which my attention span could not be even partially sustained?

Somehow, these questions were more compelling to me than the fact that the bags under my eyes looked like silver dollars or the fact that I might forget to consume anything but coffee or weed until six P.M. on any given day. The only way to stay on top of a lifetime of deadlines is to be utterly compulsive and neurotic.

But not about time management. As I think we've established, I suck quite a bit at that. And not about work-flow organization. Organization has never been my strong suit. But one must be utterly compulsive and neurotic about one's isolation, one's focus, and one's stamina. Work must not be interrupted by more than a bathroom break or a hot shower, which I substituted for sleep and exercise.

Initially, I put the gigantic paper aside and sort of secretly feared it as I worked on other stuff. As the deadline approached, I stopped taking on new assignments. I began clearing my schedule, putting aside just enough time to write a shitty book in less than seven days. Technically, I only left myself four days before the deadline. But I figured I could allow myself the cushion of an extra day based on the assumption that the client didn't plan on handing in this monstrosity the day he received it.

When the week of the beast began, I got myself a good night's sleep, woke up at nine A.M., and dove in headfirst.

It's always slow going at the start of something big. The best thing you can do with something this terrifying is break it up into a whole bunch of little pieces. I referred to the customer's instructions:

This is a doctoral level presentation. Since I have no official dissertation proposal apart from the above heading, and I am not fully aware of the exact structure and required elements of such paper, I have briefly derived unsystematically what I think should be covered by my Doctoral Dissertation, based on talks with my professor . . .

Not a lot of help there. I shit you not, this customer paid four thousand bucks (two grand to me, two grand to my employers) for a doctoral dissertation and provided me with one page of instructions. It was like buying a used car based on the specifications that it had four wheels and was blue. The customer never followed up on his order with source specifications, never checked in to find out what the primary argument of his dissertation would be, and never suggested that he had any particularly strong opinions about the work upon which his doctoral degree would be based. Don't ask me how this is possible. It's not my job to know.

In any event, once I took on the assignment, I was pretty much on my own.

So how I wrote 160 pages in five days is a story of intense, soul-crushing solitude; a haze of facts and fabrications; a foot-dragging trudge to a blurry light at the end of a long, dark chunnel. As Lao-tzu tells, the journey of a thousand miles begins with one step. This describes every beast I've ever written. As I write the first sentence on a blank page, I remind myself that I have often been at the beginning and I have always made it to the end. This beast would be no different.

Still, it takes some effort to become ensconced in something that will own you for the next several days. And I have about as much personal interest in international accounting standards as I have in being shot in the face. So I started googling and reading. The paper called for fifty sources, so I really couldn't get too caught up in reading any one thing.

You do get caught up in the subject matter from time to time. I once had to write a paper debunking the Bush administration's version of events leading up to and following 9/11. The information was so readily available, disturbing, and fascinating that I spent all day reading. It took me twelve hours to write a ten-page paper. Another time I had to write a paper on *The Adventures of*

Huckleberry Finn, and it hit me that I hadn't read the great American novel, what with it having been banned in my high school.

So I began reading. After an hour had passed, I realized that my deadline was approaching and I hadn't written a word. I put the book down and flashed out a three-pager about American culture and the romanticizing of individual freedoms. This took me about thirty minutes, made me thirty bucks, and allowed me to get back to the book. I spent the rest of the day reading instead of working.

I didn't have this sort of distraction when reading about international financial reporting standards. I would generally read a source long enough to discover a sentence or paragraph that I understood. I'm a pretty perceptive reader, but this was a complex, esoteric subject, and you couldn't just learn it in an afternoon of roughshod skimming. I knew I had to be efficient, smart, and productive—160 pages in five days.

Day 1

I developed a thesis posing an argument that global convergence to international standards would bring greater accountability for some nations but would impose great economic hardship on developing nations already struggling to adapt to the inherent inequalities in the global economy. I didn't know if this was true, in the dictionary sense of the word. It sounded true. Based on many of the sources that I had located, it seemed like a plausible argument. Whatever it was, I was going to write a gajillion words on why it was so fucking true that I had to write a whole dissertation on it. Every sentence that I pulled from every source would be placed in quotes and given an overly long, overly wordy explanation clarifying why the thing I had just written above was true and really important.

On the first day, I was easily distracted but energetic. I made my coffee, lit a stick of incense, and put on some Dave Brubeck. I opened my window a crack and let in the sweet, dewy smell of morning. I live directly across the street from an Oyster House, so later in the day it would smell of fried fish for hours. But right then, it just smelled like morning. In quiet moments like this, I actually loved my job.

The sound of people making their commute outside while I sat barefoot at my desk, the thick aromas of coffee and weed swirling around above my head, the elegant alto sax of Paul Desmond lilting through my speakers, the cursor blinking on an empty page in front of me. This was the kind of picturesque academic moment that made me inhale with vitality and exhale with a sense of contentment.

It was also the kind of environment where you sat and did nothing for a whole day. You could look up baseball stats, you could illegally download music, you could browse Internet porn, you could IM with friends who hated their jobs and did nothing but "lol" and "brb" all day long. This was usually how I spent the first day of any big project. I'd procrastinate magnificently for hours, then reward myself prematurely for finishing a few pages. After three or four pages, I'd stand up and wander around my office, playing with toys or watching old ball games on the MLB Network. God forbid I should come across reruns of *Sanford and Son*, because I swear to crap, I'd get nothing done.

Three P.M. and I'd written just under 7 pages. I sucked.

I was pretty unhappy with myself. I like sleeping late, so it's officially a waste of a morning if I've gotten up before I want to and still haven't managed to get my ass in gear. Most nights, the Phillies play at seven P.M., at which point my productivity goes out the window. Friends tend to drop by for most games. At 162 a year, this is quite a commitment, and is in a category of things that I will allow to supersede my work, joined only by Bree and my personal hygiene.

The thought of a baseball game just a few hours away filled me with joy and focus. I started to connect with the topic. There's always that moment during a long process like this, when something clicks and I begin to understand more fully what I'm writing about. I'll read a sentence that articulates perfectly what I need to understand in order to do the bare minimum, which was admittedly a lot in this case. I found that sentence in the late afternoon of Day 1. By the first pitch of the Phillies game that night, I had 22 pages. I felt OK about that. Not great but OK. I kicked off early. Only 138 pages to go.

Day 2

Day 2 was fantastic. I woke up at seven A.M. and felt a rush of clarity. I was getting it, and I was cranking. I was feeling upbeat, and as I eased my way into it, I put on Gershwin's *Rhapsody in Blue*. It has the sweeping grandness of a sunrise over the city skyline, and it makes me feel purposive, like somebody with a briefcase or a guy in a commercial about business-class air travel.

I pulled up all the shades, and spring gushed into my room. I was a young man in my prime. Nothing better than that. This was how I felt on my good days. I felt a genuine strength coursing through my wrists, disobeying the carpal tunnel stiffness and bouncing sprightly out of my fingertips. It would be a stretch to say that I was enjoying my paper on accounting, but I was feeling pretty good about my grip on it. The literature made sense, the facts were coming together, and the structure of the dissertation was laid out across a dozen separate Microsoft Word files.

My MacBook allows me to divide my screen into six separate desktop spaces. It's like being able to spin around in your chair and work on six different monitors at once. I dipped in and out of them like an octopus, plugging in a page or two for the literature review, than grabbing a source from an old paper on international trade agreements and inserting it into the background section, then taking a break from these to write an abstract. At one time, I might have had twenty files open at once and four different Web browser windows going, each with five to ten tabs open.

And of course I was running iTunes. I was no longer trying to concentrate. Now I was power-flowing. I was sprinting. I was running the decathlon. It was all coming with great ease now. I was listening to the Clash and Talking Heads and the Ramones. I had written 20 pages by the time that evening's Phillies game was about to begin.

Still, I rewarded myself for a productive day by getting lazy. I did basically nothing during the game. I got out maybe four pages in three hours. Suddenly, it was ten thirty, and I was just a shade more than halfway to where I wanted to be before I went to sleep. The day suddenly caught up with me all at once. Bree was getting ready for bed. She'd be working a double starting in the morning.

Me, I was getting ready for my third shift of the day. Kraftwerk's *Autobahn* took me into the late-night hours. It's the musical rendering of a fast drive on a neon highway. The glow from my computer screen made my eyes feel like I'd been in chlorinated water all day. They were burning and watering. The pace that I'd enjoyed for most of the day was no longer possible. I stopped after every sentence, my wrists pressing into the keyboard like paperweights. I squeezed out another drop of words . . . then stopped . . . then a few more . . . then stopped.

Then I stopped looking at the clock. I stopped looking at the page count. I determined simply to write until I could no longer make sense of my surroundings.

When I heard the tailgate of the beer delivery truck clatter open at the Oyster House, I realized the sun was rising. I had written another 26 pages. I got into bed at seven A.M. with only 92 pages to go.

Day 3

My alarm was set for nine A.M., but I snoozed until about nine fifteen. That extra fifteen minutes toyed with me. I blinked and it was gone. I pulled myself out of bed and sighed. I had nothing to look forward to that day. No sleep. No warmth. No sunshine. No time for love, Dr. Jones.

It was just me and the beast. And on that third day, I was just starting to feel off. I don't know. Maybe it was the two hours of sleep. Perhaps it was the knowledge that I had to go through this day, the day after that, and some portion of the next day too before I could be a human being again. It's conceivable that I was falling out of love with the subject matter. It was an absolute battle to get through the morning. My body ignored the coffee. It felt like

I had hot sauce on my eyelids. I spent the first half of the day on 10 pages.

By about two P.M., I was doing everything in my power to get back into it. This was no time to puss out. I put on *Fun House* by the Stooges. Iggy Pop used to pull his pants off and cut himself with broken bottles onstage. I kind of thought of him as a role model. I stood up and jumped around the house. I stretched and jogged in place and shouted profanities at the mirror. I sat back down coursing with adrenaline.

I wrote one sentence about how the plan for the U.S. GAAP to ultimately converge with the IFRS is complicated by the implications of the PCAOB and blah blah blah bling blar blar blar. By the time I got to the end of it, I was all out of piss all over again. I was running out of gas right in the middle of the race. I was going to need some help for this one.

I called my buddy Doc, who showed up in less than an hour.

"So, how's it going?" Doc asked.

"Ohhh, super," I said with the inflection of a dead man.

"Yeah?"

"Oh yeah. Totally. It's an emotional roller coaster. It's the feel-good paper of the year."

"Yeah?"

"Yeah. I want to kill myself, but in a way that's much faster than the way I'm currently doing it."

"Catch the Phils game last night?"

"Um. I think so. Was that the game where all the players melted into a single swirling ball of psychedelic fractals during the seventh-inning stretch?"

"Dude, maybe you should get some sleep."

"Nah, it's just there's so many games a year, they all sort of blend together."

Doc cut a few bumps of cocaine, and we blew them off the back of my *American Heritage Dictionary*.

"Wooohoo," I said. "This oughta help."

The coke rushed through my head, and my eyes were like tractor wheels. Doc left me with a gram and went on his way. I immediately cut another couple of lines for myself. I vacuumed them up and put on the Mahavishnu Orchestra. The fusion jazz combo is the height of anxiety. It's heavy, brooding, and hot. It gives me the jimmy leg. So I started bouncing and trembling and typing. And for a series of forty-minute bursts, I was unstoppable.

But the party ended every hour, so I had to keep ringing the bell. I'm listening to Captain Beefheart and Wu-Tang, and I'm totally relating. Hut one, hut two, hut three, hut! Ol' Dirty Bastard live and uncut! I am the Dirt Dog.

By four A.M., I'd had another 40-page day. I had no sensation in the tip of my nose, my teeth felt like they could fall out of my head, and my eyes looked deranged. I'd been running my hands furiously through my hair. I looked like the guy from A Flock of Seagulls if he'd gone ten rounds with Mike Tyson.

Fifty-two pages to go. You would have to have gone through those last three days just to know how good that actually sounded to me. I got into bed at four thirty, gnashed my teeth, and stared at the ceiling until six A.M. I fell asleep and dreamed that I was awake.

Days 4–5

I woke up at ten A.M., furious with myself for oversleeping. I took my shower and washed the dried blood from my nose. I skipped my coffee and went straight to the coke. If this was to be a bender, there was no point in pussyfooting around it. The greatest influence on my writing at this time was probably Chris Farley's E! True Hollywood Story.

And like that, I was back into it.

The deadline was ten that night, and as I had presumed right from the start, there was no earthly way I was making it. But I hadn't heard a word from this guy in months, so I wasn't too worried that he was watching the clock. My expectation was something more like the next morning, though it would all be like one big fat day for me. There would be no friends today, no fraternizing with my lady, no food, no Phillies game. I could do nothing to keep my mind from straying every fifth sentence. I was chewing on my molars and knuckling my temples, trying to force my head to find a new way to say the things I'd already said, trying to find a new avenue down which to spray my bullshit, trying to kick-start my rusted engine.

At this point, every splash of water on the face, every three-minute stretching break, every new album, every hit of weed, and every line of coke, it was all part of this never-ending struggle to trick myself into being awake. Like when your remote is dead, you know you can always open it up and flip the batteries. It tricks the remote into a few more channel changes. By midnight, my head felt like a construction site. Things were clanging and crashing, whistling and buzzing, building and breaking. I was cracked the fuck out. I felt like a really geeky version of Scarface, or at least the nerd Scarface would have gotten to do his homework. But, I was at the 140-page mark. If I, too, was to die in a hail of bullets over a bag of cocaine, let it not be said that I did not understand the basic principles of international accounting standards.

The realization that I was this close . . . that did bring me some real energy.

So I dropped the hammer down and did me some wordsmithing. When I'm motivated by the thought of being done, I'm like Eddie Van Halen. I just start riffing all up and down the place, playing fast, shredding loudly, never stopping to reflect. Spitting out a blazing chord progression as the next one formulates in my head. There was no way to know whether the words I was writing made any sense. It didn't matter anymore.

And in the end, when it was done, instead of relief, I felt like I had malaria. I couldn't even go to sleep. For about a day, I had post-traumatic stress disorder. You'd think that once you got home from the war, you'd be all "Hooray for my bed. Hooray for my refrigerator. Hooray for my TV." But no, it's not like that. Not after the things I've seen, man.

That whole next day was spent trying to reaffirm my connections to humanity, apologizing profusely to Bree for going on a secret cocaine bender, regenerating the vast economy of words that I had surrendered to this one project. And then, of course, writing a five-page paper on the Dutch East India Company and a three-pager on apartheid in South Africa. That's right. It never fucking ends. Even when you're not in the shit, you're still at war.

And then, two days later, and for the first time, I heard from my client, who for two months prior to receiving his automobile-priced paper had provided me with no instructions, no specifications, no details, and no interaction.

"Hello, I received a work with you, but this is either the wrong work, or there has been a complete misunderstanding from your side in regard to the topic of the work . . ."

Son of a bitch.

CHAPTER 13

Portrait of the Scumbag as a Young Man

I suppose there wasn't much of a chance I'd turn out any better than this.

I did deliver the senior address at my high school graduation.

I should clarify, though. I was not class president. Student government meant longer days, more hours in school, and even the commitment of some weekends. I'd sooner have stubbed cigarettes out on the back of my hand than voluntarily spent more time in school.

I also was not the valedictorian. In a class of about 450, I was ranked in the low 200s. I was right there in the middle of the pack. But I sat next to the valedictorian, second in line at high school graduation, because I had won a contest to deliver the speech. Pissed the valedictorian off something awful. She had worked way too hard her whole life to sit next to an asshole like me on the big day.

My grades were good enough to get by on. I fell in the steady C to B– range. Never got a D. But my high school was deeply competitive and frequently squawked about its graduation rates and the rates at which it sent students off to college. It was your typical wealthy suburban status school. So for a student in honors classes, I was clearly blowing it.

I didn't care.

In elementary school, I was moody and scored poorly in penmanship, but was otherwise a solid A student. While I excelled in my studies, though, I routinely earned the NI for "Needs Improvement" in Conduct. It was said of me often during regular parent-teacher conferences that I couldn't sit still. To say I was bored is an understatement. But I showed great promise. So have a lot of people.

Something evil clicked in when I got to junior high. I knew kids whose parents gave them cash money for good grades, which of course blew my mind. These kids around me had money for baseball cards and firecrackers after every report card, and I was shoplifting just so I had something to trade at lunchtime.

One day, I approached my parents on the matter. "Mom, Dad, I got straight As this time around. Don't you think this should be worth money?"

My dad examined my report card as though he were actually considering my proposal.

After a moment, he looked up at me and said, "What, no A-pluses?"

"Dad, they don't give A-pluses on report cards!"

"Well, see if you can't fix that and then we'll talk."

It was a good approach. It made me feel the arbitrariness of grades at an early age. By seventh grade, when we had all transferred from our cozy little trailer trash elementary school to the big regional junior high, I was getting hair in strange places and having confusingly vivid dreams about Denise from *The Cosby Show*.

I was also surly and suspicious of authority. It was part of my adolescent programming. In the first week at our new school, we all had one-on-one meetings with our guidance counselors.

Mr. Muscelli was a friendly little guy with a mustache. He looked at my elementary school record.

"Says here you had trouble sitting still in class."

"I'm better now."

"Great. Great. Excellent grades. Well, David . . . I don't think we'll have any trouble with you. Welcome to Carusi Junior High."

He shook my hand.

I went back to class and proceeded to deteriorate as a student, shedding any of the compliant impulses that might have survived my first ten years of schooling. The records that Mr. Muscelli had reviewed belonged to somebody else: a child eager to impress, to receive validation, to be praised. The pimply preteen mope that I had become wanted nothing to do with praise or validation.

I wanted to question; I wanted to challenge; I wanted to diverge. These impulses were largely unwelcome in junior high. There was a sit-down-and-shut-up vibe that permeated this and every school I would attend thereafter. So I quietly decided to fall through the cracks.

They did a thing at Carusi called interim reports. These were given to students who appeared to be struggling at the halfway point of a grading term. I got four that very first grading period. I was a C student.

Mr. Muscelli delivered my interim reports and said, "I'm very disappointed in you."

"Whatever, dude."

I had officially turned off. Twelve years old, and the whole world had suddenly become clear to me. I didn't know what I wanted to be or what I wanted to do. I just knew that whatever it was, there had to be a better way, that if I started out doing exactly what I was told, I was really only setting myself up to make a living doing exactly what I was told. Even at twelve (or maybe especially at twelve), that kind of a future sounded simply ridiculous to me. Whatever the alternative was—personal struggle, short-term disappointment, or long-term failure—it simply had to be better.

By the time I got to high school and saw that Pink Floyd video with the creepy masked schoolchildren marching into the meat grinder, I was long lost. I couldn't be bothered. Sixteen, seventeen, eighteen years old, and for eight hours a day, five days a week, I had to go somewhere where you couldn't take a piss without permission and a hall pass.

I thought of Gandhi and chose passive resistance as the chief mode of my rebellion. I read nothing. I took note of nothing. I studied nothing. I did nothing . . . or at least as close to nothing as possible without failing.

I would squeeze a passing grade from an exam, pepper classroom discussions with witty remarks, write essays in homeroom at the start of the day. I was good on the fly. I wrote the senior address during lunch period on the closing day of the contest and was surprised to find that my terrible personality was not enough to keep it off the graduation program. It was one long running joke about how many steps we'd taken in the halls, how many shuttlecocks we'd stroked in gym class, how many fruit cups we'd eaten in the cafeteria. I fudged the numbers, of course. It got lots of laughs, a good smattering of them over the very idea that I should be speaking at graduation. My sincerity on matters relating to school was in extreme doubt and rightfully so. My speech was not an outright affront but a gentle prodding concerning the monotony, the repetition, and the redundancy of it all.

Of course, it was nothing personal.

Even as I grew to hate school itself, I hated very few of my teachers and, at least as far as I could tell, only those who deserved it. Some, you got the impression, had gone into the education business because they simply couldn't get adults to listen to them. They would take this sense of inadequacy out on the children.

Others suffered from a critical lack of qualifications in some area, whether this was an absence of knowledge about the subject matter being taught, an incapacity to speak without triggering REM sleep in pupils, or a general distaste for humanity that made you wonder why in the hell this person had ever become an educator or anything else that forced them to interact with others.

But there were great teachers too. There were oddball widows with inexplicable mannerisms and memories stretching back to the days when you'd have to get under your desk and pray that three feet of plywood would protect you from a Russian nuclear invasion. There were middle-aged guys with sharp minds, sarcastic answers, and white spit-corners on their mouths from talking too much who probably should have been college professors but who-knows-what went wrong, and now here they were babysitting us instead. There were good-natured ladies who didn't move me too greatly to inspiration but who entertained my disillusionment, smiled at my jokes, graded me for my abilities in spite of my efforts, and made long days seem no longer than they actually were.

There were even things I liked about school itself, and there were things that, if it had been different, I could have continued to like as I got older.

I liked classroom discussion. I was a know-it-all little bastard with opinions on everything, and I loved to give them. I liked to hear what other people had to say. I liked to agree with them and disagree with them. I raised my hand frequently and tried to make people laugh whenever possible.

Once in a while, I actually liked the exams. I know that's probably not the coolest thing to say. But in practice more than principle, I enjoyed the process. It was like doing a crossword puzzle or watching *Jeopardy!* Fill in the blank, shade in the dot, circle the letter, whatever. It was like a game, and I liked getting things right, gliding through the answers, feeling certain of my rightness. More than anything, this was fifty minutes without a yammering teacher, without staring front and center, without looking at the clock. Fifty minutes to myself.

And no matter when it was, I always loved snow days. Not just the kind that got you out of school. I loved the days when it sort of snowed while you were still in school, when we sat distractedly peering out the window, wondering how bad it might get out there. It provided a feeling of collectivity, of togetherness, that I enjoyed. The darkened sky and the downy white blanket on the playground always made me feel like we were all in on something. You could even see the teacher glancing nervously out there, reminding us that this was school and that it was incumbent upon us to pay attention, but all the while with her thoughts clearly on her ice scraper, her drive home, her shovel, and her walkway.

Snow in school had an eerie half-holiday feel to it, like we were right to pay less attention, as though there was some inbuilt excuse for the usual half-in, half-out way in which most kids endured class time, as if on just this one special occasion, it was OK for us to universally acknowledge the importance of the world outside of this deeply insulated place where things were learned with increasingly more theoretical and less practicable emphasis.

And the uncertainty was a beautiful contrast to the glacial inexorability of the four-thirty bell. Were they going to let us out early? Would one of the buses break down on the way home? Would Mr.

Santiago, the janitor, have to come in and smash the side of the radiator with a wrench?

This was the kind of anticipation you couldn't experience watching a snowstorm from the comfort of your kitchen window over a cup of hot cocoa.

I guess it wasn't all bad. But the truth is, even in my earliest memories, the things I really treasured about school were those that seemed in direct contradiction to everything for which the institution stood.

I loved it when the teacher was out and we had a substitute with only a few brief instructions and a noticeably limited knowledge of the subject matter. We were given busywork and made to privately idle away the minutes without being disruptive.

And I loved lining up single file for fire drills and waiting excitedly outside while precious minutes of class time ticked away. And there was always this hope as you stood out there, knowing most of the way that this was just a practice drill, that a small stream of smoke would show itself, that a crackle would echo from the gymnasium window, that the smell of camping would fill the air, that this would be the real thing, that we wouldn't be going back inside that day after all, that we would all have to stand back to make way for the fire trucks, that we might get to watch our school be consumed by flames. I'm sorry, but when I was a kid, I thought that it was every kid's dream to see his school burn down. I never wanted to see anybody get hurt. I just wanted the place to go up, and I wanted to watch it happen.

To me, the greatest pleasures in school were always those that forced the daily plan off its runners. Anything to defy the dreadful predictability and maddening sameness of it all. Enter Ed Simon.

Ed Simon was a high school history teacher who changed my life. Mr. Simon railed vainly against the inevitable fate of our generation, empowering us to believe that we should be more than a bunch of jerks in cubicles playing solitaire and counting the seconds until Friday at five.

I haven't spoken to Mr. Simon in at least ten years. The last time I saw him, he was walking around the Cherry Hill Mall listening to his Walkman. Even in the age of CDs, itself now passed, he insisted on tapes, which he would liberally trade with inquiring students. He once traded me Muddy Waters's *At Newport 1960* for the Offspring's *Smash*. No offense to the Offspring, but clearly I got the better end of that deal.

Mr. Simon was one of the last of the hippie history teachers, a relic from the culture wars of the 1960s. Not burned-out but certainly singed at the ends. He was a hard-core caffeine addict. He would chain-drink Dunkin' Donuts coffee and chew his fingernails until you could see the bones of his fingers. His lectures were highly expressive, so he would wave his long, gnarled fingers around wildly while he ranted. One time, his finger started bleeding as he was waving it around, so without skipping a beat, he wrapped a Dunkin' Donuts napkin around it and continued to use the finger to point at things and say stuff.

Tall, lanky, somewhat underfed, with dark red hair and a dark red beard, he was intensely knowledgeable about the history of the world, about America's past, and about the culture that we were creating.

He was not particularly optimistic about where we were heading, even, we suspected, to the extent that he wanted nothing to do with it. We always pictured Mr. Simon—a confirmed if somewhat involuntary bachelor—living amid meticulously organized stacks of yellowing newspapers and Betamax cartridges.

He would tell us that our culture was too hung up on materialism, that he made a pretty decent living but did not feel compelled to own fancy clothes or a "status car." Indeed, Mr. Simon drove a rust-blue Ford Fiesta circa 1980. The driver-side door was a different color than the rest of the car. He gave me a ride home from school once. The backseats had been ripped out, and the rearview mirror was affixed with duct tape.

Mr. Simon's method of teaching spoiled me. We were in high school, but his classroom was exactly how I pictured college would be. Open discourse. Furious debate. Discussion applicable to events happening in our world right then. No multiple-choice testing. All essay writing. No formatting requirements. We were just asked to make a thoughtful argument and to demonstrate a reasonable knowledge of the subject matter. This was the class where I truly learned to express myself in spite of the restrictive nature of formal education.

Mr. Simon would come into class and say, "Today we're going to talk about the First Amendment."

We would read the language of the amendment. He would explain its intended purposes, its extrapolated purposes, and the difference between loose and strict constructionist interpretations of its meaning. He would hand out a newspaper article about the display of the Ten Commandments at a courthouse. We would read it.

Then he'd say, "Sam, what do you think about the argument made by Justice Scalia?"

"Well, for starters," Sam would reason out, "Scalia applies the First Amendment to a case that really is about the separation of church and state. The idea of displaying the Ten Commandments at a courthouse is not about freedom of expression. It's about Christian hegemony."

Mr. Simon would say, "Of course you'd say that, Sam. You're an unrepentant liberal. Let's hear from one of our conservatives. Thompson. Don't you think that what Sam just said is total crap?"

Thompson would say, "Well, not total crap. Only partial crap. I agree that this is not an issue of freedom of expression. But I also don't see how displaying the Ten Commandments violates church and state. Nobody's saying you have to look at them."

"So what's even the point of having them?" Jennifer would interject. "I mean, if it's not to enforce a Judeo-Christian value system in a public government space, what's the point? Decoration?"

Mr. Simon would step in. "Yeah, Thompson. What's the point of the Ten Commandments, then?"

"It's not about why it's necessary. It's about why it's necessary to prevent it. Who does it really bother?"

"Stein. Does it bother you?" Mr. Simon would point to Stein.

"Ummm. I guess so. Yeah."

"How come?"

" 'Cause I don't need to read stuff about how there's only one god and how I shouldn't take his name in vain every time I have to go fight a speeding ticket."

"Great point, Stein! Thompson?"

"Well, maybe you shouldn't have been speeding in the first place."

"I love it. Thompson, our law-and-order man."

Mr. Simon was brilliant at this. He'd get everybody involved. He knew us well enough, had gotten to understand our varying views of the world. He'd use these things to set us in motion with one another. He'd work us up into a frenzy.

Then he would stand back, stop calling on people, and simply let the debate unfold. He believed that in order to get to the bottom of something, you couldn't just be told about it. You had to be forced to think about it and to defend it. You had to be willing to compromise it or protect it. You had to be challenged on your assumptions, and you had to persuade others to be challenged on theirs.

By the time we left class on any given day, we'd be shouting at one another about federal funding for the arts and how the Second Amendment was archaic and should be repealed. Debates would continue into the lunchroom and even stretch across multiple days.

I asked Mr. Simon to write one of my college recommendations. Mr. Simon was famous in the little bubble of our school for his college recommendations, which may have been his finest contribution to the world. He knew his students well enough to help launch the best of them with honest evaluation and effusive praise. Toiling in obscurity as a high school teacher with professorial capabilities, he saved his greatest work, his most lucid writing, and his best efforts for the letters dispatched to countless universities on behalf of his favorite students.

We met in the lunchroom after school and bantered for three hours about music, other students in the class, and my future. This was his interview process for the recommendation.

"Seriously, Mr. Simon. I really think you should give the Yardbirds a chance. There's this hypercharged British rave-up quality about them that makes you think of women in short skirts and go-go boots."

"I just don't see the need. I can listen to Sonny Boy Williamson and Howlin' Wolf doing the real thing. A bunch of white British teens playing blues? It just seems unnecessary."

"Yeah, but that's the thing. It's not the same thing as blues. They may have recorded it with the intention of sounding like old black dudes from America, but because they're white and British, it's something completely different and worth hearing in its own right."

"Yeah, I'm not so sure."

"So if I make you the tape, you won't take it?"

"I'll listen to it. But probably not more than once."

"Fine. I'll just save myself the tape, then."

"Right. Probably a good idea. Anyway, back to the recommendation."

"Right."

"So you're going to be a writer, right?"

"I hope so."

"Good. Do it. You should. You're a good writer, or at least, I like your writing."

"Thank you."

"Yeah. So what do you think of Ms. Reiner?"

"Ms. Reiner the French teacher?"

"Yeah. What do you think of her?"

"She's pretty cool. I had her last year. She's nice. Talks about her ex-husband a bit too much in class, but I like her."

"Yeah. I like her too. I asked her on a date last year."

"Oh yeah? How'd that go?"

"Not so good. I think I kind of freaked her out. We had coffee once, and now she doesn't really seem to want to talk to me."

"Oh well . . . who knows?"

"Yeah. Who knows? What do you think about Ms. Larkin?"

Standard letter-of-recommendation stuff.

Of course, Mr. Simon was well liked by many of his fellow teachers and perceived as an annoyance by administrators. He was an educational renegade who, as the years passed, ran afoul of the curriculum police more and more. While I was there, he was frequently in skirmishes with administrators about the structure of his classes. These turned, soon after, into out-and-out battles. And a few years after I graduated, Mr. Simon finally got tired of fighting and departed from the school in silent frustration. Education was changing. It was becoming more regimented, more saturated in politicization, more structured. Less flexible, less inventive, far less fulfilling. Mr. Simon bailed while he was still in his early fifties.

In the years following my formal education, as I found myself ever more embittered with school and the things that it entailed, I thought of how I had disappointed Mr. Muscelli, how I had wished to see my school burn down, how I had spoken at graduation instead. And I thought of Mr. Simon. Often.

And when I had finally reached a breaking point as a paper writer, when I could no longer rationalize that this was a sensible way to use the irretrievable minutes of my life, I thought of him yet more often. I just couldn't articulate what I was feeling, couldn't make sense of this self-satisfaction and regret rolled into a single shapeless sentiment. My relationship with school had been a dysfunctional one. And for some reason that I couldn't quite place my finger on, I had doomed myself to life as a student.

I decided to reach out to one of the few adults I'd ever really connected with in school. Ed Simon was just the outlaw I needed to consult. So I googled him. Of course, I knew the odds were pretty low that this guy had a Facebook page. Indeed not.

Instead, I found his obituary.

Sixty years old, he was survived by his mother, a sister, and his stacks of yellowed newspapers. My understanding is that he died alone and was not found for days.

It was too late to talk to him. He was gone. School being what it had been, I could never think to love it. I could only think to resist it. Mr. Simon had found a way to do both. This was an impulse that I admired, that I wished I'd had, that I wished I could ask him about. It seemed, though, that like my schooling, like my youth, and like Mr. Simon himself, the opportunity to learn this impulse was gone forever.

CHAPTER 14

Fear of Flying

I'd never felt as much like a man as I did the day I bought Bree's engagement ring. Paid for it with cold hard cash. It was the most expensive thing I'd ever purchased. I don't think Bree had imagined I could afford such a thing, especially without missing any bills or raising any red flags.

I just worked myself double-time.

And with greater diligence came more repeat customers, more long-term projects, more advanced studies. Indeed, at this very time, I was working my way through a doctoral program in cognitive and behavioral psychology. The focus of my work was posttraumatic stress disorder. I was taking the course of study for a guy who went by only his initials. We'll call him RP.

I spent my days with RP and my nights with Bree. And one night, when she came home from work, she found the entire house dark. The stairs leading up to the bedroom were lined with candles. Neil Young played softly in the bedroom, flowers covered every surface, and a bottle of champagne waited on ice. I stood at the door, wearing my suit, clutching the little velvet box in my pocket, and waiting nervously for her to ascend.

I had planned to say some very specific things, some very specific poetic things that we would both remember forever. But when she appeared in the doorway, her eyes already welling up with tears, everything got jumbled. I tripped over my own words, and she looked at me with loving confusion. I was blowing it. So I dispensed with the setup.

I got down on one knee and pulled the ring from my pocket.

Before I could finish asking the question, she fell down to her knees and wrapped her arms around me.

"That wasn't really an answer," I said.

"Yes! Yes! Yes!"

Now that we were planning a wedding, I had to take on more work still. I wrote everything that RP could throw at me.

I've never met RP, but he had a profound impact on my life, just as I, no doubt, had a profound impact on his.

RP was well on his way to a Ph.D. For the course of at least one full year, he would do nothing but enter his credit card information into our system. He would order dozens of papers, hundreds of pages, thousands of dollars' worth, and he would request me for each and every assignment. RP would pay my rent for a year.

Now, to be clear, there is nothing that I gave to RP that he couldn't have gotten elsewhere. The university system is designed for rich, lazy, and highly ambitious people like RP. RP was a member of America's academic elite, a pillar of society, a man of letters destined to be handsomely compensated in his profession.

RP wasn't stupid. He had a basic handle on the English language. He understood the instructions. He didn't even seem that distressed. And why should he have? Unless he was pitching hay at sunrise on somebody's farm, this guy didn't do a squirt of work all year, and possibly hadn't his whole life. RP knew how to massage a bad system. By the time he reached this advanced level of his education, he had learned that it was all about two things: the money, which he had, and the grades, which he needed.

He paid for tuition. He paid for housing. He paid for books. He paid for papers. What was the difference at that point? He knew what he wanted, he did a reasonably decent job of expressing himself, and he rarely ordered anything last minute. It was as though he'd carefully laid out his entire course of study in advance so that it could be completed by somebody else. Then he'd swoop in to take credit without the tiniest objection from his conscience. He'll make a great boss some day.

I have no idea what kind of psychologist he'll make. Maybe not such a great one. He had dependency issues. He was hooked on my papers. His addiction was total, and the consequence of withdrawal would have been utter professional ruin. Goddamn the pusherman.

From November of one year to October of the next, RP commissioned me two or three times a week. As soon as I finished one assignment, he'd hit me with two more. I completed all of his homework, took all of his take-home exams, and passed all of his classes. I did everything short of laying out his jammies before bed.

RP would send me assignments like the following:

Your writing should illustrate knowledge of the concepts through an original personal and/or professional integration of the assigned text material. If vignette application is required, please use the persons and situations within the context of your answers. If you feel that you need to quote the text, this is acceptable, you still must reference the author and indicate the page number. These answers should be 1-2 pages each. 1. What do you think a theorist representing each of the following systems of psychology would say about human nature: Mentalism; Mechanism; Determinism; and Materialism? 2. Define William Wundt's tridimensional theory of feelings, and what do you see as Wundt's contribution and legacy to modern Psychology? Give examples . . . [etc.]

Piece o cake. I was actually enjoying the hell out of my doctoral courses. I was writing day in, day out about guys whose bits and pieces had been blown off in the war; about mothers with agoraphobia and hoarding disorders; about dudes with massive sexual insecurities stemming from absentee-father issues.

Maybe that doesn't exactly sound like a party. But the exercises were truly compelling. Everything was done in vignette form. It was storytelling: looking into the lives of people and trying to explain why they were the way they were. It was a lot more interesting than many of the other things I had to write about (accounting, corporate law, tax policy, call center administration, bureaucracy maintenance, etc.).

And it was actually provoking a visceral response in me, crack-ing open doors, casting faint illumination into unexplored corri-dors. It wasn't intentional at first. It just started to happen. I learned about the symptoms of panic disorders: the cold sweat, the racing pulse, the inexplicable dread, the mental prediction of some un-speakable thing just about to happen. I learned about how triggers work and how past events and self-fulfilling prophecy can snow-ball into a fear so great as to be crippling.

I knew all of these symptoms. They greeted me at the top of a mountain trail, over the edge of a balcony, and even just when I looked up at the dizzying spires while driving across a suspension bridge.

I have a terrible fear of heights. It hits me right in the stomach. If I get six rungs up a ladder, I feel like I have to drop a deuce. The fear is totally automatic. I can't do anything to talk myself out of it.

Scenic overlooks make me nervous, balconies make me anxious, and rooftops make me sweat profusely. A gentle curve on an ele-vated highway feels like a white-knuckle space adventure; a Ferris wheel, like a torture method being used to break me before inter-rogation.

Airplanes are the worst. I hate flying. Nothing could feel less natural to me. To make matters worse, I'm terrible at sleeping. When I was in high school, I could do seventy-two-hour sleepless stretches standing on my head. I'd watch Letterman into Conan into reruns of bad sitcoms from the eighties into weight-loss info-mercials into *Good Morning America*. Then I'd go to school cranky and bloodshot. If my own bed treats me so poorly, what chance do I have in the coach section of an airplane?

I'll pop a couple of Ambiens and guzzle a few glasses of Scotch at the airport bar, and I swear I'm clearheaded and conscious enough to fly the plane.

I would kill to sleep through even just takeoff, to doze off for just one hour of that interminable limbo during which my life is at the mercy of so many statistical possibilities, to close my eyes and open them to suddenly find myself advanced thousands of miles across the map.

But it's never like that. I experience every second of stricken terror. I feel turbulence like a killer receiving last rites. When the plane dips suddenly, I look around at the blank faces of snoozing businessmen and magazine readers, and I conclude that either I'm irrational or all of these people have made peace with God, themselves, and the great yawning inevitable.

Not me.

I grip the armrests, turn up my iPod, and say to myself, Enjoy it, old boy. This could be the last song you'll ever hear.

So as I wrote my way through my Ph.D., I began to think of myself as a useful case study. As I did for the imaginary clients in RP's assignments, I thought of my past in vignette form.

Bree and I love the outdoors. And for a stretch of about one year, our schedules worked out so that we could go hiking every Monday. Soaking rain, shining sun, swamp-ass hot, or balls cold, we went out every week.

On a clear spring day, we ascended a five-mile trail to the top of the highest point in Berks County, Pennsylvania. With half a mile to go, we were chugging along, getting on a pretty good sweat. You couldn't really feel the elevation except in your ears. As we got higher, the wooded trail closed in on us. The dirt path grew narrower until it was just wide enough for us to shuffle our feet one in front of the other, pushing our arms and shoulders through the brush around us.

And suddenly, a sound I've only heard in cartoons. It was right beneath me. I looked down, and there in the brush, maybe three inches from the front of my boot, was a coiled rattlesnake. Its head was raised, flattened, and ready to strike.

"Oh shit!" I reached back for Bree and started pedaling us in reverse until we were twenty-five feet back down the trail.

"What the fuck!" Bree shouted.

"Holy crap. Did you see that? Do you see that?" It was slithering down the path in our general direction, but it was a good distance away now. We stood, frozen, watching it.

"Oh my god," I said excitedly. "That was fucking amazing!"

"Was?" Bree said frantically. "It's still right there!"

"No. It's all right. He's all the way up there. It's fine. That was incredible! That was a close encounter!"

"Why are you so excited?"

"Well, no, I mean, look, we're OK. It was a close call, for sure. But we live to tell about it, right?"

"Well, it's still there, so . . ."

"We're at a safe distance now," I said.

"I won't feel safe until we're back at the car."

"Yeah, well . . . what do you want to do? We're, like, four and a half miles into a five-mile trail. Do you want to go back?"

"What!? No! That's ridiculous. We're already here."

"Well, he's in our path, so we'd better decide what we're going to do soon."

"Fine," she said, working her courage back up. "Fine. Let's walk around the trail."

"Agreed."

We cut into the woods and walked parallel to the trail, all the while peering over to keep visual contact with the snake. At this point, it seemed he couldn't have cared less about us. Still, we took paranoid steps, looking down at our feet and back to the trail, until we felt sure we had passed him. We popped back out onto the trail and watched him slither away.

"Dude!" I exclaimed. "Can we talk about that shit now?"

"No! Shut up! I feel like we're surrounded by snakes right now! Just . . . let's keep going."

We arrived at the peak, a grouping of flat, craggy rocks baking in the sun. Bree skipped up to the edge and started flashing pictures.

"Not too close!" I begged her.

Immediately, my excitement over our recent near-death experience was eclipsed by the sheer terror of the completely stable ground and the magnificent vista before us. I sat down on one of the rocks a good ten feet back from the edge and clutched things around me, expecting that at any moment the earth would shake me off like a flea.

My doctorate in psychology was coming along nicely. I had begun to understand more about myself all the time. The rattlesnake really could have done some damage. And I had respected that enough to get out of its way. But I hadn't feared it. As I came to understand further from my studies, snakes were simply not one of my triggers.

They did not possess the encompassing and ultimate quality of heights. They couldn't pull you tumbling into oblivion, with your life at the mercy of what you knew were coldhearted odds. I lacked the impulse to fear the rattlesnake, in its threatening but minuscule singularity. But gravity, the space between me and the earth, the always likely possibility that I could stumble over my own stupid feet—these were the surrounding and irresistible forces of the universe. I'm confident that the world is a place of random indifference and that I've done nothing to persuade it that I shouldn't be thrown hopelessly into its bosom. It's a very lonely feeling.

My course in cognitive psychology touched on the isolation often experienced by victims of post-traumatic stress disorder. As I proceeded with the course, the orders began to come both in greater numbers and at greater lengths. RP would contact me and say,

> Tomar: I understrand you have been are assigned to this project as I requested I have another 4 of 5 of these papers to do over the next four weeks. So as soon as you get in the groove with this one I'll send more, probably 3–4 days each. Let me know if you have any questions. RP

The assignments that succeeded such a message would be far-ranging within the field. One assignment would be a nine-page critique of an article concerning pharmaceutical-based mental health plans and panic disorders. RP would fax along the peer-reviewed article.

Another assignment would require a five-page written response to a DVD on the difficulties experienced by wounded Iraq War veterans attempting to return to normalcy following combat. RP would mail along the DVD.

Yet another assignment would present me with the hypothetical scenario of a wounded veteran, with a description of his wartime experiences, his prewar mental history, and his current health and family circumstances. In the space of twelve pages, I would be asked to evaluate the subject and present a plan for treatment. Again, my responses in scenarios like this would be at least partially presented in vignette form.

In some exercises, I would be assigned a hypothetical patient and asked to simulate the dialogue of a first appointment. Often, these dialogic exercises would reveal that the patient's combination of panic attacks, intensifying paranoia relating to the outside world, and acute stress response patterns was probably related to some repressed or underestimated trauma.

Because trauma victims will often distance themselves from the fear, pain, or dread related to the original event or series of events, it is common for the victim to begin to experience psychological symptoms after years of failing to confront the trauma. This results in the panic and anxiety disorders that are often at the root of a phobia.

For this reason, some therapists recommend exposure therapy, in which the subject is required to gradually confront the triggers of his or her panic episodes with professional support and comfort. By confronting one's fear and simultaneously reversing the conditioned responses that produce the psychological and chemical symptoms of panic, proponents of this treatment mode contend, one should be able to unravel the web woven by trauma.

Upon learning of this mode of treatment, I resolved that this was the only possible way to make peace with my own inexplicable and intensifying condition. As these things tend to, it was getting worse the more I thought about it. But I had to face it. I had to take flights. I had to go on hikes. Sometimes I had to change the lightbulb ten feet above my front stoop. Life makes no allowances for fear.

My first attempts at self-directed exposure therapy were not totally successful. I recorded this entry in my amateur psychology journal:

Our good friend Felix is a gifted photographer and offered to take engagement photos for us. Felix has a great eye for context and scouted out a few gritty South Philly locations for the shoot. We were going for something less Hallmark and more Exile on Main St.

I'll skip ahead, through the delightful part of our day, which took place on solid ground, including some cobblestone, which you are bound to find in Philadelphia. After an hour of making sexy to the camera, we followed Felix to the final and most spectacular location. It was actually less than two blocks from our house and had always filled me with curiosity. Nestled snugly between the community hockey rink and a Vietnamese noodle house is an abandoned three-story structure without walls.

A redbrick building dripping with tar and graffiti, it stands alone in a parking lot, tended to only by crackheads, homeless people, and the guys from the noodle house who heave bags into the adjacent dumpster. Believe me when I tell you that, removed from the experience, the resulting photographs are stunning.

But if you had been there as we took pictures on the perimeter in preparation for our eventual foray inside, you would have known by looking that I felt a pure dread welling up in my cockles. The plan, to which I had agreed as part of an exposure therapy process about which only I knew, was to pass through the gut of a broken metal door and climb to the top floor.

As we entered and started climbing, we stepped carefully to avoid the debris, filth, dismounted railings, and dead animals that cluttered the stairway. Each flight was covered in a muck of things I couldn't possibly describe.

As we reached the top of the first flight of stairs, I was sickened by the sight of an open portal leading to the second floor. In order to pass from the stairwell onto the second floor, one had to cross over a platform that was about the size of a TV tray and, I imagine, was encased by walls at one point in the building's history. Not so today. I could see that the platform stuck out from the stairwell wall with nothingness around and nothingness below. The portal onto the floor was three gigantic, terrifying feet away from the stairwell.

It was clear that the third story would be exactly the same except one more flight up, making the certainty of my death upon falling that much greater. We passed the second-floor portal. I glanced over at it again and considered vomiting.

I pictured myself losing my footing as I passed over the platform. I saw a bird's-eye view of myself sprawled out and splattered below. I pictured Bree and Felix during that frantic moment of realization that I was no more.

By the time we reached the third-floor platform, I was dripping with sweat and considering my obituary. My face was pale, and my insides were stewed. Exposure therapy, I kept reminding myself. Tell yourself something comforting, I thought.

OK, OK. Something comforting. Hmmm. Well, these photos should be pretty bitchin', so it's practically worth it. And besides, this is just a conditioned response. You're being irrational. We're going to be just fine. It's just a three-foot platform. You can walk three feet, can't you? No big deal. You've done that before. And pretty soon, this will all be over . . . particularly if you plunge to your bloody death less than two blocks from your own home. Oh god. I'm going to die. I don't want to die.

The third floor was even worse than I had expected. That three-foot platform looked like a high wire over a football field. It was damp and cracked and covered with algae. Bree stepped across it in her high-heeled boots like it was nothing.

This made me feel like a pretty huge pussy.

So I held my breath, hugged the wall, and slid from the stairs to the platform. I thrust myself through the portal and onto the third floor.

It was a big empty warehouse space that was open on all sides. You could see the city in all its glory. Pep Boys this way, the river that way, and nothing but beautiful highway in between. The only thing standing between us and the edge was our own judgment. The middle of the floor provided no comfort. Where an elevator had once been, there was now a gaping shaft that I envisioned swallowing us all whole and keeping it secret for one hundred years. It was surrounded by a moat of rainwater and scum.

Felix followed us in and encouraged us to walk farther out onto the floor. He had a shot in mind that he was determined to get. But as we advanced farther, my steps became more labored. Each time I put a foot down, I deliberated carefully and slowly, until eventually I could go no farther. I froze.

"Just a little more," Felix said.

I just shook my head no.

"Yeah, just back up just a little bit more."

The edge was maybe eight feet away. That was good enough. I shook my head no.

"C'mon, baby." Bree was holding my hand.

"I think I have to go. We have to get out of here," I said calmly. Felix could see that I was freaking out a little bit. My feet were planted into the floor, and everything was rubbery.

"Yeah, man. We'll get out of here. Just back up a couple more steps. We'll just get the shot and get out of here."

"Fine," I said. Exposure therapy. I tried to shuffle my feet back a few more steps. Nothing doing. All I could think about was that we had to pass over that platform again. That was exactly when I was going to die. Felix flashed a couple of pics. He looked at them on his digital screen. He looked back at us and back at the screen.

"Let's get out of here," I said.

"OK, just—"

"Yup, I gotta go. Gotta go now."

"It's OK, baby. Everything's fine." Bree had seen this before, but maybe never quite this bad.

"I have to get out of here. I have to get out of here now."

Felix could see that he was getting nothing but abject horror from me. This was not the feel we were going for. He could see there was no use being up here.

"OK, OK. Let's go. I'll go first," he offered. I rushed past him, passed over the platform, and plunged into the warm embrace of the stairwell, relieved at the decay around me. If I fell now, I'd just need a tetanus shot and a hot bath.

That's what I got for practicing psychology without a license.

By contrast, my course work was going swimmingly. As is

always the case, I was doing loads of other work at the same time. I was pulling from the typical grab bag of papers on supply chain management, Marcus Garvey, OPEC, and APEC; stuff on Bloom's taxonomy, Leonardo's *Last Supper*, O'Brien's *The Things They Carried*, and Geraldo's mustache; a design paper on a low-back Spanish chair from Ikea, an analysis of the fireworks business in China, and a brief overview of great clarinet players through history.

My life was the normal interdisciplinary jumble. But RP remained a constant.

Whatever his doctoral studies in psychology were doing for me, clearly this arrangement was working for RP. He returned to me after every filed assignment without critique, complaint, or correction. RP was clearly satisfied with the ongoing results of our transaction. I suspect he was getting pretty good grades. And even though RP's fraud was taking place across multiple semesters, in more than a dozen classes, and throughout countless personal interactions between him and his professors, at no point through this duration, it seemed, had RP's academic standing been threatened, nor had he even been given pause by the suspicion of a professor, such that he might reconsider so enthusiastically continuing to pay for my services.

And of course, RP really had no choice at this point, lest he should suddenly have to hand in an assignment in his own words. People would think he'd suffered a serious head injury.

So RP continued ordering pages by the dozens right through midterms. Stress disorders, anxiety-related insomnia, repressed trauma, and panic attacks floated in and out of my consciousness while Bree and I drove out to potential wedding venues and discussed floral arrangements.

Then I had a dream one night in which some unrecognizable person was driving and I was in the passenger seat. We came up on a curve and took it too fast. I could feel that we were taking it too fast, and I said something to the driver, but it was too late. We busted through the guardrail and into the wild blue yonder. I got a zero gravity sensation in my balls as I awaited the inevitable.

When I woke up and pieced it back together, I had an epiphany. I recorded the following vignette.

Highway 1 is beautiful and precarious. One can only imagine the carnage that went into its construction.

At the end of college, Donovan Root and I flew out to San Francisco to visit our buddy Dead Bear. It was the last time I ever flew somewhere without the fear of god inside me.

Dead Bear was an old buddy from Jersey, now living in Haight-Ashbury and working as a lawyer. We slept in his living room and did bong hits for breakfast.

We made the decision that we were going to drive up the coast on the 1 and the 101 to the town of Eureka in Humboldt County, renowned the world over for the excellence of its marijuana. We were going to find out for ourselves.

But we weren't prepared for the majesty of the drive itself. We were delayed at every turn by the stunning expanse of shimmering ocean, the rolling hills, the prehistoric enormity of the Pacific Northwest. To explain for those who haven't driven this stretch of highway where it bends and twists north of the Golden Gate Bridge, the 1 is a two-way road, one lane going each way, dynamited into the side of the mountains.

Looking to our left as we traveled north, we could see the Pacific Ocean rolling in below, crystal blue and intoxicating. I was raised on the Jersey Shore. I always just assumed the ocean was brown and ridden with medical waste.

To our right was an alternating scene. Lush moss blankets cropped up into mountains, cast their shadows on us for a mile, then dipped back into valleys. Valleys were dotted with cows and farms, shrouded in forests and sometimes a million miles below us. Sometimes there were guardrails. Sometimes there weren't. Sometimes there were signs that warned of rockslides. Sometimes there were rocks but no signs.

We paid our respects to the highway, taking many stretches as slowly as fifteen miles per hour, occasionally being passed by locals familiar with the intricacies of the snaking road. At one point, a cow wandered in front of our car. We stopped to watch it casually amble down the side of the mountain at a seventy-degree angle. The cow knew what it was doing, which was more than I could say for us.

Valleys would produce tiny towns, comprising only what we could see immediately in front of us on either side of the highway. We were so enchanted by the panoramas, charmed by the eateries, riveted by the adventure, that we stopped every few miles to play.

We stopped to get oysters from a shack perched precariously on a cliff. We stopped to buy strange objects from local merchants. We stopped to smoke a joint under a big tree. We stopped at a winery to watch the sunset.

Then we got back in the car, and suddenly it was getting dark. And then it started to drizzle. And we looked at the clock and we looked at the map and we looked at where we were. Suddenly, it was night, and we were hours from our destination in Eureka.

Donovan Root took over driving. Dead Bear had taken us much of the way in his car, Cosmic Charlie. Cosmic Charlie was getting tired, and everybody inside was getting tense. The road that had been so inspiring just an hour before was now a harrowing and endless thing. There was no way out of this. Valleys became chasms and vistas became abysses.

At one point, I watched our tire roll across the white line and brush the empty space of air where a bit of highway had fallen out. I gasped.

"What's that?" Donovan asked.

"Youuu . . . really don't want to know."

We had listened to the Grateful Dead most of the way. There are few bands or musicians who have so evocatively summoned in sonic textures the brilliant colors of Northern California. But now it was night, and it was time for a change. We put on Bob Dylan's Blonde on Blonde and proceeded on our journey, holding our collective breath and hoping for a happy ending.

Dylan had gotten no further than "Pledging My Time" when the car that had inched along all day and into the evening suddenly started to pick up speed. It was an alarming sensation. I was in the backseat. Dead Bear was in the passenger seat. Bob Dylan carried on. "They called for the ambulance and one was sent. Somebody got lucky, but it was an accident."

The car was going into a steep decline with a guardrail directly ahead and a hairpin turn right after. Here, the road twisted back on itself while continuing its decline. Suddenly the guardrail was coming on in a hurry.

"Donovan! Slow down!" Dead Bear shouted.

Donovan couldn't even form the words to tell us he couldn't. His mouth was frozen, his foot pumping the break, the break responding by doing nothing at all. We were in free fall. It was an agonizing second, not nearly long enough for us to say good-bye. And suddenly, time stood still.

The car jammed to a halt. Bob Dylan stopped singing. Nobody moved a muscle.

"Donovan! What the fuck, man!" Dead Bear screamed.

"I . . . I don't know what happened."

"OK, OK," I said. "I think we're OK, right? Everybody's OK?"

"Yeah, I think so."

"Yeah, I'm fine."

"OK, good. Let's get out and assess the situation."

The situation was that Cosmic Charlie's front bumper was hanging over the edge of a cliff. The guardrail was bowed below it. A patch of dirt roughly the size of a healthy bull turd, used to lodge the guardrail in the embankment, had grabbed one of our tires and held us back from the great unknown ever after. Our tire was jammed into the mud, and we couldn't back it out. We were stuck.

And we were nowhere. Our cell phones were inoperable. What's more, we were huddled up together on a slick pile of grass inhospitably located at the bottom of the first steep decline and at the top of the whole rest of the world. We conferred and concluded that there was little to guarantee that another car wouldn't make the same mistake we had and finish the job that the mountain had failed to complete on its first swipe.

So when a car passed after about five minutes, Dead Bear boldly volunteered to get in. As he pulled away in a minivan, Donovan and I watched, quite certain that this would be the last time we ever saw him.

When he returned twenty minutes later in the cab of a California Highway Patrol tow truck, our reunion was joyful. He had been taken to what would probably better be termed a settlement than a town, where he had been left to a pay phone and his own resources.

When he called 911 and they asked for a landmark, he replied, "The phone booth is the landmark."

Now please understand that as a resident of New Jersey, famous for the corruption and racial profiling of its police officers, I have always been skeptical of law enforcement, and of people in general. But god bless the officers who were dispatched to us that night. They yanked our car out of the mud, they comforted us, and they told us that we were lucky. This was the worst spot out here, they told us. The guardrail had been replaced only that month after a previous accident.

"We fished that guy out of the ravine with a helicopter," they told us. One of the cops pointed his Maglite down into the valley. Nothing but treetops below.

Cosmic Charlie had sustained minimal damage. A headlight was hanging out of its socket. One of the cops grabbed some twine from his car, rigged up the headlight, and scraped the dirt from Charlie's grill, an act of decency unlike any I had ever seen in all my years of being pulled over and illegally searched on the New Jersey Turnpike.

The car was running fine, but now there was the whole new dilemma of still being stuck out on this godforsaken highway without a place to roost for the night. One of the cops said, "Head on down the highway for just another ten miles or so. There's a bed-and-breakfast up in the first town you'll hit. You can't miss it. Go in and ask for Terry."

"Ummmm, OK," Dead Bear said as we got back into the car. We were a bit shell-shocked from all the unsolicited kindness.

Dead Bear drove at the speed of a shopping cart for that ten miles, until we got to a place with a little wooden sign that read "No Vacancies."

We walked in anyway. A slim middle-aged woman welcomed us into a tavern that doubled as the reservation desk. Terry.

"You the boys that lost it around the curve?" she asked. Apparently the officer had phoned ahead on our behalf.

"Uhhhh, yeah," said Dead Bear. "Yeah. We, uhh, we saw that you had no vacancies, but we're kind of stuck right now and . . ."

"OK. That's OK. We'll get to that. First things first. Have you boys had anything to eat?"

We all shook our heads no. She led us to a table and sat us down. While we were waiting for her to come back, a gentleman with an Australian accent approached us and introduced himself as Geoffrey. He regaled us with stories about his half-wolf/half-dog, about chicken-thieving coyotes, about mountain lions, about the storm brewing in the clouds. We were silent and enraptured. This guy was straight out of Tolkien.

Terry came back with a basket of bread, a bottle of red, and three bowls of clam chowder "fresh from the ocean out back."

As we drank and ate and came to our senses, it became clear to us what had transpired. We were safe now. But we had almost died, and less than an hour before this meal. Without words, we sat and shook our heads and exhaled brazenly. We were alive, but we had almost died. A patch of dirt had been the difference between our lives and the obvious alternative. A patch of dirt. A piece of the earth several inches wide and freshly packed less than a month prior, but not nearly so heroic to the last poor bastard to hydroplane on a killer hairpin turn. It really is all up to chance, now, isn't it?

Incidentally, the chowder was transcendent. As we ate, Terry came back and said, "Here's the deal. We have a cottage with three beds, but the lock doesn't work. So we want you to stay the night free of charge. Breakfast will be on your porch in the morning. Just be sure to tip your chambermaid generously."

This just kept getting weirder.

Terry sold us a six-pack of beer from the microbrewer the next town over. Geoffrey told us about a little hidden trail just down the road, said that it led to the beach.

After a meal and bottle of wine for which we were not charged, Terry led us to our cottage. It was beautiful. It was a one-room house with a claw-foot tub and a potbelly stove in the middle. We *weren't, the three of us, looking for a romantic getaway together per se, but this was the sweetest place we'd ever been. We thanked Terry profusely, told her we'd be happy to pay for a room like this. She refused.*

Then there was silence as we tried to register this generosity. We stood confounded, looking at one another.

"All right," Terry said. "All right. Come here." She beckoned Dead Bear forward and hugged him. Then she hugged Donovan and me and departed. The whole thing really shook me up.

After she left, we cleaned ourselves up, rolled a few joints, grabbed the six-pack, and left our cottage. As to the name of the town, we were sworn to secrecy in exchange for its bounteous and beautiful hospitality. But I can say that it was one of those that exist for only a half mile on either side of the 1 and that I'm not even really sure it would actually be there if I went looking for it today. That night, we walked back up the highway that only a few hours before had tried to kill us.

We wobbled along the yellow line, ensconced in warmth. Bullfrogs croaked, and the smell of lavender was thick in the air. We pondered the possibility that we had in fact died and that this was what had awaited us on the other side: a magnanimous innkeeper, a six-pack of beer, and everything for free so long as you tipped generously. We found Geoffrey's trail and stumbled down to the moonlit beach. We made a bonfire and climbed up on the giant redwood stumps that were washed up all over the beach like dinosaur bones. We watched the ocean and wondered if we were still alive.

So, that's what I got from my doctoral studies. This had been the last time I had faced a height without fear, a moment upon which I had reflected endlessly in the years since but which I had never previously identified as traumatic. But by god it had been. Chance is a hairpin turn and a pile of dirt, and now I knew that. It was a lot to absorb.

On the other hand, that I should have lived, and not only that, that I should have lived to marry the woman I'd loved since I was just a dumb sixteen-year-old kid, that was a lot to absorb too. For all the questionable things I'd done, to what did I owe my great fortune? And what had I done to live up to it?

I have to admit, RP's course of study helped me to face these questions, to identify my fears, and even to begin making peace with my more encompassing anger and sense of displacement. For all of its concrete challenges, even growing up is just a matter of perspective. My fear, my anger, and my alienation remained powerful forces, but ones that I was beginning to understand and even control. And to these accomplishments, I can say that RP's course of study was a major contributor, that my years of postgraduate study in general had been a major contributor, that the educational experience that had so cruelly eluded me in school and that had been readily available to me in my profession had been a major contributor.

RP would be committing fraud every single time he introduced himself as Dr. So-and-So. But me, I was learning, I was growing, and I was grateful for it.

CHAPTER 15

Graduation

After a long day of paper writing, suddenly it was the evening, and the Phillies game was starting, Doc Halladay taking the mound. I picked Bree up from work, we threw our bags in the car, and she drove us down the shore. Larry Andersen and Scott Franzke called the game on the radio. I wrote a five-page paper about the scriptures of the Sikh religion on the way.

Once there, we unpacked, and I wrote a four-page paper about how music makes me feel. As I did, I pitied the jackass who couldn't write that one on his own. But great for me. Work was scarce, and I had a wedding to pay for. It took me all of ten seconds to write a paper about why the Beatles are awesome.

It was the end of the month again, and since my company paid monthly, I was getting in everything I could. I was planning on spitting out another three-pager about the administrative skills required to be a good elementary school principal over the course of the next twenty-five minutes, getting some sleep, and popping back up at seven for a couple more papers. We had a nice day at the beach planned, so the goal was to finish everything before Bree got up.

Nothing big, really. Two pages on "a controversial issue." I love "pick your own" papers. If I'm feeling randy, I tend to reward the customer's faith in my discretion by making the controversial issue something like "the use of sock garters in professional sports" or "Hall versus Oates." But my primary goal was to write this one in under twenty minutes, so I would throw together the standard fare about abortion.

After that, I had a two-page assignment with the following directions: "University Level / Clear Conclusion / Professional language / No repetition." The subject was listed as "not specified." I hadn't decided yet, but I would probably write about the high price of shower caps these days.

When I was a kid, I had the same recurring night terror for years and most especially in the early summer. In my dream, I would know it was summer, but I would get up to the sound of my alarm anyway, I would put on my clothes, and I would eat a cranky breakfast. I would catch the bus to school, and everybody would seem fine with all of this. I would quietly ride to school, and then suddenly, as I sat in the classroom waiting for the start of the school day, I would look out the window and remember the meaning of summer.

"What are we doing here?!" I would inquire madly. "It's summer. We don't have to be here!" And nobody would say or do a thing, and there we would be, stuck in an endless loop of schoolwork, homework, and busywork with no end in sight. Then I'd wake up. "Thank goodness," I would say to myself, "it was only a dream."

But was it? Or was it a prognostication?

I'd taken longer to graduate than anybody in history. It was absurd. I was in my thirties, my hairline was receding, and I was regularly passing myself off as a kid in school. I felt like Dylan from *Beverly Hills, 90210*.

Morning after morning, I was waking up to these pedantic little nonsense assignments about how business ethics are a key to success in the business world (knowing this was bullshit), about how one of the best ways to create better classroom results is to promote more individualized learning strategies (recognizing that education was increasingly standardized), about how there needs to be a more meaningful push for a sustainable way of life in America (knowing full well that only a breakdown in civil order could facilitate this change). Basically, it was all theory and no exercise.

I was stuck here just like I was at the industrial cleaning supply company. Even writing papers had become a menial, formulaic task. It was as rote and thoughtless as anything. Still exhausting as a way of making a living, but plodding and predictable like one never-ending day at the hubcapping plant or the chewing gum factory. This was how I reached that point; this was how I got to that place where my head went on vacation and my fingers just wrote. This was how my closest friends had come to know me, with my hands connected to the keyboard and my head turned slightly toward the people in the room, conversing and typing at once.

I always wished I had been born a musician like Tom W. What he does blows my mind. Performs, moves, sings, sneers, punches, and kicks the piano all in seamless coordination, all parts of the body doing different things at once.

My curse is that I was born with this same skill, but I can only apply it to something that you do in the privacy of your home rather than in front of thousands of drunk, leering, panty-throwing domestic types.

So the intellectual luster had left this work. The artistic excitement was getting harder to summon all the time. I didn't care what my output looked like. It only mattered that I completed it. I had reached the limits of what my profession could teach me. I had started to feel more and more like a guy who only read the inside jacket of the book, the back cover of the DVD, the little blurb in *TV Guide*. You get the idea.

I had never left school. What the hell was I still doing here? What the hell was I afraid of that I hadn't taken any greater a leap than this? And how the fuck was I thirty? I'd been stuck here for a long time, engaging in theoretical exercise, wading ankle-deep in ideas but never swimming in them.

And then, here, in this suspended state, I started to notice things. A blemish on my hip. What the fuck is that? I never had one of those before. Then a new tuft of hair in a place that I couldn't style, like my shoulder or my lower back. My god! That sprouted overnight! When did I become a Chia Pet?

I was getting older. I was getting looser around the middle, thinner up top, tougher to look at, just generally not what I pictured myself to be.

And it wasn't just looks. I was getting more sentimental too. As

Bree and I planned the details of our wedding, the very thought of it would overcome me with a new kind of sensation, a euphoric rush of emotion so overwhelming that it just had to come out of my eyeballs. Until I was in my late twenties, I don't think I could have cried even if you had run over my foot with a Zamboni.

But now, everything set me off so that I welled up with tears. Adult contemporary pop songs about true love; commercials about how good wireless roaming plans bring families together; episodes of *The Golden Girls* where the ladies boldly faced the terrifying realities of aging.

I was hopelessly nostalgic for my youth, and in a way that seemed totally inconsistent with how I remembered feeling about things all the way back then. I wasn't just nostalgic for the smell of cold weather on NFL Sundays, or the houses that I'd once lived in, or the friends I'd once had.

I was getting nostalgic for things that had sucked, like doing suicide sprints in wrestling practice, like missing an elementary school field trip because of the chicken pox, like old breakups. I wasn't nostalgic for the girl, mind you, but the actual breakup. I was having weird sentimentality for all the kinds of feelings that I could remember, including heartbreak and misery. I had no sense of longing to go back to this time. There was just a realization that I was getting older and that all the things I'd lost with age couldn't be gotten back.

Bree threw a party for me on my thirtieth birthday.

Fifty of my friends were there. They all brought me bottles of Scotch and blunts. They lit the candles on my cookie cake and sang a loud, drunken, raucous "Happy Birthday to You." Someone shouted, "Make a wish."

I couldn't think of anything that I wanted, at least nothing that I thought I needed to wish for. I loved my friends. I loved my family. I was standing beside the woman I was going to marry. I was my own boss. I called no man "sir." I was living the sweet life.

I said, getting a little choked up, "I can't think of a thing. I've got everything I need right here."

One of my friends shouted, "Pussy!"

I guess I deserved that.

I had never pictured this guy at thirty: happily coupled, fully socialized, and at least personally, if not professionally, content. I had never pictured that.

But then, I had never pictured myself at thirty . . . at all. In episode 5F18 of *The Simpsons*, Marge, in one of her many moments of tempered marital discontent, asks Homer, "When we got married, is this how you thought we'd be spending our Saturdays? Driving out to the boondocks to trade in a refrigerator motor?"

Homer replies, "Eh, I never thought I'd live this long."

I know this feeling. I was pretty sure I was destined to flame out young. Of course, relatively speaking, it's not too late for that. But still, looking at myself in the mirror, I can't help feeling that I've already exceeded the life expectancy of twenty-year-old me, who was pretty sure he'd have choked to death on his own vomit well before thirty.

When I started writing papers for a living, I never pictured a future. I never pictured having to earn the lifelong respect of my wife, having to look my children in the eyes and explain how I made a living, having to decide how to educate them.

I never pictured any of this. It wasn't for lack of inspiration. I thought I'd be great at something. But I also figured that I might simply be dead. I don't know why. Call it youthful nihilism, or a sense that it probably wouldn't matter a whole lot either way, but that's what I thought. So as I wrote papers for the leaders of an American future in which I anticipated playing no part, and as I considered that future for a generation of children to which I intended to contribute no seed, I thought nothing of the years ahead.

To me, they were as unlikely as the idea of making an honest living.

It was a selfish way to live. Not simply hoarding knowledge and making it no benefit to civilization, but also assuming from a young age that I'd take this knowledge to the grave. What the hell good was I to anybody or anything? Not that I was suicidal or even morbid. I loved life. I treasured every moment. But I also figured that this attitude would be the death of me. No respect for the future. No sense of consequence. No plan.

No regrets . . .

And now, not only was I not dead but I was happy, healthy, and housebroken. A few years ago, owning a paper towel holder would have seemed out of my reach. Now I had a cheese board and table runners and a credenza. I had different glasses for different types of beverages. Bree and I would go antiquing in the spring and apple picking in the fall. We avoided eating anything with trans fats in it and took fish oil capsules daily for the omega-3 fatty acids. I was a few bad sweaters and a Rod Stewart record away from being the perfect model of domesticity.

And then there was my work. Why was I still in school? For so long, school had been my archnemesis: my Moby Dick, my Professor Moriarty, my Sideshow Bob. Could it be, then, that I needed it? There was no denying it. I had come to depend on it over the better part of a decade, even though as a younger man I'd dreamed of being freed from it. I had found a sick, dysfunctional symbiosis with school, like fungus spreading out over the decay it created. School's shortcomings allowed me to do what I did.

And what of school? Did it need me? How many of its shortcomings had I helped to obscure? And how many of these did I have the power to expose? Could it be that school needed me, that our purposes were somehow intertwined?

I don't mean this in an arrogant way. Over the years, I had stopped being angry. I was just working now. This was what I did for a living. I had nothing to do with school. It had nothing to do with me. Professionally speaking, I was just a lone wolf set on survival. Nothing to see here. I went about my business quietly, without the resentment of my youth, with the patience of maturity, with fairness to my clientele, diligently, determinedly intent on making the work pay until I found a way to depart amicably.

But I was a petty bandit sneaking through the halls of the universities, committing misdemeanors left and right. And from this position of concealment, tiptoeing from one class to another, from one major to another, from one degree to another, from one university to another, from one country to another, I could see the same thing everywhere.

Brochures may be designed to hide university shortcomings from parents. Statistical smoke screens can be cast to hide the declining value of a higher education from the buying public. Promises soon to be broken about awaiting opportunities may be sold to next year's graduates. But nothing is done to patch up the cracks that I have gotten to see as I have moved about invisibly.

I admit it. I was in there to steal shit. But if you skulk in and out long enough and see enough of the same things, you realize that our greatest national resource—the young people who make up tomorrow's workers, professionals, and leaders—is being deprived of everything it needs to flourish. And as with so many of the challenges before America, greed is a major cause. A crime of that magnitude can be humbling even to the petty bandit.

Around this time, I wrote a paper on Plato's "Allegory of the Cave," a parable that I had read many times. This turned out to be a particularly valuable reading.

The professor's instructions were as follows: "Describe and explain what you would consider to be, for yourself, an ideal education. This paper can be in first person, since it is mostly based on your opinion. The entire paper is based on Plato's 'Allegory of the Cave' . . . No internet sources can be used. Need work cited. One of the sources needs to be the actual 'The Allegory of the Cave' "

Right. No Internet sources. Schmuck.

Anyway, I got down to business and wrote the paper. Basically, Plato's allegory describes a bunch of people who are born chained to the ground in the back of a cave, with shackles binding them at the arms and neck. They can't see anything but a fire in front of them and a wall just beyond the mouth of the cave. The fire casts shadows on the wall, so that they have only a vague sense of life beyond the cave and an indefinable awareness of the shadowy figures that pass by without restraints. As Plato tells, "To them . . . the truth would be literally nothing but the shadows of the images."

In Plato's allegory, one man is freed from bondage and struck by a revelation that he at once fears and knows he must share with the others in the cave. Plato describes the experience.

At first, when any of them is liberated and compelled suddenly
to stand up and turn his neck round and walk and look towards

the light, he will suffer sharp pains; the glare will distress him, and he will be unable to see the realities of which in his former state he had seen the shadows; and then conceive some one saying to him, that what he saw before was an illusion, but that now, when he is approaching nearer to being and his eye is turned towards more real existence, he has a clearer vision.[1]

I was particularly moved by the idea of a "more real existence." Something new was becoming apparent to me. As usual, my assignment seemed to accidentally comment on the life I was living. To do anything short of sharing everything I'd learned moving among the shadowy objects began to strike me as irresponsible.

The time had come, the age in my life had arrived when I might finally do something responsible. What kind of future did I want for myself, for my family, for those around me whom I loved with all my heart? I no longer wanted to be a part of the destruction. I wanted to stand up to it. I wanted to shine an exploding white light into the cave.

I was beginning to look forward to a day when I could be done with this way of working, with immersing myself so constantly in thoughts, ideas, theories, studies, and arguments that I couldn't find a second to reflect on them all. I began to think that someday I could put all these things together and make of myself some singularly unified Renaissance man. That day could never come so long as I was in the trenches.

How much could I learn of self-betterment, of the human condition, of the struggle between good and evil, when I persisted in living amorally, as an unfeeling siphon pumping productivity from the muck? How could I read history's great thinkers and assess history's great villains; how could I come to understand the reasons men suffer and kill one another; how could I come to learn of all the ways that we can right a wrongheaded ship and continue to respond only with hostile opportunism? How could I learn so much of virtue when I had none of my own? How could I ever shine a light on anybody else when I remained chained down in a cave of my own design?

Maybe these questions should have been obvious to me from the beginning. But they weren't. And now they were cascading before me.

I had to be done with it, and now I knew it. I remembered quitting my old job at the industrial cleaning supply company and how nobody had really cared. The lack of closure had haunted me. There are so many things that one thinks and never gets to say out loud. And these things persist, and get louder and larger, and become part of some much grander treatise that the brain thinks it needs to deliver in order to find peace.

But all of this is, of course, totally secondary to the unending pressure just to get by. Now that I had finally gotten to a place of paying the bills and living in relative comfort, I had a wedding to pay for, and then maybe a house and some kids and a large automobile and all that other stuff.

Even at this late stage in the game, even with everything I had learned up to this point, the way out was no clearer. Every day would be this intense, nauseating maze of assignments, and every night would be this uneasy pool of sleepless sweat.

So I worked, in spite of a mounting certainty that this work was now out of step with whatever it was I hoped to be as a man.

I called my parents, and I apologized to them. I told them I was sorry for being a generally rotten kid, a spiteful teenager, and a financial liability as a young adult. I apologized for my anger and told them that I wasn't angry anymore, that I was actually optimistic and hopeful. I told them that I was a man, that I intended to start a family of my own, and that I appreciated everything they had done for me.

My mother thanked me, but she didn't let me get by on just that. "You'd better mean it," she said.

And after that, I knew I had to come clean. Reconciliation felt good. But I had always loved my parents. I had a lot longer way to go with schools. And I started to think that they might be interested in knowing some of the things that I knew. I decided it would make a tremendous commencement speech.

I decided to tell them the things that I had come to know, with the hope that it could help all of us. Of course, the last word on this is far from spoken. More questions than answers lurk in the pages of this book. At this stage—which the optimistic franchise might characterize as a rebuilding season—it could be no other way.

Suffice it to say, we all have a lot to learn.

Acknowledgments

Much credit belongs to the incredible people around me who have supported and encouraged me, both through the process of writing this book and through the course of a career that has not always appeared to be headed anywhere.

Thanks to those who provided me with pertinent news stories, feature articles, and Web links throughout the process. You were instrumental in helping me formulate the arguments driving this book: Adam Dembowitz, Lauren Dembowitz, David Pinzur, Avi Lebovic, Hilary Stiebel, Matthew Tanzer, Jamie Brotz, Michelle Neff, Nicholas Schorn, and Mary Bronfenbrenner. An additional thanks to Ms. Bronfenbrenner and her class for their ongoing support and dialogue.

Additional thanks to those who played a critical support role in the process of writing this book: Brett Lean, Lori Lean, Casey Jones, Rich Miller, Bill Serotta, Howard Ross, Emad Hasan, Janene Hasan, D. Jones, Matt Young, Hilary Siegel, Jon Adler, Chris Hezel, Lisa Hezel, Glenn Oettinger, Mike Stiebel, Kellen Sporney, Phil Brown, Jess Lauer, Rachel Lauer, Kelani Edmonson, Mike Thomas, Lily Thomas, Aaron Vill, Ari Rom, Lauren Tanzer, Kelly Schorn, Low Cut Connie, Emily Pinzur, Adriana Sabatini, Dena Lebovic, Cary Neff, Wendi Snyder, and Jodi Kratchman.

Thanks also to those upon whom I called for editorial notes, fact-checking, and feedback: Adam Weiner, Brian Schorn, Michael Kratchman, Daniel Swerdlin, Dave Lauer, and Ian Snyder. Particular thanks to Dave and Ian, who served a primary role in supporting the text with key figures, findings, ideas, and insights. Sorry, guys, but your fingerprints are all over this thing.

Thanks to Liz McMillen, editor at the *Chronicle of Higher Education*. Ms. McMillen and staff provided a respectable forum, a receptive environment, and a perceptive editorial process for the initial "Shadow Scholar" article. Ms. McMillen's support, boldness, and energy were essential to the article's success and to the opportunity for me to tell my story here.

An enormous debt of gratitude is owed to Sydelle Kramer and Susan Rabiner of the Rabiner Literary Agency. I have been blessed with agency representation that is smart, patient, and perfectionist. Sydelle and Susan have battled on my behalf and deserve tremendous credit for putting me in a position to write this book.

Likewise, I am deeply indebted to Benjamin Adams and the staff at Bloomsbury USA. Ben's sharp editorial eye and intuitive reading are as much on display here as is my own work. I am particularly grateful to Ben for his fearlessness in allowing this story to evolve organically and for allowing it to be told in a way that is frank and accurate. Thanks also to managing editor Lisa Silverman and legal counselor Alan Kaufman for their critical input.

An unparalleled gratitude is also owed to my longtime friend and colleague Howard Megdal. Editor in chief of *The Perpetual Post* and author of the devastating Madoff-era e-book *Wilpon's Folly*, Howard is a writer and reporter of boundless energy and unimpeachable integrity. His eternal advocacy of, enthusiasm for, and confidence in my work have long been sources of determination for me even when at my most disenchanted.

Thanks to the poker boys, the finest bunch of degenerate gamblers that a guy could know.

Thanks to my sisters, Jen, Heather, and Meredith, for never failing to keep me humble.

Thanks to Debbie, Lionel, Joel, and Linda. I hate to defy reliable old stereotypes about how in-laws are supposed to suck, but you guys are pretty much the coolest people I know.

Thanks to Grandma for always asking me how "the book" was going, even during the many years that I wasn't writing any book at all. That's the kind of motivation that gets your ass in gear.

To my parents: I can't imagine the frustration that it must have been to raise me. Thank you for not drowning me in the tub when you had the chance. More important, thank you for giving me the gifts of love, humor, and self-reliance. I value these things above all others.

To my wife, my soul mate, my best friend, my B: I'm a better man because of you. Our kind of love never seems to get old. It's better than silver and gold.

Notes

Chapter 2: Rich Kid Sid

1. Deborah Frett, "Fact or Fiction: Is Gen Y Lazy?" *Huffington Post*, April 22, 2010, www.huffingtonpost/deborah-frett/fact-or-fiction -is-gen-y_b_547883.html.
2. Mark Scott, "Retirement: Gen Y's Empty Piggy Bank," *Bloomberg Businessweek*, July 15, 2010, www.businessweek.com/investor/ content/jul2010/pi20100715_116291.htm.
3. Jenny Anderson, "L.I. Inquiry on Cheating Now Covers Five Schools," *New York Times*, November 9, 2011, www.nytimes.com/ 2011/11/10/nyregion/sat-cheating-inquiry-on-long-island-expands -to-include-act.html.
4. James Ford, "DA: Teens Paid College Student Thousands to Take SATs," WPIX 11, September 28, 2011, www.wpix.com/news/wpix -seven-arrested-in-sat-cheating-ring-20110927,0,3389576.story.
5. Gianna Palmer, "Students Prosecuted for Cheating on College Entrance Exam," Reuters, November 22, 2011, www.reuters.com/ article/2011/11/22/us-education-cheating-idUSTRE7AL2UT 20111122.

Chapter 3: The RU Screw

1. Curtis Eichelberger and Oliver Staley, "Rutgers Athletics Grow at Expense of Academics Unlike at Texas," Bloomberg.com, Au-

gust 16, 2011, www.bloomberg.com/news/2011-08-16/rutgers-boost
ing-athletics-at-expense-of-academics-fails-to-emulate-texas.html.
2. Ibid.
3. Mary Beth Marklein, "4-Year Colleges Graduate 53% of Students
    in 6 Years," *USA Today*, June 3, 2009, www.usatoday.com/news/
    education/2009-06-03-diploma-graduation-rate_N.htm.

Chapter 5: Twenty Years of Schooling . . .

1. Robert Applebaum, "Here's a Demand: Forgive Student Loan Debt,"
    Guardian, October 3, 2011, www.guardian.co.uk/commentisfree/
    cifamerica/2011/oct/03/demand-forgive-student-loan-debt.
2. Mac McClelland, "Stat of the Day: Don't-Lend-College-Students-
    Money Edition," *Mother Jones*, October 5, 2011, motherjones.
    com/rights-stuff/2011/09/stat-day-dont-lend-college-students-
    money-edition.
3. Ezra Klein, "Who Are the 99 Percent?" Wonkblog, *Washington Post*,
    October 4, 2011, www.washingtonpost.com/blogs/ezra-klein/post/
    who-are-the-99-percent/2011/08/25/gIQAt87jKL_blog.html.
4. Peter J. Henning, "Crisis May Seem Criminal, but Try Making a
    Case," DealBook (blog), *New York Times*, January 28, 2011, deal
    book.nytimes.com/2011/01/28/crisis-may-seem-criminal-but-try
    -making-a-case/.
5. Jesse Bricker et al., *Surveying the Aftermath of the Storm: Changes
    in Family Finances from 2007 to 2009*, Board of Governors of the
    Federal Reserve System, 2011, p. 7, www.federalreserve.gov/pubs/
    feds/2011/201117/index.html.
6. Paul R. La Monica, "Big Bonuses Alive on Wall Street. Why?" The
    Buzz (blog), *CNNMoney*, October 18, 2011, money.cnn.com/2011/
    10/18/markets/thebuzz/index.htm.
7. Annalyn Censky, "Surging College Costs Price Out Middle Class,"
    CNNMoney, June 13, 2011, money.cnn.com/2011/06/13/news/
    economy/college_tuition_middle_class/index.htm.
8. Heidi Shierholz, "New College Grads Losing Ground on Wages,"
    Economic Policy Institute, August 31, 2011, www.epi.org/publica
    tion/new_college_grads_losing_ground_on_wages/.

9.   Censky, "Surging College Costs."

10. Bureau of Labor Statistics, "Unemployment Demographics," 2011, www.deptofnumbers.com/unemployment/demographics.

11. Mary Pilon, "Student-Loan Debt Surpasses Credit Cards," Real Time Economics (blog), *Wall Street Journal*, August 9, 2010, blogs.wsj.com/economics/2010/08/09/student-loan-debt-surpasses-credit-cards/.

12. "The Fraud at the Heart of Student Lending Exposed—the One Sentence Everyone Should Read," *Zero Hedge*, October 18, 2011, www.zerohedge.com/news/fraud-heart-student-lending-exposed -one-sentence-everyone-should-read.

13. Catherine Rampell, "Many with New College Degree Find the Job Market Humbling," *New York Times*, May 18, 2011, www.nytimes .com/2011/05/19/business/economy/19grads.html.

Chapter 7: Thanksgiving and the Great Depression

1.   Shelley Emling, "'Boomerang' Children: When the Nest Isn't Empty Anymore," *New York Times*, June 25, 2005, www.nytimes.com/2005/06/24/your-money/24iht-mboom.html?pagewanted=all.

2.   Mark Trumbull, "Boomerang Kids: Recession Sends More Young Adults Back Home," *Christian Science Monitor*, November 29, 2009, www.csmonitor.com/Business/2009/1124/boomerang-kids-reces sion-sends-more-young-adults-back-home.

3.   Christine Hassler, "Cockpit Parents: How They're Flying 20-Somethings into the Ground," *Huffington Post*, March 18, 2011, www.huffingtonpost.com/christine-hassler/cockpit-parents_b _836914.html.

Chapter 8: Ain't No Love in the Heart of the City

1.   U.S. Department of Education, "Highlights from PISA 2009: Per- formance of U.S. 15-Year-Old Students in Reading, Mathematics, and Science Literacy in an International Context," National Center for Educational Statistics, December 2010, www.nces.ed.gov/pub search/pubsinfo.asp?pubid=2011004.

Chapter 9: Degree Mill University

1. John Lauerman, "For-Profit Colleges Face State Crackdowns as U.S. Rules Delayed," *Bloomberg Businessweek*, April 7, 2011, www.businessweek.com/news/2011-04-07/for-profit-colleges-face-state-crackdowns-as-u-s-rules-delayed.html.
2. Chris Kirkham, "At Kaplan University, 'Guerrilla Registration' Leaves Students Deep in Debt," *Huffington Post*, December 22, 2010, www.huffingtonpost.com/2010/12/22/kaplan-university-guerilla-registration_n_799741.html.
3. Chris Kirkham, "For-Profit College Recruiters Taught to Use 'Pain,' 'Fear,' Internal Documents Show," *Huffington Post*, February 8, 2011, www.huffingtonpost.com/2011/02/08/for-profit-college-recruiters-documents_n_820337.html.
4. Ibid.
5. U.S. Department of Education, "Highlights from PISA 2009: Performance of U.S. 15-Year-Old Students in Reading, Mathematics, and Science Literacy in an International Context," National Center for Educational Statistics, December 2010, www.nces.ed.gov/pub search/pubsinfo.asp?pubid=2011004.
6. Ibid.

Chapter 11: Tunneling Out

1. U.S. Census Bureau, "Students Who Are Foreign Born or Who Have Foreign-Born Parents," *Statistical Abstract of the United States*, 2012, www.census.gov/compendia/statab/2012/tables/12s0228.pdf.
2. Carola Suárez-Orozco et al., "Academic Trajectories of Newcomer Immigrant Youth," *Developmental Psychology* 46, no. 3 (2010): 608.

Chapter 15: Graduation

1. Plato, *The Republic*, trans. Benjamin Jowett, available at Internet Classics Archive, classics.mit.edu/Plato/republic.html.

Bibliography

Alaya, Ana M. "Rutgers Approves 8.5 Percent Tuition Hike." NJ.com, July 17, 2008. www.nj.com/news/index.ssf/2008/07/rutgers_approve _budget_to_incr.html.

Anderson, Jenny. "L.I. Inquiry on Cheating Now Covers Five Schools." *New York Times*, November 9, 2011. www.nytimes.com/2011/11/ 10/nyregion/sat-cheating-inquiry-on-long-island-expands-to-include -act.html.

Applebaum, Robert. "Here's a Demand: Forgive Student Loan Debt." *Guardian*, October 3, 2011. www.guardian.co.uk/commentisfree/cif america/2011/oct/03/demand-forgive-student-loan-debt.

Archibald, Robert B., and David H. Feldman. "Why Does College Cost So Much?" *Forbes*, August 11, 2010. www.forbes.com/2010/08/01/rising -cost-education-opinions-best-colleges-10-feldman-archibald.html.

Associated Press. "Rutgers University Proposes 3-Percent Hikes in Student Costs." *NJ.com*, July 14, 2011. www.nj.com/news/index.ssf/2011/07/ rutgers_proposes_3-percent_hik.html.

Bartz, Diane. "Lawmakers Protest For-Profit Schools Rule." Reuters, April 27, 2011. mobile.reuters.com/article/politicsNews/idUSTRE73 Q9AH20110427?irpc=932.

Bartz, Diane, and A. Ananthalakshmi. "For-Profit Education Rule Heads for Final U.S. Review." Reuters, May 3, 2011. www.reuters.com/ article/2011/05/03/us-education-forprofiteducation-idUSTRE7425 RY20110503.

Berrett, Dan. "Cheating and the Generational Divide." *Inside Higher Ed*, November 17, 2010. www.insidehighered.com/news/2010/11/17/ cheating.

Bricker, Jesse, B. Bucks, A. Kennickell, T. Mach, and K. Moore. *Surveying the Aftermath of the Storm: Changes in Family Finances from 2007 to 2009*. Board of Governors of the Federal Reserve System, 2011. www.federalreserve.gov/pubs/feds/2011/201117/index.html.

Bureau of Labor Statistics. *The Employment Situation—September 2011*. www.bls.gov/news.release/archives/empsit_10072011.pdf.

———. "Unemployment Demographics." 2011. www.deptofnumbers .com/unemployment/demographics.

Censky, Annalyn. "Surging College Costs Price Out Middle Class." *CNNMoney*, June 13, 2010. money.cnn.com/2011/06/13/news/ economy/college_tuition_middle_class/index.htm.

Coleman, Matt. "For-Profit Colleges Wary of Proposed Gainful Employment Regulations." *Florida-Times Union*, October 15, 2010. jacksonville.com/news/metro/2010-10-16/story/profit-colleges-wary -proposed-gainful-employment-regulations.

Doyle, Larry. "Are Student Loans an Impending Bubble? Is Higher Education a Scam?" *Business Insider*, May 2, 2011. articles.business insider.com/2011-05-02/wall_street/30065150_1_higher-education -student-loans-housing-nightmare.

Eichelberger, Curtis, and Oliver Staley. "Rutgers Athletics Grow at Expense of Academics Unlike at Texas." Bloomberg.com, August 16, 2011. www.bloomberg.com/news/2011-08-16/rutgers-boosting -athletics-at-expense-of-academics-fails-to-emulate-texas.html.

Ellis, Blake. "Class of 2011: Your Paychecks Will Be Bigger." *CNNMoney*, February 10, 2011. money.cnn.com/2011/02/10/pf/college_graduates _salaries/index.html.

Emling, Shelley. "'Boomerang' Children: When the Nest Isn't Empty Anymore." *New York Times*, June 25, 2005. www.nytimes.com/2005/ 06/24/your-money/24iht-mboom.html?_r=1&pagewanted=all.

Fischer, Karin. "American Universities Have Major Stake in Immigration Reform, Speaker Says." *Chronicle of Higher Education*, February 22, 2011. chronicle.com/article/American-Universities-Have/126474/.

Ford, James. "DA: Teens Paid College Student Thousands to Take SATs." WPIX 11, September 28, 2011. www.wpix.com/news/wpix-seven -arrested-in-sat-cheating-ring-20110927,0,3389576.story.

Frett, Deborah. "Fact or Fiction: Is Gen Y Lazy?" *Huffington Post*, Ap-

ril 22, 2010. www.huffingtonpost.com/deborah-frett/fact-or-fiction
-is-gen-y_b_547883.html.

Gabriel, Trip. "To Stop Cheats, Colleges Learn Their Trickery." *New York Times*, July 5, 2010. www.nytimes.com-2010/07/06/education/ 06cheat.html?pagewanted-all.

Geiger, Roger L., and Donald E. Heller. *Financial Trends in Higher Education: The United States*. Penn State Center for the Study of Higher Education, 2011. www.ed.psu.edu/educ/cshe/working-papers/ WP%236.

Hassler, Christine. "Cockpit Parents: How They're Flying 20-Somethings into the Ground." *Huffington Post*, March 18, 2011. www.huffington post.com/christine-hassler/cockpit-parents_b_836914.html.

Henning, Peter J. "Crisis May Seem Criminal, but Try Making a Case." DealBook (blog), *New York Times*, January 28, 2011. dealbook.ny times.com/2011/01/28/crisis-may-seem-criminal-but-try-making -a-case.

Indiviglio, Daniel. "Chart of the Day: Student Loans Have Grown 511% Since 1999." *Atlantic*, August 18, 2011. www.theatlantic.com/busi ness/archive/2011/08/chart-of-the-day-student-loans-have-grown -511-since-1999/243821/.

Jones, Sydney, and Susannah Fox. *Generations Online in 2009*. Pew Internet and American Life Project, January 28, 2009. www.pewinternet .org/Reports/2009/Generations-Online-in-2009.aspx.

Kirkham, Chris. "At Kaplan University, 'Guerrilla Registration' Leaves Students Deep in Debt." *Huffington Post*, December 22, 2010. www .huffingtonpost.com/2010/12/22/kaplan-university-guerilla-registra tion_n_799741.html.

———. "For-Profit College Recruiters Taught to Use 'Pain,' 'Fear,' Internal Documents Show." *Huffington Post*, February 8, 2011. www.huffing tonpost.com/2011/02/08/for-profit-college-recruiters-documents_n _820337.html.

———. "For-Profit Colleges Evade Stricter Rules by Courting Powerful Allies in Washington." *Huffington Post*, December 12, 2011. www .huffingtonpost.com/2011/12/12/for-profit-college-regulations_n _1144792.html.

Klein, Ezra. "Who Are the 99 Percent?" Wonkblog, *Washington Post*,

October 4, 2011. www.washingtonpost.com/blogs/ezra-klein/post/
who-are-the-99-percent/2011/08/25/gIQAt87jKL_blog.html.

La Monica, Paul R. "Big Bonuses Alive on Wall Street. Why?" *CNNMoney*,
October 18, 2011. money.cnn.com/2011/10/18/markets/thebuzz/
index.htm.

Lauerman, John. "For-Profit Colleges Face State Crackdowns as U.S.
Rules Delayed." *Bloomberg Businessweek*, April 17, 2011. www.busi
nessweek.com/news/2011-04-07/for-profit-colleges-face-state-crack
downs-as-u-s-rules-delayed.html.

Lewin, Tamar. "Burden of College Loans on Graduates Grows." *New
York Times*, April 11, 2011. www.nytimes.com/2011/04/12/education/
12college.html.

Lowrey, Annie. "Is College a Rotten Investment?" *Slate*, May 11, 2011.
www.slate.com/articles/business/moneybox/2011/05/is_college_a_rot
ten_investment.html.

Marklein, Mary Beth. "4-Year Colleges Graduate 53% of Students in 6
Years." *USA Today*, June 3, 2009. www.usatoday.com/news/educa
tion/2009-06-03-diploma-graduation-rate_N.htm.

McClelland, Mac. "Stat of the Day: Don't-Lend-College-Students-Money
Edition." *Mother Jones*, October 5, 2011. motherjones.com/rights
-stuff/2011/09/stat-day-dont-lend-college-students-money-edition.

McPherson, Sam. "Is Forgiving Student-Loan Debt the Answer to Fixing
the Ailing Economy?" *Examiner*, September 16, 2011. www.examiner
.com/college-in-oakland/is-forgiving-student-loan-debt-the-answer-to
-fix-the-ailing-economy.

Murray, Sara. "The Curse of the Class of 2009." *Wall Street Journal*, May
9, 2009. online.wsj.com/article/SB124181970915002009.html.

Nies, Yunji de, and Karen Russo. "University of Central Florida Cheating
Scandal Prompts Professor to Issue Ultimatum." ABC News, November 10, 2010. abcnews.go.com/Business/widespread-cheating-scandal
-prompts-florida-professor-issues-ultimatum/story?id=11737137
#.T0pozsw89sU.

Palmer, Gianna. "Students Prosecuted for Cheating on College Entrance
Exam." Reuters, November 22, 2011. www.reuters.com/article/2011/
11/22/us-education-cheating-idUSTRE7AL2UT20111122.

Pilon, Mary. "Student-Loan Debt Surpasses Credit Cards." *Wall Street*

Journal, August 9, 2010. blogs.wsj.com/economics/2010/08/09/ student-loan-debt-surpasses-credit-cards.

Plato. *The Republic*. Trans. Benjamin Jowett. Internet Classics Archive. classics.mit.edu/Plato/republic.html.

Primack, Dan. "Occupation: From Wall Street to the University." *CNNMoney*, October 5, 2011. finace.fortune.cnn.com/2011/10/05/ occupation-from-wall-street-to-the-university/.

Princeton Review. "Rutgers, the State University of New Jersey—New Brunswick." 2011. www.princetonreview.com/RutgersTheStateUniver sityofNewJerseyNewBrunswick.aspx.

Rampell, Catherine. "Many with New College Degree Find the Job Market Humbling." *New York Times*, May 18, 2011. www.nytimes.com/ 2011/05/19/business/economy/19grads.html.

Rutgers University, Division of Grant and Contract Accounting. Rutgers University Financial Statements. postaward.rutgers.edu/reports .htm.

Scott, Mark. "Retirement: Gen Y's Empty Piggy Bank." *Bloomberg Businessweek*, July 15, 2010. www.businessweek.com/investor/content/ jul2010/pi20100715_116291.htm.

Shierholz, Heidi. "New College Grads Losing Ground on Wages." Economic Policy Institute, August 31, 2011. www.epi.org/publication/ new_college_grads_losing_ground_on_wages/.

Star-Ledger staff. "Rutgers Leads Nation in Athletics Subsidies Among Public Schools, Report Says." *NJ.com*, June 27, 2011. www.nj.com/ rutgers/index.ssf/2011/06/rutgers_leads_nation_in_atheletic_spend ing_among_public_schools_report_says.html.

Suárez-Orozco, Carola, F. X. Gaytan, H. J. Bang, J. Pakes, E. O'Connor, and J. Rhodes. "Academic Trajectories of Newcomer Immigrant Youth." *Developmental Psychology* 46, no. 3: 602–18.

Tarrazi, A. "$3M in Parking Tickets Left Unpaid." *Daily Targum*, 2006. www.dailytargum.com/2.4985/3m-in-parking-tickets-left-upaid-1 .1505593.

Teranishi, Robert T., C. Suárez-Orozco, and M. Suárez-Orozco. "Immigrants in Community Colleges." *Immigrant Children* 21, no. 1 (Spring 2011): 153–69.

Tompor, Susan. "Student Loan Debt Exceeds Credit Card Debt in USA."

USA Today, September 10, 2010. www.usatoday.com/money/perfi/
college/2010-09-10-student-loan-debt_N.htm.

Trumbull, Mark. "Boomerang Kids: Recession Sends More Young Adults
Back Home." *Christian Science Monitor*, November 29, 2009. www
.csmonitor.com/Business/2009/1124/boomerang-kids-recession-sends
-more-young-adults-back-home.

"UCF Professor Richard Quinn Accuses Class of Cheating." YouTube.
www.youtube.com/watch?v-rbzJTTDO9f4.

U.S. Census Bureau. "Students Who Are Foreign Born or Who Have
Foreign-Born Parents." *Statistical Abstract of the United States*, 2012.
www.census.gov/compendia/statab/2012/tables/12s0228.pdf.

U.S. Department of Education. "Highlights from PISA 2009: Performance
of U.S. 15-Year-Old Students in Reading, Mathematics, and Science
Literacy in an International Context." National Center for Educational Statistics, December 2010. www.nces.ed.gov/pubsearch/pubs
info.asp?pubid=2011004.

———. *Student Loan Default Rates Increase*. Press release, September
13, 2010. www.ed.gov/news/press-releases/student-loan-default-rates
-increase-0.

William & Mary. "Honor System." www.wm.edu/offices/deanofstudents/
services/studentconduct/studenthandbook/honor_system/index.php
(accessed 2011).

"The Fraud at the Heart of Student Lending Exposed—the One Sentence Everyone Should Read." *Zero Hedge*, October 18, 2011. www
.zerohedge.com/news/fraud-heart-student-lending-exposed-one
-sentence-everyone-should-read.

Index

politics, xiii, 58, 62
post-traumatic stress disorder,
    203–204
poverty, 55
pragmatism, 16–21
prep school, 10
Princeton Review, 23, 24
Princeton University, 30, 170
professors, 23–24, 47, 64, 75,
    79–81, 96, 189
  vs. Internet, 79–88, 222
  role of, 79
  Rutgers, 23–24, 30
  salaries, 30, 31–32
promotion system, 66
psychology, 42, 197–215
public-school education, 15
punctuation, 12

Quinn, Richard, 79–81, 86

radio, ix, x
Ramones, 180
reading, 108
real-estate industry, 57–58, 59
  subprime mortgage crisis,
    57–58, 62
reality TV, 13, 14, 157
recession, of 2008–2009, 30,
    55–60, 137
recruiting, college, 121–38
recycled papers, 124–25
reference materials, 73–74
references, 78, 157
Renaissance, 223
research, 88
  formal process of, 86–87
restaurants, 64
résumé, 41

Reuters, 19
revisions, 16, 20, 76–77, 100,
    102–107, 111, 119–20,
    146–52, 154–55
Rice, Kathleen, 19
Roosevelt, Franklin D., 70
RU Screw, 24–39
Rutgers University, 4–8, 20,
    22–39, 113
  athletics, 31, 31n., 32
  bureaucracy, 6, 22–39
  class size, 6, 30
  corporate sponsors, 25
  Expository Writing, 9, 11–13,
    17–18
  financial aid, 23
  financial problems, 30–36
  freshmen, 9, 24
  graduation, 37–39
  History Department, 30
  housing, 5
  parking and transportation,
    5–6, 7, 22, 26, 28–29,
    32–36
  professors, 23–24, 30
  RU Screw, 24–39
  tuition, 4–5, 30

salary, 13–14
Sampson, Vince, 62
SATs, 18–19, 24
  cheating scandal, 18–19
Saudi Arabia, 68
Sawyer, Diane, x, xii
Scalia, Antonin, 193
Schiano, Greg, 31, 31n.
science, 108, 158
seasonal depression, 52
self-esteem, 68

A Note on the Author

Dave Tomar is a Philadelphia-based freelance writer and a graduate of Rutgers University in New Brunswick, New Jersey. In 2010, he authored an article titled "The Shadow Scholar" under the pseudonym Ed Dante. The article, detailing his decade of experience as an academic ghostwriter, highlighted the issues of cheating and the need for reform in higher education. "The Shadow Scholar" became the most read article in the history of the *Chronicle of Higher Education* and received special citation from the Education Writers Association. Dave Tomar has also been a regular contributor to the *Perpetual Post*.